PERSPECTIVES ON GREEK PHILOSOPHY

In commemoration of the philosophical interests of Stanley Victor Keeling, the annual lectures in his memory highlight the interest and importance of ancient philosophy for contemporary study of the subject. This volume brings together the Keeling lectures from leading international figures in ancient and modern philosophy, presented between 1992 and 2002. Including contributions from Bernard Williams and Martha Nussbaum, lectures range across topics such as Intrinsic Goodness, Necessity, Fate and Determinism and Quality of Life, extending from Plato through Aristotle to the Stoics. Edited and with a preface by R. W. Sharples.

ASHGATE KEELING SERIES IN ANCIENT PHILOSOPHY

The *Ashgate Keeling Series in Ancient Philosophy* presents edited collections of leading international research which illustrate and explore ways in which ancient and modern philosophy interact. Drawing on original papers presented at the S.V. Keeling Memorial Lectures and Colloquia at University College London, this series incorporates contributions from the Anglo-American philosophical tradition and from continental Europe, and brings together scholars internationally recognised for their work on ancient philosophy as well as those whose primary work in contemporary philosophy speaks of the importance of ancient philosophy in modern philosophical research and study. Each book in the series will appeal to upper-level and graduate students and academic researchers worldwide – both those who are interested in ancient philosophy and those who are working in the relevant areas of contemporary philosophy.

Perspectives on Greek Philosophy

S.V. Keeling Memorial Lectures in Ancient Philosophy
1992-2002

Edited by

R.W. SHARPLES
University College London

ASHGATE

Published by
Ashgate Publishing Limited
Gower House
Croft Road
Aldershot
Hampshire GU11 3HR
England

Ashgate Publishing Company
Suite 420
101 Cherry Street
Burlington, VT 05401-4405
USA

Ashgate website: http://www.ashgate.com

British Library Cataloguing in Publication Data
Perspectives on Greek philosophy : S.V. Keeling memorial
  lectures in ancient philosophy 1992-2002. - (Ashgate
  Keeling series in ancient philosophy)
  1. Philosophy, Ancient
  I. Sharples, R.W.
  180

Library of Congress Cataloging-in-Publication Data
Perspectives on Greek philosophy : S.V. Keeling memorial lectures in ancient
philosophy, 1992-2002 / edited by R.W. Sharples
        p. cm. -- (Ashgate Keeling series in ancient philosophy)
    Includes bibliographical references and indexes.
    ISBN 0-7546-3279-2 (alk. paper)
        1. Philosophy, Ancient. I. Sharples, R.W. II. Keeling, S.V. (Stanley Victor),
    1894-1979. III. Series.

B171 .P48 2003
180--dc21

                                                                        2002034528

ISBN 0 7546 3279 2

Printed and bound in Great Britain by MPG Books Ltd, Bodmin, Cornwall

Contents

List of Contributors

Sarah Broadie is Professor of Moral Philosophy at the University of St. Andrews.

Jacques Brunschwig is Professor of the History of Ancient Philosophy, Emeritus, at the University of Paris I Panthéon-Sorbonne.

David Charles is Fellow and Tutor in Philosophy at Oriel College, Oxford.

John M. Cooper is Stuart Professor of Philosophy at Princeton University.

David Furley is Professor of Classics, Emeritus, at Princeton University, and an Honorary Fellow of Jesus College, Cambridge.

T.H. Irwin is Susan Linn Sage Professor of Philosophy at Cornell University.

Martha Nussbaum is Ernst Freund Distinguished Service Professor of Law and Ethics at the University of Chicago.

Günther Patzig is Professor of Philosophy, Emeritus, at the Georg-August-Universität, Göttingen.

Bernard Williams is Deutsch Professor of Philosophy at the University of California, Berkeley, and a Fellow of All Souls College, Oxford.

Preface

This volume contains nine of the ten Stanley Victor Keeling Memorial Lectures given at University College London in the years 1992-2002 inclusive.[1] The tenth, given in 1999, was by Professor Myles Burnyeat of All Souls College, Oxford, on 'Plato and Aristotle on the Pleasures of Philosophy'.

Stanley Victor Keeling (1894-1979) was Lecturer and then Reader in Philosophy at University College London; upon his retirement in 1954 he went to live in Paris, where he died in 1979.[2] While his principal published works were on Descartes and McTaggart,[3] he also taught ancient philosophy, and wrote of his desire to ensure that the study of Greek philosophy 'should assume in our university courses a position commensurate with its importance'. It was with this in mind that, when an anonymous donor set up the endowment that funds the Keeling Lecture (and subsequently also the biennial Colloquia[4] and a Scholarship) it was laid down that the subject of the Lecture should be ancient Greek philosophy. The inclusion in this volume of a lecture by Professor Jacques Brunschwig recognizes Keeling's interest in France (he studied for his doctorate at the Universities of Toulouse and Montpellier, and lived in Paris after his retirement).

The lectures published or reprinted here have been arranged in the (approximate) chronological order of the topics covered, rather than in the order in which they were given. My thanks as editor are due to the lecturers, and to the publishers in the case of lectures published elsewhere, for permission to print or reprint the lectures. (Specific acknowledgements of permissions to reprint are given at the start of each lecture.) My thanks are also due to Ashgate Publishing for undertaking the publication of this volume and indeed of the *Keeling Series in Ancient Philosophy*,

---

[1]   Nine of the lectures from the first ten were published in R.W. Sharples (ed.), *Ancient Thinkers and Modern Thinkers: The Stanley Victor Keeling Memorial Lectures 1981-1991*, London: UCL Press, 1993.

[2]   See the 'Biographical Sketch' by E. Senior, with a bibliography of Keeling's publications, in S.V. Keeling, *Time and Duration*, ed. G. Rochelle, Lewiston: Edwin Mellon Press, 1992.

[3]   S.V. Keeling, *Descartes*, London: Ernest Benn, 1934, 2nd, revised ed., London: Oxford University Press, 1968; J.M.E. Mactaggart, *Philosophical Studies*, edited with an introduction by S.V. Keeling, London: E. Arnold, 1934. In 1948 Keeling gave the British Academy annual Master Mind lecture on Descartes (*Proceedings of the British Academy* 34 [1948] 57-80).

[4]   Of which the following have so far been published: R. Heinaman (ed.), *Aristotle and Moral Realism*, London: UCL Press, 1995; R.W. Sharples (ed.), *Whose Aristotle? Whose Aristotelianism?*, Aldershot: Ashgate, 2001.

and to my colleagues in the Keeling Committee, Professor Gerard O'Daly and Dr Bob Heinaman; Dr Heinaman has undertaken most of the work of inviting lecturers and organizing lectures in the period covered by this volume.

Bob Sharples
Department of Greek and Latin,
University College London

Chapter One

Plato's Construction of Intrinsic Goodness*

Bernard Williams

I

Thrasymachus says in Book I of the *Republic* that justice is 'the advantage of the stronger' (338C). This is not offered as a λόγος or definition of justice: if it were, it would lead to the conclusion that since the stronger certainly pursues his own advantage, he must pursue justice, which Thrasymachus of course denies. Closer to what he principally wants to say is his later statement (343C) that justice is an ἀλλότριον ἀγαθόν, something that always does somebody else some good. Thrasymachus' own account operates at the very primitive level of dividing agents (whether they be individual people or cities) into two types, the strong and the weak, and identifying justice simply as a device used by the strong to exploit the weak. This immediately raises the question of what makes one agent stronger than another. In particular, what makes a collective agent, such as a city or a group of bandits, strong? Indeed, what makes it a collective agent at all? The answer, as Socrates points out at 351 seq, must be, to a significant degree, the practice of justice between the individuals who form the collective agent. So Thrasymachus' primitive model must be wrong.

This implies, further, that we cannot go on saying simply that justice 'always does someone else some good.' Thrasymachus himself, when he said this, did not mean that the benefits secured by any just act were uniquely benefits to someone other than the agent. He did not deny that when the weaker party acts in accordance with justice, he secures a benefit for himself; he claimed that when this is so, it is only because of power possessed by someone else who is stronger and who also gains a benefit. Justice is always in someone else's interest, because when an agent has an

* Some passages in this paper are reprinted or adapted, by permission of the publishers which we gratefully acknowledge, from B. Williams, 'Plato against the Immoralist', in O. Höffe, ed., *Platons Politeia*, Berlin: Akademie Verlag, 1997, 55-67, and B. Williams, *Plato: The Invention of Philosophy*, London: Phoenix, 1998.

interest in doing some just act, it is always (leaving aside errors, which are discussed at 339ff.) because it is in someone else's interest that this itself should be so.

However, not even this much will be true, once we accept that justice helps to make collective agents strong. In place of Thrasymachus' view, that justice is a device used by the strong to exploit the weak, we have the idea put forward by Glaucon in Book II, that it is a device of the (individually) weak to make themselves (collectively) strong – to make themselves stronger, in fact, than those who, before this association, were individually strong. On this account, Thrasymachus' first formulation, that justice is the interest of the stronger, might be replaced with an equally crude slogan to the effect that it is the interest of the weaker. When the association of the (previously) weak is formed, and the collective agent comes into being, justice does each of the participants some good in a way that does not depend on its doing some other, exploiting, party some good.

Expressed in these terms, Thrasymachus' and Glaucon's accounts seem to be opposed to one another. It is not simply that they can easily be formulated in terms that are contrary to one another: to us, the opposition may seem to extend to their ethical value. The Thrasymachean account, to the extent that it can be made coherent at all, is fiercely reductive and 'unmasks' justice as an exploitative device. Glaucon's theory, on the other hand, is the ancestor of honourable contractualist accounts which show why justice is the basis of collective endeavours and the division of labour, and why it is of great value to human beings.

Granted these differences, it is significant that every party to the discussion in the *Republic* treats Glaucon's position (and its elaboration by Adeimantus) as essentially a somewhat refined version of Thrasymachus'. 'I shall renew Thrasymachus' argument,' Glaucon says (358B-C); and Adeimantus, who, like his brother, does not accept this outlook himself but wants to hear it refuted by Socrates, says that he has put as strongly as he can the view of Thrasymachus and others who agree with him (367B). The reason for this is, at one level, obvious. There is an opinion about justice that Thrasymachus on the one hand, and Glaucon and Adeimantus on the other, certainly share, despite their other differences: that the life of justice[1] is in some sense *a second best*. This is the issue that is picked out at the beginning of Book II, when the distinction is made between things that are valued in themselves, things that are valued for their consequences, and things that are valued for both (357-8).[2] What Socrates is encouraged to show, contrary to the common opinion which has been expressed in different ways by Thrasymachus and by Glaucon, is that justice falls into the third class. It is obvious that this is the issue, but there is another question to

---

[1]   Granted the wide range of the term δικαιοσύνη in the *Republic*, the issue under discussion can be taken to be the general value of ethical constraints on one's relations to other people. 'Justice' is the only appropriate translation of the term, and I shall stay with it, but the broad scope of the issue must be kept in mind.

[2]   'Consequences' translates more than one expression: τὰ ἀποβαίνοντα 357B6; ὅσα γίγνεται ἀπ' αὐτῶν D1, 358B6. There are also, of course, various references to specific consequences of justice, or rather of the reputation for it.

which the answer is rather less obvious: why should the discussion take this form? Why are the standards for the value of justice raised so high?

The first point to emphasize is how radically individualistic, at this stage of the discussion, the issue is taken to be. Glaucon's account might be said to show that we have an interest in pursuing justice, and if we assume that 'we' is taken collectively, this is straightforwardly true. Indeed, as we have already seen, granted the collective 'we', justice does not even come out as a second best – without justice there will be no collective 'we'. But the collective 'we' has a tendency to unravel, and in the discussion with Thrasymachus we are not allowed to assume it. The question whether *we* have reason to pursue justice is taken, by Socrates as it is by Thrasymachus, to refer to each of us. The question each of us must ask is 'what reason do I have to be just?', 'what does justice do for me?'. This is the force of Socrates' earlier remark (352D): our discussion is not about a trivial matter, but about how one should live.[3]

The question, then, is about the best life for the individual, and already at 347E Socrates has said that he regards it as an issue 'bigger' than Thrasymachus' first formulations, whether he was right in thinking that the life of the unjust person was better[4] than that of the just. A closely related idea is that no-one would choose to be just if he had an alternative ('no-one is willingly just,' 360C.) The force of this is supposedly given to us by the two thought-experiments that Glaucon presents, the ring of invisibility (359D-360) and that in which we are invited to think about two men, one of whom has all the social rewards of justice without being really just, while the other has genuine justice and none of its conventional rewards (360E-361D).

There are difficulties with each of the thought-experiments: the second, because it is not clear what exactly we are invited to suppose,[5] and the first, because it is unclear what it could tell us about real life. But they are intended, in any case, to sharpen the question 'do you value justice for its own sake or for the sake of the rewards and the reputation that conventionally go with it?' The question gains in force when we take into account Adeimantus' contribution. The general effect of that contribution is to reinforce Glaucon's insistence that we should 'take away

---

[3]   χρὴ ζῆν: for the force of χρή, cf B. Williams, *Shame and Necessity*, Berkeley: California University Press, 1993, 184 n.57, and materials cited there. By the time of Plato, the term bears a certain contrast with δεῖ, which introduces rather a notion of (relatively) external necessity. So in the *Republic*, the idea that the just life is a life one 'should' (χρή) live is contrasted with the idea that one 'has to', is 'forced to', live it: cf. 358C, people pursue justice as necessary, not as good.

[4]   κρείττω; ἀμείνων 358C.

[5]   It is not clear, in particular, whether the genuinely just man 'appears' unjust because he has an unconventional notion of justice, so that the world judges unfavourably the character he really has; or because the world factually misunderstands what his character is. I have discussed the passage in *Shame and Necessity*, 98f. with n.46; and see n.47 for the point that the reference to Aeschylus does not help.

reputation' (367B), and we may wonder why he says that the argument has not been adequately expressed by Glaucon, and that 'what most needed saying has not been said' (362D). His point is that as Glaucon has put it, it is the enemies of justice such as Thrasymachus who emphasize the idea that people pursue justice for the sake of the conventional rewards. On the contrary, Adeimantus says, the real problem is that the friends of justice, people who are trying to encourage the young to be just, themselves emphasize those rewards, and so sell justice short; and he cites passages from the poets to this effect (prefiguring some of the objections that will be brought against them later in the dialogue).

II

All this, then, gives some sense to the idea of pursuing, and praising, justice 'for its own sake'. But now we must ask why Plato thinks it so important that we should value justice in this way. What is the point of insisting that one does not value justice properly unless one values it, in this sense, for its own sake? A modern reader may easily be misled at this point, and take the answer to this question to be more familiar than it is. He or she may take Plato to be thinking of a pure, self-sufficient moral motivation, in terms of which the agent does good or right actions simply because that is what they are, and for no other reason. On this conception, if one reflects on the value of a moral life, one will insist simply on its moral value: this is what it is to be concerned with justice and other moral values for their own sake, and it is contrasted with relating those values to anything else at all, such as one's own happiness. But this, certainly, is not Plato's concern. His argument can be formulated only because there is one, univocal, kind of question in practical reason, 'how should I live?', 'what is the best life?', 'how shall I do best?', to which Thrasymachus and his friends give the wrong answer, and Socrates, on behalf of justice, will give the right answer. It is not that the pursuit of justice 'for its own sake' has a quite special, moral, value which vindicates itself. The question of its value, rather, is the question of what makes a life worth living, a question to which other 'non-moral' goods might in principle, as the others suggest, provide the answer.

Another way of putting the point is that the idea of 'pursuing justice for its own sake' occurs in Socrates' answer to the question, not in the question itself. The question is not 'What is the value of justice pursued for its own sake, as opposed to the sake of its consequences?' The question is: 'What is the value of justice?', and Socrates' answer is: 'It has no value (really), unless it has value when it is pursued for its own sake.' So the question remains: why does Plato's Socrates think this? Why does he raise the standards for the vindication of justice so high?

The question has been put in terms of someone's desiring or valuing or pursuing justice for its own sake. This might equally be expressed in terms of justice being valued or pursued as an end, or as a final good. This, so far, does not give us a sense for justice *being* a final good, as distinct from some agent's pursuing it as a final good, but the discussion between Socrates and the Thrasymachean party already suggests a direction in which one might get to that notion: what was to be the Aristotelian way, to the effect that justice is a final good if a rational, reflective, or wise person would pursue it as a final good. We shall need to keep this idea in mind.

However, my title uses a different phrase, 'intrinsic goodness', and we must not assume that this is the same idea. Christine Korsgaard has pointed out[6] that the standard contrast to 'final' is 'instrumental', while the contrast to 'intrinsic' is 'extrinsic', and you need a theory to show that these two distinctions come to the same thing. Korsgaard makes several important points, but I do not want simply to accept her account as the basis of my discussion. She writes:

> To say that something is intrinsically good is not by definition to say that it is valued for its own sake: it is to say that it has its goodness in itself. It refers to the location or source of the value rather than the way we value the thing.

Extrinsic goodness, on the other hand, is value that something gets from some other source.

One consideration that Korsgaard uses in separating the intrinsic/extrinsic distinction from the final/instrumental distinction does not seem to me to have the effect that her account requires. There are, as she says, various ways in which the goodness of one thing can be dependent on the goodness of another without the first being a means to the second. But many of these possibilities apply to practical reason itself. As David Wiggins and others have pointed out in discussing Aristotle, one may value going to the concert as a way of, not as a causal condition of, having a good evening. This kind of example is among those that Korsgaard uses to distinguish extrinsic from instrumental value. But these examples need not lead us to a notion which, in contrast to the final/instrumental distinction, refers to 'the source of the value rather than the way we value the thing'. It need lead us only to the conclusion that even within the scope of practical reason, or again, 'the way we value' something, the contrast to 'final' should be something broader than 'instrumental'; there are various ways of pursuing something 'derivatively', as we might say, as opposed to pursuing it as an end or final good, and one species of this is pursuing it as a means or instrument.

There is a second question about Korsgaard's account of these distinctions which is very relevant to the present discussion. As Korsgaard formulates her central point:

> One [distinction is that] between things valued for their own sakes and things valued for the sake of something else – between ends and means, or final and instrumental

6 'Two Distinctions in Goodness', *Phil. Rev.* 92 (1983); reprinted in *Creating the Kingdom of Ends*, Cambridge: Cambridge University Press, 1996. The quotation, and the one that follows, occur in the reprint at p. 250.

goods. The other is the distinction between things which have their value in
themselves and things which derive their value from some other source: intrinsically
good things versus extrinsically good things.

But we do not need Aristotle to remind us that a rational or wise person can pursue
or value a certain thing both for its own sake and for the sake of something else.
We have already seen that what Socrates wants to show, and will claim in the end
to have shown, is that justice should be valued both for itself and for its
consequences – that it is both a final and an instrumental good. Let us take 'a good'
to be some type or general object of pursuit or valuation, such as justice, or honour,
or pleasure. (This is the sense in which two rival politicians each of whom is
pursuing honour are both pursuing the same good.) If one and the same good can
be both final and instrumental, then *that* distinction is not one between different
classes of goods; it is a distinction between kinds of goodness or ways in which
things may be found good, and not, as Korsgaard puts it, a distinction between
different things. But the intrinsic/extrinsic distinction, as she explains it, *must* be a
distinction between things: if something 'has its value in itself' – whatever exactly
that means – it presumably cannot also 'derive its value from some other source'.
This shows that we are not merely taking apart two distinctions that operate in the
same field.

I do not propose to pursue the idea of intrinsic goodness, as distinct from final
goodness or goodness as an end, directly. My aim is to work round, in Plato's
thought, to a certain idea of intrinsic goodness and to see what function it performs
there. At the end of the paper I shall suggest that we need, for our purposes, an idea
of intrinsic goodness which is rather different from the one that we shall have
ascribed to Plato; rather paradoxically, it is Plato's own argument that will have
helped to make this clear.

For the immediate discussion of Plato, at any rate, there are three ideas which I
should like us to keep in mind from Korsgaard's formulations and the discussion of
them. The first is Korsgaard's own point that we cannot assume that a notion of
intrinsic goodness must be the same as that of final goodness or goodness as an
end. The second idea, which we may take from Korsgaard's language of 'sources',
is that the notions of intrinsic and extrinsic goodness have something to do with the
ways in which the goodness of various things is explained; and, closely connected
with this, that the notion of something intrinsically good is that of a thing whose
goodness is in some sense self-explanatory. Third, there is an obscurity about what
it is that these distinctions serve to distinguish: in particular, whether they
distinguish good things, or ways in which good things are conceived or valued.

III

Now I should like to start again, from a different point in Plato's work – Diotima's
speech in the *Symposium*.

The symposiasts have been talking about what ἔρως is, what it is to be a lover. We know that the lover has desires. We know that the lover and his desires have some relation to τὸ καλόν or καλά, beauty or beautiful things; in particular, beautiful young men. Now we learn more precisely what these desires are, and what their relation is to the beautiful. It is certainly not – as opposed to what some earlier speeches said – that the desire itself is beautiful. Nor is the desire a desire for the beautiful, at least in any sense that it is at all transparent: (206E2-5) 'love is not love of the beautiful, as you think. – What is it, then? – Of reproduction and birth in the beautiful.' This desire itself turns out to be an expression, or form, of a desire to be immortal.[7]

Now this provides a schema, to put it in rather formal terms, which can be filled out differently for different types of ἔρως. A man's ἔρως for a woman defines birth, τόκος, literally; ἐν, 'in association with', is sexual; and the immortality in question is genetic. But a man may bring forth or generate not babies but ideas or poems, and live for ever (or at least for longer) through those. The beauty in question may now be that of a particular youth, or something more general – as we might say, youthful beauty; again, that may be beauty of soul rather than of body. There is nothing in all this to imply that the various refinements, as perhaps we may call them, necessarily keep step with one another. Socrates has been disposed to generate ideas and good thoughts but in association with youths who had beautiful bodies; though he may have got at least some of the way towards being 'a lover of all beautiful bodies' (210B), rather than being obsessed with one person. Conversely, Alcibiades, we learn later, is drawn to Socrates' beautiful soul (215-217), but he has little idea of what an appropriate τόκος would be.[8]

Then Diotima gives her account of the end of the progress, to the 'final and highest mysteries of love' (210A), which she doubts that Socrates can achieve. Here, in a famous passage, the lover is said to turn to the great sea of beauty, and will come to see something 'wonderfully beautiful in its nature', which

> always is and neither comes to be nor passes away, neither waxes nor wanes; it is not beautiful in one way and ugly in another, nor beautiful at one time and not at another, nor beautiful in relation to one thing and ugly in relation to another, nor beautiful in one place and ugly in another, as it would be if it were beautiful to some people and ugly to others;

and it is not embodied in any face or body, or idea, or knowledge, or, indeed, in anything. This culminating, ultimately fulfilling, encounter still fits the original schema. This would indeed be a worthwhile life for a man (212A); he would bring

---

[7] The dialogue may suggest that this itself is an expression of the desire that the good should be with one for ever, 206A. I shall not take this up here.

[8] This helps to answer the question which dogs Plato's account of Socrates, why being loved by Socrates did not transform Alcibiades: it is loving Socrates that should have done that, and he did not know how to do it.

forth, not images of virtue, but true virtue, and his relation to τὸ καλόν, which is now the item that has just been described, would be that of seeing it and being with it, words reminiscent of the language originally applied to sexual relations with a beautiful person.

There are several things which, it is important to see, this account does not imply. It has been thought to imply that no-one ever really loves a particular person, but only the beauty in that person, a beauty of which that person is at best a poor exemplar. On the contrary, the account gives a sense to loving a particular person, in the form of a range of different contents laid down by the schema, and it denies that love is for beauty itself. Moreover, there is no suggestion that the particulars, these bodies or souls, were only seemingly or illusorily beautiful. They are indeed not unconditionally, or unqualifiedly, or perhaps we can say (as opposed to 'relatively') absolutely, beautiful, which is what the item of the final vision is. Indeed, retrospectively from the point of view of the vision, human bodies and colours and other such things are said to be merely 'mortal nonsense', but that is a comparative judgement of value, and it does not imply that it was simply a mistake to have thought that those things were beautiful, or even that one was mistaken to have pursued them. We may say that it is like a growth in aesthetic taste, from kitschy music, say, to more interesting music. It does not altogether deny the point or the object of the earlier taste, and indeed the earlier taste is a condition of the process, which is a progress rather than the mere detection of error or the elimination of a misunderstanding.

Diotima says that the earlier pursuits were 'for the sake of' (ἕνεκα) the final secrets, 210A, and she also says of one who comes to the vision that he is coming to the τέλος of the erotic, which may imply a similar idea, though it need not. But, emphatically and several times, she says that this is so only for one who is going about the erotic in the right way.[9] This does not mean that unless the ultimate state is reached, the earlier states are pointless. It means that from the later perspective we can see a point to them which they do not reveal at all to some people, and reveal only imperfectly even to those who are going about them in the right way. For those who do go about them in the right way, that imperfection is expressed in an obscure unsatisfactoriness or incompleteness in those relationships, which can be traced to their failure to express adequately the desire to have the good for ever.[10]

Diotima at some points makes it seem that once one has got going in the right way the ascent or refinement is almost inevitable: (210B) 'if one is to pursue beauty of form, it would great foolishness not to recognize that the beauty in all bodies is one and the same.' Yet she also describes the ascent as involving tasks (E6). All

[9] 210A2; A4; E3; 211B5.
[10] How far, and in what ways, such a feeling may come, in an uninterpreted form, even to those who are not going about the erotic in the right way, is a question to which the earlier speeches suggest answers.

this refers to the higher levels of the progress, above the point which she is doubtful that Socrates himself will be able to pass. Now Socrates is not liable to great foolishness, and what is to come later, the speech of Alcibiades, will show that he is not incapable of ethical tasks which may be involved. I take it that we are being told that Socrates was not in a position really to 'pursue beauty of form', and that the discovery of the sea of beauty, the final vision, involves intellectual tasks that were formulated by Plato himself.

The object of the final vision is absolutely or unconditionally beautiful. If we associate the idea of the intrinsic with a notion of explanation, we may also say that this object is intrinsically beautiful; although Plato does not make much of it in the *Symposium*, he certainly thought that this object would explain, in some sense, why anything, including itself, was beautiful. The object is also, I suppose, a good thing: to reach it was the τέλος of a progress inspired by the desire to have the good for ever. However, just in virtue of the account (or, rather, the apology for an account) which we have suggested for 'intrinsic', we must not suppose that because this object is intrinsically beautiful, and it is good, it is intrinsically good. If it were intrinsically good, its goodness would not be explained by anything else. But we know, not from the *Symposium* but from the *Republic*, that its goodness is explained by something else, the Form of the Good, which explains the goodness of everything including itself (as the sun enables everything including itself to be seen, 508B.) On the provisional account of intrinsic goodness, the Form of the Good is, for Plato, the only intrinsically good thing.

There are significant differences of tone between the *Symposium* and the *Republic*. The *Symposium* more emphasizes the pathos of the finite, the attractiveness of the contingently and transitorily beautiful which nevertheless carries with it a yearning for something the beauty of which will not be transitory, something to which some people may be able to ascend. The ascent of course has parallels in the *Republic*, but many of that dialogue's most powerful images are those of descent, which convey the regret of the return to the cave, of leaving the unconditioned for the conditioned. Relatedly, the *Republic* makes more of the idea that the contrast between the conditioned and the unconditioned is a contrast between appearance and reality, and its images of the contingent, particularly in relation to the Cave and in the discussions of art, are of illusion, deceit and dreams (476C); even though, when Socrates in Book V (479A) explains why the 'lovers of sights' are in a state of belief (δόξα), the 'appearances' he cites are in fact matters of comparison or relativity.[11]

Yet the end of the educational story that the *Republic* tells, the vision it offers, is strikingly similar to that of the *Symposium*. The Guardians are drawn to the intellectual world by love: they love study which tells them about being (485B), and the Form of the Good is the 'greatest study' (505A2). 'And so we shall say that

---

[11] A6 τῶν πολλῶν καλῶν μῶν τι ἔστιν ὃ οὐκ αἰσχρὸν φανήσεται; means '...will not appear as ugly', not '...will not appear to be ugly'.

they will admire and love (ἀσπάζεσθαί τε καὶ φιλεῖν) the things of which there is knowledge' (479 fin), and notably at 490B we are told that

> the genuine lover of learning...would go on and would not be discouraged and would not cease from ἔρως until he seized with the appropriate part of his soul each thing that by its nature is, and drawing near to what really is and being united with it (μιγεὶς), he would bring forth reason and truth, he would know and would live in truth, and would be nourished and so would cease from his painful labour. ... [12]

The intrinsically beautiful in the *Symposium* was not something that it would make sense to want: what one wanted was to generate the right kind of offspring (virtue, in fact) in its presence, which means in its cognitive presence. In exactly the same way, the Form of the Good, that which is, and alone is, intrinsically good in an explanatory sense, is not anything that one wants: what one wants is to generate reason and truth in its presence – that is to say, in its cognitive presence and by its intellectual light.

IV

Aristotle famously said (*EN* 1096b33-5) that if there were a separate and absolute Good, 'it is obvious that it could not be achieved or possessed by man; but it is to something of that sort that our inquiry is directed.' If Aristotle means by this (he may not) that Plato unfortunately overlooked this feature of the Form of the Good, that it is not achievable in action, he has missed the point: it would be a category mistake to suppose that it could be any such thing. If he means (equally, he may not) that Plato introduced the Form of the Good, a supposedly self-explanatory intrinsically good thing, in place of a final good, which is what Aristotle himself was looking for, then he is also mistaken. Plato has more than one final good, and the most significant is the life of the intellect – living, as he put it, in the presence of Forms – and this involves living in the light of the Form of the Good. So there is a final good, one among others, which is related to the intrinsic self-explanatory good, but it is not the same as that good, and it would not make sense to suppose that it was.

For reasons that Aristotle gave, and which Plato began to explore in his later work, there are grave problems in even understanding the notion of something that is absolutely good or beautiful in the sense of the *Symposium* and the *Republic*. The problems do not come simply from the idea that the goodness or beauty of such a thing must be self-explanatory. A major problem is that the thing is meant to explain the goodness or beauty of everything else which is good or beautiful; hence that it cannot be any specific sort of good or beautiful thing; hence that there is

---

[12] For ᾧ προσήκει ψυχῆς, cf *Symp.* 212A1, ᾧ δεῖ.

nothing else about it which explains its goodness or beauty; and hence, seemingly, that it is good or beautiful and nothing else at all. This is surely unintelligible.

Some of the notorious problems, then, come from the idea that there is just one intrinsically good item which is both self-explanatory and other-explanatory. Yet some of the recalcitrance of the Form of the Good, the difficulty in saying anything about it, would surely arise also with a larger class of self-explanatory intrinsic goods, forming a class of objects whose goodness was to be explained in advance of any human valuation. Such items (unlike the Form of the Good) will have other properties, and the sense in which their goodness will be self-explanatory is, presumably, that it will be explained by those properties. But then what is the nature of the a priori guarantee (as it will have to be) that such an explanation cannot refer to something else: for instance, that it might not be *improved* by referring to something else? Might it not be improved, for instance, by relating these properties to things that we value? Moreover, what is the a priori guarantee that some of those same properties could not causally depend on some other intrinsically good thing, as they cannot, if intrinsic goods and extrinsic goods are to form two disjunct classes? I shall not try to explore these questions here, but I find it hard to believe that the problems posed by Plato's Form of the Good are entirely due to its special role as a unique and explanatorily very ambitious intrinsic good.

The main point I want to emphasize, however, is not how hard it is for Plato to specify the Form of the Good, but how much he manages to say without specifying it. The criticism of Plato in Aristotelian style, to the effect that his account of the good is too intellectualist and inadequate to the claims of practical reason, is likely to distract us from a rather obvious feature of the *Republic*, that a lot of what it actually tells us about the Form of the Good consists of considerations that relate it to practical reason. It tells us almost nothing about the intellectual content of encountering the Form of the Good; it leaves us uncertain how much Socrates himself knows about it, and certain that he cannot at this point explain whatever he does know about it (506E, 517B, 532-3). Yet Socrates is supposed, by the end of the dialogue, to have met fully the challenge set in Book II; so it must be possible to understand why justice is a final good without understanding adequately, or barely at all, what the one and only intrinsic good is, or what is involved in its theoretical contemplation. We can understand Socrates' answer because we can gather from his account at least the following: that the wise or rational person needs to regard justice as a final good, and that he can make sense of it as a final good. We can take away some more as well, about the role of the Form of the Good in this, and I shall come back to that, but the central point is that we can take away these two conclusions.

The first conclusion, that the rational person needs to regard justice as a final good, has both an individual and a political form. In its individual form it is implicit in the description of the divisions of the soul in Book IV, and in the associated account of the various virtues. A less schematic expression of it occurs in the studies of degeneration in Books VIII and IX, but it may be less easy to see, partly because those studies, for obvious reasons, tend to mix psychological and political considerations, and partly because the story of degeneration is shaped by comparisons with a completed state of justice which by this stage is taken for granted, and so the story may not help us to see what exactly the individual's need for justice is. To get a slightly different view of Plato's account of this, it may be helpful to look outside the *Republic* again, to a dialogue which has many of the same preoccupations, the *Gorgias*.

V

This dialogue presents conversations that Socrates has with three speakers, Gorgias, Polus, and Callicles, who take in succession increasingly radical positions. The discussions are structured by the use that is made of three distinct value-oppositions. One is the contrast between δίκαιον and ἄδικον, the just and the unjust: this relates, as in the *Republic*, to values that concern fair dealing with others, respect for their persons and their property, and generally a prohibition on exploiting them. The terms of the second distinction, καλόν and αἰσχρόν, are understood here not in their directly aesthetic sense as in the *Symposium*, but in their connection with action and character, where they relate to honour and shame. I take it, as I have argued elsewhere, that this is not merely a matter of one's reputation; the distinction is one between things that agents can be proud of, and think well of themselves for having done or been, as opposed to things for which they despise themselves, feel ashamed or embarrassed or contemptible.[13]

The last contrast, between ἀγαθόν and κακόν, good and bad, is often, in the *Gorgias* as elsewhere, interpreted in terms of self-interest: one seeks the ἀγαθόν in seeking what is best for oneself. The basic idea, however, is something more general and abstract, the idea of what an agent has good reason to pursue or not. These are the terms which are, throughout these conversations, unquestionably tied to the conclusions of practical reason, and it makes no sense in this context to say that an agent knows that something is (on balance) κακόν, and that he has decided that this is what (on balance) he has reason to pursue.

Gorgias, the first speaker, accepts the conventional idea that all these values go together, so that what is δίκαιον is also καλόν and ἀγαθόν: we have reason to pursue the just and should think well of ourselves and others for doing so. It is in these terms that he defends his practice of rhetoric. Polus enters the discussion to offer a more radical position, which separates δίκαιον and ἀγαθόν: we should stop thinking that the δίκαιον is what we have reason to do. However, he treats the dimension of καλόν and αἰσχρόν in a less radical way, and is manoeuvred by Socrates into claiming both that to behave unjustly is αἰσχρόν, and that what is αἰσχρόν is κακόν −

---

[13] For the role of shame in Greek (and, indeed, our own) ethical experience, see *Shame and Necessity*, above n.3, in particular chapter IV and Endnote 1.

that is to say, that we have reason to avoid it.[14] This is inconsistent with his attempt to hold that injustice is not κακόν.

Polus' mistake is to sustain at once a conventional link between δίκαιον and καλόν (just behaviour is admired, injustice is something to be ashamed of), and a natural link between καλόν and ἀγαθόν (we have reason to do what will make us admired, no reason to do what will make us ashamed of ourselves). The last speaker, Callicles, sees Polus' mistake, and, takes the further step of denying the conventional link between δίκαιον and καλόν. In doing this, he wants to keep the link between καλόν and ἀγαθόν: the rational person will want to be admired and envied, to think well of himself, and not to be an object of contempt, but he will bring this about, Callicles urges, through power and the exploitation of others, having no concern for considerations of justice.[15]

Callicles is a more powerfully eloquent, and in some ways more sophisticated, version of Thrasymachus. He is supposedly refuted, but it is easy to feel that Plato has deliberately dealt him a hand of losing cards. Although there are several complexities in the argument, Callicles effectively ends up (from about *Gorg.* 491 onwards) defending a crudely gluttonous form of hedonistic activity, which not many are likely to envy. But this was not supposed to be the idea. The successfully unjust man was supposed to be a rather grand, powerful, stylish figure (the aesthetic echoes of καλός are relevant here) whom others, if they were honest, could admire and envy; but he has ended up, in Socrates' refutation, as a low addict or at best a heartlessly boring *bon viveur*, whom anyone with any taste would despise. It is easy to think that Socrates wins the argument only by changing the subject.

However, there is more to the strategy than this suggests. Callicles (491B) wants to say that the successful unjust man will be καλός, and admirable in recognizable ways: he will, for instance, be intelligent and brave. But the direction of Socrates' argument, which brings it close to the concerns of the *Republic*, is to suggest that Callicles has no right to suppose that, on the assumptions he and his unjust man are left with, there could be a basis either for admiring virtues such as intelligence and courage, or for thinking that the unjust man could actually sustain them. How does Callicles explain the values of courage and intelligence? He may do so in terms of political power: but quite early in their discussion (488-489), Socrates shows that there is a conflict between such a political conception and Callicles' ideal of an individual person who is 'better', since political power is a collective enterprise, in which the individuals are not going to be in his sense

---

[14] *Gorg.* 474C seq. κακόν and αἰσχρόν mostly appear in this discussion in their comparative forms.

[15] My very bare summary follows what I take to be the points in the dialogue that are most significant for the present question. Needless to say, other important patterns can be extracted from what is a very rich set of arguments.

'better', above all in a democracy.[16] The alternative is that he explains the value of these human qualities simply in terms of the satisfaction of desire – that is to say, as Plato puts it, in terms of pleasure. But that is not convincing, since someone can think of himself as καλός only if he can admire himself, and that implies grounds on which others can admire him, which implies more generally that one person can admire another.[17] A criterion that consists merely in the individual's desires being satisfied provides no basis for admiration at all. All that is left is hedonism.

Socrates in the *Gorgias* argues that any basis of admiration implies τάξις and κόσμος (503D seq), order and discipline, and that these, applied to the soul, constitute justice. The argument for this, which in the *Gorgias* could politely be called schematic, is strengthened in the *Republic*, with its account of the parts of the soul and their functions. At the same time, the *Republic*'s account is more complex, since it allows types of individual between the perfectly just person and the democratic or, worse, tyrannical person to whom Callicles' ideal, according to the *Gorgias*, must inevitably be reduced. But of course the *Republic* claims to show that the intermediate types are not as they would wish to be if they understood their natures better; and even they must, to some extent, regard justice as a final good.

Moreover, we need there to be people who regard justice as a final good if there is to be any stability for anyone. This is the political aspect of the argument. The 'analogy' between the individual and the city which is introduced at *Rep.* 368D is officially put forward to help us understand justice in the individual: it is as though the same message were written in larger letters. In fact, the way in which the *Republic* proceeds means that justice in the city and in the individual cannot be separated from one another, and the answers that the dialogue eventually gives to Thrasymachus and to the questions of Glaucon and Adeimantus are essentially political.

Whatever exactly the state of the lower classes in the city is meant to be,[18] it is certainly true that they are like the lower sections of the soul in this respect, that they cannot look after themselves: they have no inherent principles of order and discipline. The order and discipline that they need come from elsewhere, from the Guardians. This means that the Guardians must be ethically self-sufficient, and this means that they must be able to see that justice is worth pursuing for its own sake.

---

[16] In connection with the later discussion of Pericles, Socrates is in effect presenting Callicles with a dilemma for the aristocratic or oligarchic amoralist: the Athenian empire, which was run in ways he should admire, was run by a democracy.

[17] It is a Calliclean idea, obvious in his opening speech about nature and convention (482E seq), that the respectable secretly admire the ruthless, unless they have been intimidated into not doing so. This is very close to the inspiration of the Gyges' ring story in the *Republic*.

[18] I have discussed a difficulty about this, implicit in the supposed analogy, in 'The Analogy of City and Soul in Plato's *Republic*', in E.N. Lee, A.P.D. Mourelatos and A.O. Rorty eds., *Exegesis and Argument: Studies in Greek Philosophy presented to Gregory Vlastos*, Assen: van Gorcum, 1973, 196-206.

If justice were, as Glaucon argued, valuable only as a second-best, there would be no motive for the Guardians to be just, since they are not in anyone else's power. The constitution of Plato's city essentially depends on its rulers seeing justice as good in itself, or for its own sake, and if it is to be more than a virtuous tyranny, the lower classes will have to have some kind of belief to the same effect.

Plato could not use this conclusion, of course, to *demonstrate* that justice was good in itself. Those who accept Glaucon's account will reasonably not trust Plato's constitution. For them, a just city will reject ethical aristocracy and will consist of imperfect citizens keeping an eye on each other. This is why the ethical and the political parts of Plato's enterprise help each other. The ethical argument we have already followed suggests that people's lives will be incoherent if they are the sort of people who (the political analogy suggests) form the lower two classes of the city, and if, in addition, they try to be ethically self-sufficient. Democracy, in particular, is the project of such people trying to be ethically self-sufficient as a collective, and that is a doomed venture which ends in tyranny, just as Callicles, though he would like to be a free spirit who admires and is admired by some other free spirits, can in the end be nothing but a sordid slave of desire.

The city needs just people as rulers, but, equally, just people need the city. This is to some degree concealed by the downward movement of the *Republic*, which emphasizes the sacrifice of the Guardians in becoming rulers. But the question of that sacrifice can come up only in a context in which the able young have received an education which enables them to be Guardians, that is to say, the education offered in a just city. Guardians will not emerge, and young people will not become fully just, unless the institutions replicate themselves (which is what, the tale of decline tells us, will eventually fail to happen); and it is precisely the strongest spirits that will be corrupted without those institutions (492). So not only does the city need people who will see justice as a final end; such people, and young people who would like to become such people but do not yet fully understand what is involved, need the just city, or some approximation to it which can also bring it about that there will be such people.

So we can reply to the challenge of Book II. The rational person needs to regard justice as a final good. Moreover, he, and we, can make sense of regarding it as a final good, because that is exactly what the various arguments of the *Republic* have enabled us to do. These were the two conclusions that I said we would be able to take away from Socrates' argument. If we accept them, then, I suggest, we have been shown that justice *is* a final good.

VI

The Form of the Good, the item that we identified as being, on Plato's account, the one and only intrinsic good, has played a role in this account, but it is significant what a very small role it is. We are told that if we were to grasp it and work down again from it, we would understand the point of all the virtues, as well as of everything else. But as I have already said, the really significant thing is that Socrates has been able to meet the challenge of Book II, and get us to understand his answer, without any of us getting a glimpse of the Form of the Good. There is indeed an element which is essential to the answer even as we, or Glaucon and Adeimantus, understand it, an element in which the Form of the Good is mentioned. This is the motivation of the Guardians, which makes them reluctant, and hence uniquely reliable, rulers: they are driven by the love of truth, which, Plato tells us, expels other wants (485), with the result that they want no rewards, and so will not squabble or conspire as other rulers do (520 seq). The search for truth, Plato seems to think, is the only genuinely selfless motive; at the same time, it is connected with the truth-seeker's own self, since it is only as a mind seeking truth that one can fully satisfy the desire for immortality. The Form of the Good is the ultimate object of this search for truth. But once again, it is significant how little difference it would make to the argument if it were not. For the Guardians to have what, on Plato's account of things, is this essential motive, they need to have in mind a certain final good, the aim of understanding; perhaps, given his ideas of immortality, this must be, more specifically, the aim of understanding eternal reality. It makes no difference to this whether or not this reality has as its highest element the one and only intrinsic good.

It is just because the Form of the Good, which for Plato is the uniquely intrinsic good, is so retiring and inexplicable, that Plato's account of justice as a good, and, more generally, of what should concern one who is living the best possible life, has so little to do with it. He can answer the basic challenge of the *Republic*, to show that justice is a final good, and answer it in a way which he can reasonably suppose we shall understand, without his doing much more than to salute the intrinsic good. This is paradoxical, and the paradox suggests some lessons for the way in which we should think about these notions. They are no more than suggestions, but I think that both the failures and the successes of Plato's enterprise should encourage us to take them seriously.

First, we should abandon the idea that the distinction between intrinsic and extrinsic goodness determines two classes of things. I have already suggested that this idea contributed to the opaque and unhelpful character of absolute beauty and the Form of the Good. If we accept that one and the same thing can be both intrinsically and extrinsically good, then we can, to this extent, bring the intrinsic/extrinsic distinction into line with the final/instrumental distinction.

The next suggestion is that we should take a further step in the same direction, and treat final goods as a species of intrinsic goods. I argued earlier, in criticism of Christine Korsgaard, that the contrasting term to 'final' need not be merely 'instrumental', but something more general: I proposed the label 'derivative'. This, in itself, was intended to be a fairly uncontentious proposal. It is more contentious to suggest, as I am now suggesting, that the final/instrumental distinction altogether should be understood as an application of a more fundamental distinction between intrinsic and – using the term now more broadly than before – derivative goodness. The reason why this proposal is more contentious relates to a point about final goodness which we have accepted throughout the discussion: that the basic notion in this connection is that of someone's wanting or pursuing something as an end or final good, and that the notion of something's *being* a final good is to be explained in terms of this, for instance as what a wise or rational person would pursue as an end.

On the present proposal, intrinsic goodness will be treated in a similar way. The notion of something's being an intrinsic good will be explained in terms of a more basic notion of someone's valuing something as an intrinsic good.[19] It is important that this does not imply that all valuing is reducible to practical attitudes: 'valuing' does not entail 'wanting' or 'pursuing' or 'trying to bring about' (or a disjunction of them). This is particularly significant for us who, unlike Plato, regard a range of things in the world as having intrinsic goodness, although they are not ends or final goods: works of art, for instance, or natural beauty. Valuing such things cannot be reduced to practical attitudes. It can of course, in various connexions, be expressed in practical attitudes, and it would be an empty thing if it could not be expressed in such attitudes, even if there are some circumstances in which it can be expressed in no more than wishing. What exactly valuing involves in various circumstances, including what practical attitudes it may involve, is a significant question, and we should expect the answers to it to be fairly open-ended. This is indeed part of the point of the very abstract notion of 'valuing'.

There should be answers to this question, of what is involved in valuing a certain thing as an intrinsic good. There should be an answer, too, to the further significant question, of why we should value it in this way. This leads to the place of explanation among these notions. It is common to all accounts, presumably, that the extrinsic or derivative is explained in terms of the intrinsic. The interesting questions concern the explanation of the intrinsic. Up to now we have assumed, as Plato assumed when he was concerned with the Form of the Good, that intrinsic goodness should be self-explanatory. This idea turned out to be unfruitful. However, when we considered Plato's account of the final good of justice, we found that (relative to his own assumptions) he was able to explain it in terms of our needing to treat justice as a final good, and our being able to make sense of our doing so.

My last suggestion is that we should extend this schema to intrinsic goodness in general. We give up the unrewarding idea of intrinsic goodness being self-explanatory. We say that something is intrinsically good if we need to value it as intrinsically good, and we can make sense of our doing so.[20] The formula 'we can

---

[19]   This means, of course, that we cannot explain 'we value X as an intrinsic good' as 'we value X because we believe that it is an intrinsic good'.

[20]   I do not think that 'need to' is too strong, granted that an account is being given of 'X is an intrinsic good'. The account leaves room for people to treat something as an intrinsic good (for instance, as an end) without their having to claim that it is an intrinsic good *überhaupt*.

make sense of our doing so' is intended to secure a place in this discussion for something that is almost always a good idea in philosophy, explanation without reduction.

We may take the case of trust, or, more generally, honest relations between people.[21] This is widely regarded as a good thing, and there is quite a lot to be said about why it is a good thing. The value of trust and trustworthiness is not self-explanatory, and to claim that it was would be to leave it unexplained, an object of blank intuition. Yet the goodness of these things is not merely derivative, either. We do regard it as intrinsic. Moreover, we have to regard these things as intrinsically good if they are even to be derivatively good, since many of their good effects, and indeed their existence, depend on their being valued as intrinsic goods. So what is needed for us to be able to make sense of them as intrinsic goods? We have to be able to think reflectively about trust and trustworthiness as fitting into a structure of human qualities and social relations, in a way that relates them to other things that we value, and which does not reduce them to a device for maximizing utility or for getting out of the Prisoners' Dilemma. If they appeared to reflective understanding as simply such a device, the idea that they were intrinsically good would unravel, and we could not make sense of them as intrinsic goods. If we can make sense of these things as intrinsic goods, we are not *pretending* that they are intrinsic goods. That would be something else: it would be to pretend that we needed them, or to pretend that we could make sense of them as intrinsic goods, and neither of these things need be so. If we can make sense of trustworthiness in such terms, then we shall have *constructed* an intrinsic good.

Plato's Form of the Good is a peculiar and very extreme example what an intrinsic good has to be if it is regarded as a kind of thing that presents itself as self-explanatorily good, prior to any considerations of how we might value it. We have seen how little it contributes to Plato's enterprise. On the other hand, we have seen how much Plato achieves, in his own terms, by asking the questions 'do we need to value justice as a final good?' and 'can we make sense of our doing so?' If we use 'intrinsic' in the new and broader way, Plato will be asking these questions about justice as intrinsically good, and in answering them, he will have constructed an intrinsic good.

---

[21] I discuss in detail this example of constructing an intrinsic good in *Truth and Truthfulness*, Princeton: Princeton University Press, 2002.

Chapter Two

Morality and Immutability: a Platonic contribution to meta-ethics*

T.H. Irwin

I

In Plato's *Euthyphro* (10A-11B) Socrates argues against Euthyphro's suggestion that piety is what all the gods love. His argument, sometimes known simply as 'the Euthyphro Argument', is the source of a long sequence of philosophical reflections on definition, and on related issues in meta-ethics. I want to discuss one part of this sequence, beginning with Cudworth's revival of the Euthyphro Argument in the late 17th century. Cudworth and his successors exploit the Euthyphro Argument to introduce questions about realism, anti-realism, and response-dependence.[1]

Plato's argument is brief. Some crucial premises and presuppositions are taken for granted, and the point of the conclusion may be interpreted in different ways. Different views on these questions suggest different views about how the argument affects Plato's criteria for definition and their relevance to meta-ethics. I will raise these issues about the Euthyphro Argument before turning to later versions of it.[2]

---

*   An earlier version of most of this paper was presented as the Keeling Lecture at University College, London, in 1996. Some of it was presented at a conference in Ancient Philosophy in Chicago in 1997, and as an Erskine Lecture at the University of Canterbury, Christchurch, in 2000. Sections 1-3 overlap in part with 'Socrates and Euthyphro: the argument and its revival', presented to a conference on Socrates in Athens and Delphi in 2001, and forthcoming in V. Karasmanis, ed., *Socrates 2400 years from his Death*, Athens: European Cultural Centre at Delphi, 2003. I have benefited from the discussion on these occasions. In particular I received helpful comments by Richard Kraut, Stephen Gardiner, and Andrew Mason.

[1]   For recent discussion of these issues see, e.g., Crispin Wright, *Truth and Objectivity*, Cambridge, Mass.: Harvard University Press, 1992, 109-39 (section entitled 'The Euthy-phro Contrast').

[2]   I say more about the *Euthyphro* and related aspects of Plato in 'Socrates and Euthyphro' (see n.* above).

II

Socrates concedes to Euthyphro that the two predicates 'pious' and 'god-beloved' are coextensive, but he still argues against Euthyphro's definition.[3] His argument is this:

1. The god-beloved is god-beloved because the gods love it, and it is not the case that the gods love the god-beloved because it is god-beloved (10D9-10, E5-7).
2. The gods love the pious because it is pious, and it is not the case that the pious is pious because the gods love it. (10D1-7, E2-3).
3. Hence the pious and the god-beloved are not identical.
4. Hence the pious is not correctly defined as what the gods love.

The argument reveals two assumptions about definition:

(a) If we try to answer Socrates' question 'What is the F', by 'The F is the G', where the F and the G are co-extensive, that is not sufficient for an appropriate answer.
(b) 'The F is the G' is an appropriate answer if and only if F things are F because they are G.

These assumptions deserve further discussion. What does Plato mean by them? Does he consistently stick to them in his different comments on definition and its objects?

Plato's acceptance of the first condition is not always clear. Socrates' most familiar refutations of his interlocutors involve counter-examples. He argues that, for instance, Laches' accounts of bravery and Charmides' accounts of bravery do not pick out a property with the right extension (*La.* 191A8-B6; *Ch.* 159B7-161B2). Plato seems to have the same point in mind when he argues, in the middle dialogues, that sensibles are in flux. By 'flux' Plato means not change in particular sensible objects, but the fact that (for instance) a certain type of action changes from being just in some circumstances to being unjust in others.[4] This fact reveals instability in some sensible properties. Repaying what was borrowed is sometimes just and sometimes unjust, so that it (the action type) changes from being just to being unjust. Hence the property of being a repayment of what was borrowed changes from making an action just to failing to make an action just. Since the property of being just always makes an action just, justice cannot undergo

---

3   For full and careful discussions of the argument see S.M. Cohen, 'Socrates on the defini-
    tion of piety' in G. Vlastos, ed., *The Philosophy of Socrates*, Garden City, N.Y: Double-
    day, 1971, chapter 8, from *Journal of the History of Philosophy* 9 (1971) 1-13; R.
    Sharvy, '*Euthyphro* 9d-11b: analysis and definition in Plato and others', *Nous* 6 (1972)
    119-37. Some of the philosophical issues are discussed by W.E. Mann, 'Piety; lending a
    hand to Euthyphro', *Philosophy and Phenomenological Research* 58 (1998) 123-42.
4   This interpretation probably goes back to Alexander, *In Met.* 83.9. See G. Fine, *On Ideas*,
    Oxford: Clarendon Press, 1993, 152f.

the sort of change that is undergone by repaying what was borrowed.[5] The properties that are wrongly identified with justice have the wrong extension. These are 'the many justs' that the sight-lovers of *Republic* 5 identify with justice.

But if a successful answer to the question about definition ('What is the F?') must simply identify a property that is free of flux (and so does not change from being F to not being F), that still does not seem to satisfy the demand in the *Euthyphro*. For Socrates first makes his normal point about counter-examples, and then waives it. The answer 'The pious is what gods love and the impious is what they hate' faces counter-examples, since different gods love and hate different things. But Socrates does not rest content with this objection (*Eu.* 9C-E). He allows, for the sake of argument, that there are some things that all the gods love, and he does not deny that these are all and only the pious things. The *Euthyphro* points out that the predicates 'F' and 'G' do not pick out the same property simply by having the same extension.[6]

The *Euthyphro* does not stand alone in saying that co-extensiveness is not enough for a successful definition. In the *Meno*, Socrates asks for an account of the form of F because of which F things are F (*Meno* 72C6-D1). Meno finds it difficult to provide an account that is even extensionally adequate, and so Socrates says he would be 'content' (ἀγαπᾶν) if Meno could find an account providing a co-extensive property (75B11-C1). He does not concede that such an account would answer the original demand for an explanatory account. The *Phaedo* affirms the same explanatory condition. Plato argues that Forms are 'causes'; a correct account of them must explain the relevant features of things. The beautiful is not the same as the bright coloured, because bright colour is not what makes things beautiful (*Phd.* 101C9-E3).

III

So far, we have found that, in Plato's view (at least sometimes), an adequate definition cannot be merely co-extensive with the definiendum. If the F is properly defined as the G, 'G' must be interchangeable with 'F' in explanatory contexts, those that are introduced by 'because' or 'by' or 'in virtue of'. If x is loved by the gods because it is pious, and the pious is the god-beloved, x must be loved by the

---

[5] This interpretation of the arguments for Forms, and their relation to claims about flux, in the middle dialogues is controversial. I defend it in *Plato's Ethics*, Oxford: Oxford University Press, 1995, ch. 10 (where I do not pay enough attention to the explanatory condition).

[6] I am assuming, without trying to resolve controversial issues, that the things Socrates is looking for (the pious, the just, and the other things mentioned in the 'What is the F?' question) are properties.

gods because it is god-beloved. Since this last claim is false, the pious cannot be the same as the god-beloved.

Socrates' example may be misleading because it contains two expressions that introduce non-extensional contexts. 'Loved' introduces an non-extensional context in the same way as other verbs referring to mental states do. If John loves Chianti, and Chianti is a wine full of rat poison, it does not follow that John loves wine full of rat poison, though it is true of a wine full of rat poison that John loves it. But a second source of a non-extensional context is 'because', which introduces the non-extensionality of explanatory contexts. This second source of non-extensionality is the one that primarily concerns Socrates in this case.

The non-extensionality of explanatory contexts is sometimes contrasted with the extensionality of causal contexts.[7] If a strong earthquake caused devastation in Peru, and the earthquake is the first event reported in *The Times*, then the first event reported in *The Times* caused devastation in Peru. But one might hesitate to say that the first event reported in *The Times* explained the devastation in Peru. At any rate, the first event reported in *The Times* did not explain the devastation by being (in virtue of being; in so far as it was) the first event reported in *The Times*, but by being a very strong earthquake. In such cases 'by', 'in virtue of', and so on introduce the explanatory property, and thereby introduce a non-extensional context.

This explanatory character of a definition is the feature that Socrates seems to identify in claiming that if 'The F is the G' is a correct definition, then things that are F by being F must thereby be F by being G. Euthyphro's proposed definition of the pious fails this test.

In saying that an adequate definition of the F must identify the property that explains an F thing's being F, or the property in virtue of which an F thing is F, we have not made Socrates' demand completely clear. What more can we say about the relation picked out by 'explains', 'because', 'by', 'in virtue of', and similar terms? One thing we can say is that explanation is in some way asymmetrical; in the respect in which being G explains being F, being G is in some way more basic, or more intelligible, than being F. An 'explanation' that appealed to some event or property that is less intelligible than the phenomenon to be explained would not be a real explanation. A genuine explanation should increase our understanding of the phenomenon to be explained in connexion with related phenomena. Whether or not an explanation always involves a law, it should normally connect phenomena that would otherwise appear to be unrelated; discovering the explanation is discovering a respect of genuine similarity.

Even these elementary observations about explanation help us to understand why Plato takes it to be important in the search for definitions. We may take one of his best-known examples. Justice cannot be identified with giving back what you

---

[7] This contrast is partly derived from D. Davidson, *Essays on Actions and Events*, 2nd edn., Oxford: Oxford University Press, 2001, Essays 1, 7.

have borrowed; for this is not the respect that is basically relevant in deciding whether an action would be just, or in seeing what just actions have in common. We can see this by noticing that we can think of circumstances in which it would not be just to return what we have borrowed; in these circumstances the relevant features of justice explain why it would not be just to return our friend's gun if he is threatening to shoot himself.

This example suggests that Plato's references to flux may express a more basic concern with explanatory properties. The fact that a given property changes from being just to being unjust exposes the fact that it does not explain why a given action is just. The same point holds even if the flux is purely counterfactual. We might introduce flux to express Socrates' objection to Euthyphro.

1. If the gods were to love unjust action, unjust action would be pious.
2. But it is impossible for unjust action to be pious.
3. Therefore the god-beloved is sometimes pious and sometimes impious.
4. Therefore it changes from being pious to being impious.
5. Therefore the god-beloved is not the pious.

The third and fourth steps express the facts in (1) and (2), using Plato's terms for flux. But the 'sometimes' in (3) must be taken to include counterfactual as well as actual situations, and hence the 'change' mentioned in (4) is also counterfactual.

Though Plato's emphasis on flux is understandable, it is misleading. To see what type of flux, and in what circumstances, he has in mind, we should take his basic question to be the explanatory question raised in the *Euthyphro*. The explanatory role of Forms underlies their freedom from the kind of flux that Plato has in mind; if we do not attend to this role, we will not look for the relevant kind of flux.

It is difficult to say whether Plato sees that his claims about flux depend on his claims about explanation. If he had offered an example of flux such as the one I have just offered, where the property that is in flux is allowed to be necessarily co-extensive with the property to be defined, we would know for sure that he does not take flux to require actual change from F to not F. As it is, we can only infer that he takes this view of flux from the fact that he does not suggest that the explanatory role of Forms and their freedom from flux lead to different conclusions about Forms. If we are right, the explanatory role is primary.

IV

These questions about Plato are equally relevant to Cudworth's revival of the Euthyphro Argument.[8] The very title of his work, *A Treatise on Eternal and*

---

8   In this paper I pass over relevant mediaeval discussions about morality and divine commands. I have said something about them in 'Socrates and Euthyphro (see n.* above).

Immutable Morality,[9] suggests that he is concerned with Platonic questions about change and stability. His use of these questions in his arguments about morality throws some light on the significance of the Euthyphro Argument.

Cudworth argues that some influential views of the nature of moral principles and moral obligations fail to take proper account of the fact that morality is eternal and immutable. Cudworth attacks two views about moral properties: (1) He rejects the 'positivist' view that identifies morality with the requirements of some positive law.[10] He finds the ancient sources of this view of morality in the philosophers who assert that moral properties rest on convention (νόμῳ) and not on nature (φύσει). He finds this opinion asserted by Protagoras in Plato's *Theaetetus* (167C). Among modern moralists he find the opinion in Hobbes.[11] (2) He believes that his objection to moral positivism applies with equal force to views, inspired by theological voluntarism, that identify morality with the commands of God.[12]

In arguing against both positivism and theological voluntarism Cudworth suggests that Plato's position is more unified than we might have gathered from Plato himself. Plato opposes both accounts of morality, but he does not say that they both make the same mistake. His discussion of the Protagorean position on moral properties is part of a general discussion of Protagoras; he does not describe Protagoras' error in ethics as another instance of the error that he finds in theological voluntarism. Theological voluntarism is his target in the Euthyphro Argument; if, then, the Protagorean position is an instance of the same error, the

---

[9]   *Eternal and Immutable Morality*, ed. S. Hutton, Cambridge: Cambridge University Press, 1996). I cite, as far as possible, by sections in the selection by D.D. Raphael, *British Moralists, 1650-1800*, 2 vols., Oxford: Clarendon Press, 1969 (cited as 'R') or by sections in *British Moralists*, ed. L.A. Selby-Bigge, Oxford: Clarendon Press, 1897 (cited as 'SB').

[10] 'As the vulgar generally look no higher for the original of moral good and evil, just and unjust, than the codes and pandects, the tables and laws of their country and religion; so there have not wanted pretended philosophers in all ages who have asserted nothing to be good and evil, just and unjust, naturally and immutably; but that all these things were positive, arbitrary and factitious only.' (R 119)

[11] He quotes: '... there are no authentical doctrines concerning just and unjust, good and evil, except the laws which are established in every city: and that it concerns none to inquire whether an action shall be reputed just or unjust, good or evil, except such only whom the community have appointed to be the interpreters of their laws.' (*EIM* i 1, p. 8) (Quoted from Hobbes, *De Cive*, Preface §8.)

[12] '... certain it is, that divers modern theologers do not only seriously, but zealously contend in like manner, that there is nothing absolutely, intrinsically and naturally good and evil, just and unjust, antecedently to any positive command or prohibition of God; but that the arbitrary will and pleasure of God (that is, an omnipotent being devoid of all essential and natural justice) by its commands and prohibitions, is the first and only rule and measure thereof.' (R 119).

Euthyphro Argument ought to be applicable to it. Plato does not apply the Euthyphro Argument to Protagoras, but Cudworth applies it.

V

To understand Cudworth's use of the Euthyphro Argument, we should first consider his claims about immutability. Morality is mutable in relation to whatever properties are responsible for changes in something's moral rightness or wrongness. Cudworth, then accepts these two conditionals:

(1) If F-ness is identical to rightness, then if x were to change from being F to being not-F, x would cease to be right. In that case, rightness is mutable in relation to F-ness.

(2) If it is not the case that if x were to change from being F to being not F, x would cease to be right, then F-ness is not identical to rightness. In that case, rightness is not mutable in relation to F-ness.

When Cudworth claims that other theorists make morality mutable, he means that they imply that moral rightness and wrongness are mutable in relation to properties in relation to which they are not in fact mutable.

These claims about the immutability of morality can be expressed in Plato's terms as claims about flux in properties that are wrongly identified with moral properties. If justice is returning deposits, actions would not be just if they were not instances of returning deposits, and hence justice would be mutable in relation to returning deposits. In fact, however, returning deposits is both just and unjust; hence some actions are just even if they are not instances of returning deposits; hence justice is not mutable in relation to returning deposits. Though Cudworth does not contrast the immutability of moral properties (in relation to properties alleged to define them) with the mutability (in relation to the moral properties) of properties alleged to define them, it is easy to express his views by reference to this contrast, and thereby to express them in Platonic terms.

VI

What is the connection between this claim about immutability and Cudworth's appeal to the Euthyphro Argument? It is easy to see why he thinks a positivist view makes morality mutable; he objects that a positivist view implies that morality changes with the provisions of positive law in different places and times. This account of mutability, however, does not work for theological voluntarism, which regards morality as the unchanging commands of an eternal legislator. Why does theological voluntarism not ensure that morality is immutable?

Cudworth answers that such theories ensure only that morality is unchanging, not that it is immutable.[13] The theological voluntarist, no less than the positivist, is committed to the counterfactual claim that if the relevant legislator's command were to change, right and wrong would change too. Cudworth assumes, therefore, that immutability requires freedom from changes in certain counterfactual circumstances, not only in the actual world.

Why must moral properties be free from counterfactual changes? Cudworth's answer shows that the explanatory role of moral properties is primary. He makes this clear in his argument against positivist theories that make right and wrong the products of legislation.[14] In ordinary cases of legislation, legislation alone does not create right and wrong. Legislation is necessary but not sufficient to make it wrong to drive on the right in Britain and on the left in the USA. If it is wrong for me to drive on the left in the USA, then (i) the legislator must have prohibited it, and (ii) it must be right to obey the legislator. The second condition depends on what is right in itself, apart from any legislation. The rightness of obedience cannot itself be the result of legislation or command;[15] for if the legislator commanded us to obey his commands, that second-order command itself would have no moral authority unless it were already right to obey the legislator.[16] The idea of creating moral obligation simply from commands involves a vicious regress.

---

[13] He quotes and criticizes Descartes' attempt to safeguard immutability: '[Descartes:] "I do not think that the essences of things, and those mathematical truths which can be known of them, are independent on God; but I think nevertheless that because God so willed, and so ordered, therefore they are immutable and eternal"; [Cudworth replies] which is plainly to make them in their own nature mutable.' (SB 824)

[14] 'For though it will be objected here, that when God or civil powers command a thing to be done, that was not before obligatory or unlawful, the thing willed or commanded doth forthwith become obligatory; that which ought to be done by creatures and subjects respectively; in which the nature of moral good or evil is commonly conceived to consist. And therefore if all good or evil, just or unjust be not the creatures of will (as many assert) yet at lest positive things must needs owe all their morality, their good and evil to mere will without nature: Yet notwithstanding, if we well consider it, we shall find that even in positive commands themselves, mere will doth not make the thing commanded just or obligatory, but that it is natural justice or equity, which gives to one the right or authority of commanding, and begets in another duty and obligation to obedience.' (R 122)

[15] Command and legislation are different, for reasons brought out in Hart's critique of Austin in *The Concept of Law*, Oxford: Oxford University Press, 1961, chs. 3-6 (which is at several points parallel to Cudworth's critique of Hobbes – not surprisingly, given the Hobbesian character of Austin's view). No unfairness to Hobbes, however, results if we fail to distinguish command from legislation.

[16] 'And if it should be imagined, that any one should make a positive law to require that others should be obliged, or bound to obey him, every one would think such a law ridicu-lous and absurd; for if they were obliged before, then the law would be in vain, and to no purpose; and if they were not before obliged, then they could not be obliged by any

The regress cannot be ended by a command telling people that they are obliged to obey the orders of the commander. Such a command cannot create the obligation to obey it. For anyone can issue commands of this sort, but they are legitimate commands imposing obligation on us only if the commander has the authority to issue them. Hence not all obligation can be entirely the result of commands. The attempt to generate obligation entirely from promises displays the same prospect of a vicious regress.[17] A's promise to B creates an obligation for A not simply because A has made the promise, but because it is already true that we are obliged to keep promises; and similarly B's giving A an order imposes an obligation on A to carry out this particular order only if B is a legitimate commander with the proper authority that A has already recognized independently of being told to recognize it by B.[18] So far from command creating all obligations of morality, it could not create any unless there were some obligations antecedent to any command.

Cudworth can safely concede, therefore, that some aspects of right and wrong are mutable in relation to legislation; for he has shown that these mutable aspects presuppose the existence of immutable rightness and wrongness – more precisely, rightness and wrongness that are immutable in relation to legislation – determining whether or not it is right to obey a legislator or this particular legislator. He has defeated the legislative theorists on their own ground; for if they are to maintain that things can become right by being legislated, they must also concede that some things are non-legislatively right and wrong. A purely legislative theory, therefore, is self-defeating.

Another way to express Cudworth's objection would be to say that he points to an 'open question' arising from Hobbes' account of obligation.[19] To show that something meets Hobbesian sufficient conditions for placing us under a moral obligation is not sufficient to close the question about whether we really are placed

---

positive law, because they were not previously bound to obey such a person's command.' (R 122)

[17] 'As for example, *to keep faith and perform covenants*, is that which natural justice obligeth to absolutely; therefore upon the supposition that any one maketh a promise, which is a voluntary act of his own, to do something which he was not before obliged to by natural justice, upon the intervention of this voluntary act of his own, that indifferent thing promised falling now under something absolutely good, and becoming the matter of promise and covenant, standeth for the present in a new relation to the rational nature of the promiser, and becometh for the time a thing which ought to be done by him, or which he is obliged to do.' (R 123)

[18] 'And that is not the mere will of the commander, that makes these positive things to oblige or become due, but the nature of things; appears evidently from hence, because it is not the volition of every one that obligeth, but of a person rightly qualified and invested with lawful authority.' (R 124)

[19] In speaking of an open question, I intend to suggest a partial analogy between Cudworth's argument and Moore's argument to show that attempted definitions of goodness commit the naturalistic fallacy. I do not mean to suggest that Cudworth's argument is the same as Moore's.

under a moral obligation; the question about whether we are under a moral obligation is still left open, and something beyond Hobbesian considerations is needed to answer it. In the Hobbesian case, it is right to obey a commander only if the commander has a moral right to obedience; this further question is not settled by the fact that the commander issued a command.

Recognition of the open question rests on a claim about explanation. Cudworth argues that if what a legislator commands is right, that is not because it has been commanded, but because it has been commanded by a legislator with the appropriate authority; hence commands do not by themselves explain why an action is right. This diagnosis of the explanatory failure of a positivist account of moral properties applies equally to theological voluntarism. Hence Cudworth relies on the Euthyphro Argument both to refute positivism and to refute theological voluntarism.

The relevance of the Euthyphro Argument is noticed not by Cudworth, but by Clarke in his recapitulation of Cudworth's argument against Hobbes.[20] Clarke quotes the relevant passage of the *Euthyphro* to show what is wrong with Hobbes' claim that the laws of nature are laws because they are commanded by God.[21] Agreeing with Cudworth, he takes positivism (referring to human legislation) and theological voluntarism to make the same mistake. He suggests that the necessary co-extensiveness of what is divinely commanded with what is morally right does not make moral rightness immutable in the right way. He must believe, as Cudworth does, that counterfactual mutability suffices to show that a theological voluntarism makes rightness inappropriately mutable. This counterfactual mutability rests on explanatory inadequacy.

We may try, therefore, to express Cudworth's basic point about immutability as a claim about the explanatory role of moral properties. To claim that moral rightness and wrongness are immutable is to claim that they belong immutably to the nature of things. They are therefore mutable only in relation to the nature of things, not in relation to anyone's judgments or beliefs or desires. To make them mutable in relation to anything other than the nature of things is to make ourselves unable to explain what makes actions right and wrong.

---

[20] Cudworth cites and paraphrases the Euthyphro Argument elsewhere. See C.A. Patrides, ed., *The Cambridge Platonists*, Cambridge, Mass.: Harvard University Press, 1970, 102. (I owe the reference to Terry Penner.) As far as we know, Clarke did not know *Eternal and Immutable Morality* directly (it was not published until 1731).

[21] 'As this law of nature is infinitely superior to all authority of men, and independent on it, so its obligation, primarily and originally, is antecedent also even to this consideration, of its being the positive will or command of God himself... As in matters of sense, the reason why a thing is visible is not because it is seen, but it is therefore seen because it is visible, so in matters of natural reason and morality, that which is holy and good ... is not therefore holy and good because it is commanded to be done, but is therefore commanded of God because it is holy and good.' (Clarke, *Discourse upon Natural Religion*, SB 507.) In a footnote Clarke cites *Euthyphro* 10-11.

Theological voluntarism about moral properties illustrates this issue about mutability and explanation. To say that moral rightness consists in being willed by God is to make it mutable in relation to the will of God. But we can see that it is not mutable in this respect. For if nothing about the nature of things were different, but the will of God were different from what it is, God would will what is wrong rather than what is right. If God were to will injustice and hatred rather than justice and love, and nothing were different about the nature of human beings and their environment, God would will wrong actions rather than right ones. Since we can recognize that what God willed in these conditions would be wrong, we can see that being right does not consist in being willed by God.

This argument retains its force even if it relies on an impossible supposition. The voluntarist may argue that God cannot will otherwise than he wills without the nature of other things being different, because the nature of other things depends on God the creator. But even if this is true, it is still reasonable for Cudworth to ask whether right would be different if God's will were different and the nature of other things were the same. If voluntarists reply that God always wills what is right because the nature of other things depends on God as creator, they must accept Cudworth's basic point about explanation; for they concede that it is the difference in the nature of things that makes different things right, not a difference in the will of God by itself.

Cudworth's objection to Hobbes' claims about the legislator is a special case of this general point about immutability and explanation. Against the claim that a legislator or commander can create, without any prior moral basis that makes him a legitimate authority, rightness and wrongness, Cudworth argues that we can recognize the difference between a command's being backed by overwhelming force and its being morally justified, and that in the first case we do not think it necessarily includes moral obligation. A defender of Hobbes might claim that though we think we see this difference, there really is no difference. To take this view is to reject the intuitive beliefs that make the difference clear to us in the cases that Cudworth describes. From Cudworth's point of view, the Hobbesian position is bound to be mistaken about what makes it right, when it is right, to obey the commands of an authority.

Cudworth's argument, therefore, is powerful, even if it will not appear to decisive to all possible opponents. It appeals to reasonable assumptions about the explanatory character of moral properties, and to reasonable assumptions about the appropriate method for moral theory in relation to metaphysics. It shows that anyone who wants to revise moral theory in a Hobbesian or a theological voluntarist direction must pay a price that is steep enough to raise legitimate questions about whether the assumptions underlying the revision are as plausible as they might at first have seemed. For this reason, his argument is a source of important objections to anti-objectivist views of various types.

VII

Cudworth's argument would be useful, but limited, if it applied only to Hobbes and to theological voluntarism. Sentimentalists, including Shaftesbury, Hutcheson, and Hume, agree in rejecting these views, and propose a 'moral sense' theory as an alternative.[22] Rationalists, especially Burnet, Balguy, and Price, deploy Cudworth's argument to refute sentimentalism. If they succeed, then Cudworth proves more than we might suppose if we simply focused on his criticism of Hobbes.

Balguy recognizes that Hutcheson seeks to avoid one of Cudworth's objections to Hobbes.[23] Hutcheson, no less than Cudworth, rejects the view that morality is simply the product of law, convention, or artifice. Still, Balguy believes that Hutcheson has not gone far enough in rejecting a purely positive conception of morality. According to Hobbes, morality does not accord with human nature in itself, regardless of circumstances, but only accords with human nature in the specific circumstances of the commonwealth. The sentimentalists seek to show that morality has a deeper ground in human nature; they argue that even when circumstances do not make morality beneficial for us (conceiving our benefit in a self-confined sense), we still have a sufficiently strong motive to act morally. In appealing to our actual motives and inclinations, they accept Hobbes' view about what is required to show that something is natural; for they seek to show that we often have a predominant desire to do what is morally right, even apart from any further benefit we gain from it.

Balguy answers this defence of the natural character of morality by arguing that it does not answer the objections that Cudworth raises against Hobbes.[24] For, according to the sentimentalists, what is morally right is right in so far as it appeals to our sympathetic and benevolent feelings. It would change if our feelings changed. To make morality mutable in relation to our feelings is to distort the character of moral principles and our reason for observing them.[25] It implies, for instance, that nothing would be morally right or wrong if we lacked sympathetic feelings, that fewer things would be right and wrong if these feelings were evoked

---

[22] This is at best an over-simplified description of Shaftesbury's position.

[23] 'I am as unwilling, as our author can be, that virtue should be looked upon as wholly artificial. Let it by all means be represented as natural to us; let it take its rise, and flow unalterably from the nature of men and things, and then it will appear not only natural but necessary.' (SB 527)

[24] Balguy does not mention Cudworth, but he is an enthusiastic follower of Clarke. Hence we can safely assume that he is influenced by Clarke's use of Cudworth's argument.

[25] '... it seems an insuperable difficulty in our author's scheme, that virtue appears in it to be of an arbitrary and positive nature; as entirely depending upon instincts, that might originally have been otherwise, or even contrary to what they are now, and may at any time be altered or inverted if the Creator pleases. If our affections constitute the honestum of a morality, and do not presuppose it, it is natural to ask, what it was that determined the Deity to plant in us those affections rather than any other?' (R 438)

less often, and that different things would be right and wrong if the objects of these feelings were different.

This objection to the moral sense assumes that the judgments of the moral sense are, in certain counterfactual conditions at least, corrigible. Questions about corrigibility are raised more directly by Burnet in his objections to Hutcheson's conception of the moral sense. Burnet argues that the pleasure we feel when the moral sense reacts to a person or action is an appropriate basis for moral judgment only if the pleasure is reasonable and appropriate.[26] He implies that there is room for appeal beyond the reactions of the moral sense to further rational reflection. If this is right, the moral sense cannot be the only source of moral judgments. It must be corrigible by reflection on whether it accurately represents the properties it purports to represent. We can ask, as Cudworth points out, whether a commander's order is valid, because we can ask whether the commander has the right to command. Similarly, we can ask whether the moral sense is reliable enough to justify our reliance on it.

Hutcheson argues that corrigibility does not refute his claims about the moral sense, since the very same points about corrigibility apply to the ordinary senses. Hutcheson assumes that sensory properties – colours, sounds, and so on – are not objective properties of external objects, but ideas in the mind of the perceiver who is aware of external objects. The fact that sight is corrigible, he argues, does not show that colours are not essentially the objects of a sense. Hence the corrigibility of the moral sense does not undermine the claim that moral properties are essentially the objects of a sense.[27]

This reply is effective only if the type of corrigibility that Hutcheson attributes to the ordinary senses is the same as the type that Burnet attributes to the moral sense. In correcting a sense we may simply refer to the perceptions of healthy or normal perceivers. This is what we do when we agree that jokes are not really funny if they strike some people, but not most people, as funny; we do not imagine that we are pointing out some feature of the joke that is independent of the reactions of hearers. In this case the person who originally found a joke funny does not necessarily find it any less funny, but simply recognizes that it affects other people differently. This sort of corrigibility raises no difficulty for Hutcheson. He

---

[26] 'The perception of pleasure, therefore, which is the description this author has given of the moral sense, seems to me not to be a certain enough rule to follow. There must be, I should think, something antecedent to justify it and to render it a real good. It must be a reasonable pleasure before it be a right one or fit to be encouraged or listened to.' (Gilbert Burnet, in Hutcheson, *Illustrations on the Moral Sense*, ed. B. Peach, Cambridge, Mass.: Harvard University Press, 1971, 204.)

[27] 'We do not denominate objects from our perceptions during the disorder, but according to our ordinary perceptions, or those of others in good health. Yet nobody imagines that therefore colours, sounds, tastes, are not sensible ideas.' (Hutcheson, *IMS* 163) 'Our reason often corrects the report of our senses about the natural tendency of the external action and corrects rash conclusions about the affections of the agent.' (*IMS* 164)

believes that the secondary qualities accessible to the senses are not objective properties of the external objects at all, and so he must understand the corrigibility of the senses in the way we have understood a sense of humour.

This is not, however, how we normally think of correcting our judgments about colours. We take the 'healthy' perceiver to be not the usual type of perceiver, but the type of perceiver who is best at detecting actual redness (whatever exactly we take this to be). It is quite possible that most people are a little colour-blind to differences between, say, red and green. But if they are, we do not infer that the colours of red and green traffic lights are the same; we defer to the judgments of the people we take to be better at detecting red and green. If this is so, red and green are not objects of the senses alone; we have access to them independently of the senses, and we can use this access to correct the senses.

If we think moral judgments are corrigible in the way our judgments about colour are corrigible, their corrigibility raises a difficulty for Hutcheson. In trying to correct someone's judgment, we are not simply try to align it with the judgment of normal moral judges; we are trying to align it with the judgment of good moral judges, on the assumption that they recognize the relevant properties. If that is so, then moral properties are not essentially what the moral sense says they are.

This argument against Hutcheson does not challenge his claim that we have a moral sense. It grants that we are aware of moral qualities in the way we are aware of sensory qualities, and argues that, even so, we ought not to regard moral goodness as essentially being what is approved by the moral sense. The argument confronts Hutcheson with a dilemma. Either (i) he can give a plausible account of corrigibility and maintain a plausible parallel with the ordinary senses, at the cost of allowing that we have cognitive access to moral properties that exist independently of the moral sense; or (ii) he can maintain his conception of the moral sense as the sole means of cognitive access to moral properties, at the cost of failing to give an adequate account of correction.

The objection to Hutcheson's views on corrigibility, however, does not depend on belief in the objectivity of sensory qualities. If we decide that Hutcheson's conception of sensory qualities is more nearly correct than the one assumed by the objection, then the fact that moral judgments are corrigible in ways that Hutcheson cannot accept constitutes an objection to his belief in a moral sense. In either case, the rationalist seems to have the better of this argument. According to Burnet, we justifiably accept the reactions of our moral sense because we believe, for independent reasons, that it gives us broadly accurate answers. Since we can assess the correctness of our affective reactions by principles that do not seem to depend on our affective reactions, moral approval does not seem to be simply the concern of the moral sense. On the contrary, we can adapt Cudworth's objection to Hobbes, and argue that the moral sense by itself cannot impose an obligation. We can recognize that the moral sense makes our obligations clear to us if we have some reason for believing it to be authoritative (to the appropriate degree); and to discover that, we must appeal to normative judgments outside the moral sense.

VIII

Balguy believes that the argument against Euthyphro can also be used against Hutcheson's attempt to appeal to God in support of his claims about the moral sense. According to Balguy, Hutcheson makes virtue depend on instincts that might have been different, and might be altered at God's pleasure,[28] so that he makes morality mutable in the wrong way. Hutcheson denies this charge; he answers that our moral sense is not mutable, because it reflects the choice of a benevolent creator (*IMS* 136-8).[29]

It is understandable that Hutcheson disavows the position that Cudworth and Clarke criticize in Hobbes. He does not believe that it is simply God's arbitrary will and inclination that makes it right to do what promotes the good of humanity. He agrees in speaking of natural law antecedent to any positive legislation by God or by human legislators. The first principles of natural law are eternal and immutable, and, contrary to Hobbes, natural law imposes obligations even in the state of nature.[30] Nor are they the result of the arbitrary choice of God. God approves of the actions he approves of precisely because they benefit humanity. God is himself benevolent, and approves of benevolence; that is why he makes us care about benevolent action.[31]

Balguy answers that this claim about God does not take Hutcheson far enough away from Euthyphro. We should be able to explain why God is better with these benevolent inclinations than he would be with others. Hutcheson cannot explain this; if God's being good consists in his being approved either by our or by his moral sense, there is nothing further that explains why our or his actual moral sense is better than any other one would be. In Balguy's view, however, there must be a further explanation; this will give us the genuine basis for judgments about moral goodness, independent of any moral sense. In Balguy's view, the argument that leads Hutcheson to disagree with Hobbes ought to have led Hutcheson to reject a moral sense theory too.[32] Since the fact that makes God's laws just is not simply the

---

[28] See n. 25 above.

[29] See R 366, which, however, omits the long footnote that Hutcheson added to the second edition in reply to Balguy.

[30] See Hutcheson, *System of Moral Philosophy*, 2 vols. Glasgow: Foulis, 1755, i 273, 281.

[31] Hutcheson emphasizes benevolence among God's attributes. He argues that we must attribute something like a moral sense to God (*System*, 175).

[32] 'Our author ... has made the following observation, that our first ideas of moral good depend not on laws, may plainly appear from our constant inquiries into the justice of laws themselves; and that not only of human laws, but also of the divine. What else can be the meaning of that universal opinion, that the laws of God are just, and holy, and good? Very right. But I wonder much this sentiment should not have led the author to the true original idea of moral goodness. For after we have made such inquiries, do we find reason to conclude, that any laws are good, merely from their being conformable to the affections of the legislator?' (SB 529)

fact that they correspond to God's moral sense, or to ours, moral goodness or rightness does not consist simply in being approved by the moral sense.

This argument shows that Hutcheson cannot answer the charge of arbitrariness and positivity by appealing to God; he cannot say that the moral sense is reliable because God has given it to us out of his goodness. If God's goodness is simply his having the qualities that his moral sense approves, then the resort to God simply pushes the arbitrariness back a step. If this is not the right account of God's goodness, then the claim that goodness is simply what elicits the approval of the moral sense is mistaken.

Balguy develops this objection by arguing that Hutcheson cannot appeal to God to explain why the moral sense is uniform. We might think we can answer the objection about the variability of the moral sense by arguing that God communicates his moral sense to us.[33] But why, Balguy asks, does God do this? If we claim God necessarily communicates his moral sense to us, then we deny divine freedom; but if he does not do this necessarily, we make the moral sense objectionably mutable and we make God's choice arbitrary.

We might wonder why the same objection does not arise to Balguy's own view. He does not believe it is possible, given the nature of God, for God to approve of what is evil. Must he not, then, also agree that God necessarily communicates his moral sense to us? If Hutcheson's position implies the denial of divine freedom, must Balguy's position not imply it too?

To answer this counter-attack on behalf of Hutcheson, Balguy needs to say that God's recognizing a truth independent of his will does not limit his freedom. Given the nature of God, he has every reason to choose freely to act according to true principles of right. But if he is necessitated, because of a fact about his nature independent of his judgments of truth and right, then he is not free. It would not help Hutcheson to answer this point by claiming that God is free not to communicate his moral sense to us. For then Balguy might reasonably ask why God chooses to communicate his moral sense to us. The answer cannot be that God sees that this is the right thing to do, since what is right (according to Hutcheson) is simply what is approved by the moral sense. It must, then, be an arbitrary choice by God.

If this argument is fair, it confirms Balguy's objection that Hutcheson does not really escape Cudworth's and Clarke's criticisms of Hobbes. Appealing to the divine moral sense rather than to divine commands does not explain why God deserves to be obeyed, or why the moral sense he has given us deserves to be followed. In so far as these are reasonable questions to ask about moral principles and about a moral sense, Hobbes and Hutcheson are wrong; they fail even to

---

[33]   'But will not that disposition, and that principle in the Deity, which are supposed to correspond to our natural affections, and moral sense, certainly induce him universally to communicate and continue the same sense to all rational agents?' (*Foundations of Moral Goodness*, ii 21 = *Tracts, Moral and Theological*, London, 1734, 163.)

recognize the legitimacy of questions that we recognize as legitimate. They speak as though certain questions (Why should we obey God's commands? Why should we listen to the moral sense?) were closed that seem to us to be open. Balguy argues that, since these questions seem to be open, we must reject both Hobbesian and sentimentalist theories.

On the ground that he has chosen, Balguy's objections are powerful. They are especially powerful against Hutcheson, since Hutcheson speaks as though he accepts the rationalist criticisms of Hobbes' positivism. If he is to answer Balguy, Hutcheson needs to disavow some of the intuitive judgments that underlie objections to Hobbes. Balguy assumes that moral properties cannot be arbitrary or mutable in certain ways, because we can give a further reason, in the nature of the properties themselves, for judging the moral sense to be right or wrong.

IX

Price follows Balguy in believing that Cudworth's claim that morality is eternal and immutable rules out Hutcheson's moral sense theory.[34] Hutcheson's view implies, given Hutcheson's conception of a sense and its objects, that moral properties are mutable in relation to the reactions of observers.[35] To show that this is the wrong kind of mutability, Price maintains that moral properties really belong to actions in themselves, not simply to our reactions to them.[36]

---

[34] See Price, *A Review of the Principal Questions in Morals*, ed. D.D. Raphael, 2nd edn, Oxford: Oxford University Press, 1974.

[35] 'For the term *sense*, which he applies to it, from the rejection of all the arguments that have been used to prove it to be an intellectual power, and from the whole of his language on this subject; it is evident, he considered it as the effect of a positive constitution of our minds, or as an implanted and arbitrary principle by which a relish is given us for certain moral objects and forms and aversion to others, similar to the relishes and aversions created by any of our other senses.' (*Review*, 14). 'Virtue (as those who embrace this scheme say) is an affair of taste. Moral right and wrong, signify nothing in the objects themselves to which they are applied, any more an agreeable and harsh; sweet and bitter; pleasant and painful; but only certain effects in us.' (15)

[36] 'Or is it no determination of judgment at all, but a species of mental taste? Are not such actions really right? Or is every apprehension of rectitude in them false and delusive, just as the like apprehension is concerning the effects of external and internal sensation, when taken to belong to the causes producing them?' (45) 'How strange would it be to maintain, that there is no possibility of mistaking with respect to right and wrong; that the apprehensions of all beings, on this subject, are alike just, since all sensation must be alike true sensation? Is there a greater absurdity, than to suppose, that the moral rectitude of an action is nothing absolute and unvarying; but capable, like all the modifications of pleasure and pain, of being intended and remitted, of increasing and lessening, or rising and sinking with the force and liveliness of our feelings?' (47)

Some of Price's arguments turn on questions about corrigibility that we have already discussed. He adds an argument about the non-optional character of moral judgments, to show that rejection of objectivism implies the wrong sort of mutability. In his view, rejection of objectivism commits us to the view that all actions are indifferent in their own right.[37] If we accept this view, then we have no reason not to alter our reactions so that we do not care about doing what we at present take to be right.[38] Rejection of objective right and wrong removes our reason for resisting any anti-moral tendencies.

Anti-objectivists might resist this effort by Price to blacken them as enemies of morality. Hutcheson recognizes that our moral reactions have a non-optional character that is inconsistent with the view that we are simply aiming at pleasure and the absence of pain.[39] We do not take the attitude to our moral reactions that we might take to feelings of pain that we would rather get rid of. Hutcheson can therefore answer Price by pointing out that our moral outlook itself treats our moral judgments as having the non-optional character that Price seeks to trace to an objectivist conception of them. If this is right, then we need not believe in objective moral properties in order to treat our moral judgments as non-optional.

Price, however, might reasonably be dissatisfied with this reply on behalf of Hutcheson. The moral sense theorist can show that it is psychologically possible to regard our moral judgments as non-optional. But this proof (if we concede it) of psychological possibility does not capture the reason we think we have for regarding our judgments as non-optional. Price points out that sometimes we regard our judgment as non-optional because it is constrained by the nature of the things we are making the judgment about.[40] A psychological explanation of why we regard judgments about triangles as non-optional would miss the point; for we regard the non-optional character of the judgment as the result of a fact about triangles. Price argues that in the same way we regard the non-optional character of our moral

---

[37] ' ... if no actions are, in themselves, either right or wrong, or any thing of a moral and obligatory nature, which can be an object to the understanding; it follows that, in themselves, they are all indifferent. This is what is essentially true of them, and this is what all understandings, that perceive right, must perceive them to be.' (48)

[38] 'If this is judging truly; how obvious is it to infer, that it signifies not what we do; and that the determination to think otherwise, is an imposition upon rational creatures? Why then should they not labour to suppress in themselves this determination, and to extirpate from their natures all the delusive ideas of morality, worth, and virtue? What though the ruin of the world should follow? There would be nothing really wrong in this.' (48)

[39] 'If our sole intention, in compassion or pity, was the removal of our pain, we should run away, shut our eyes, divert our thoughts from the miserable object, to avoid the pain of compassion, which we seldom do: nay, we crowd about such objects, and voluntarily expose ourselves to pain ....' (SB 104)

[40] 'Whatever any thing is, that it is, not by will, or decree, or power, but by nature and necessity. Whatever a triangle or circle is, that it is unchangeably and eternally. It depends upon no will or power, whether the three angles of a triangle and two right ones shall be equal ...' (50)

judgments as the result of facts about right and wrong actions themselves. Changing our moral judgments at will would be misguided because it would lead us away from being guided by the facts about the actions. The moral sense theorist's explanation gets things the wrong way round.

Even if we allow that Price has over-simplified some aspects of his opponents' position, his criticism seems quite cogent. Hutcheson certainly does not believe that the moral sense is purely arbitrary, or that it detects no genuine feature of actions. He believes that it responds to benevolence; to this extent it is guided by objective properties of actions. Still, he fails to satisfy a condition that Price imposes on an adequate account of moral judgment; he not does explain why the moral sense focuses on benevolence. One might reply that benevolence is the quality that really deserves approval, but Price points out that this reply is not open to Hutcheson, who cannot say that any quality of the action itself is the one that really deserves approval.

X

This continuous pattern of argument from Cudworth to Price shows both that the Euthyphro Argument has significantly influenced the development of meta-ethical discussion in modern philosophy, and – more important – that it raises some fundamental questions about conditions of adequacy for an account of moral properties. I have tried to expound the later applications of the Euthyphro Argument sympathetically, to suggest that they present powerful objections to positivism, voluntarism, and sentimentalism. I have left to one side some further issues. I have not, for instance, fully examined possible replies, on behalf of Hobbes or Hutcheson, to criticisms based on the Euthyphro Argument, and so I have not tried to decide how conclusive a case Cudworth and his successors have constructed. Nor have I considered what accounts of moral properties might satisfy the explanatory constraints imposed by the Euthyphro Argument, or whether these are reasonable accounts. Still, the very fact that the Euthyphro Argument raises these further issues is further evidence of its historical and philosophical significance.

Chapter Three

Quality of Life in Plato and Aristotle*

Günther Patzig

It may be thought that it is somewhat anachronistic to use the expression 'Quality of Life' in connection with ancient Greek philosophical theories. The concept of 'Quality of Life', in German 'Lebensqualität', is used vaguely and in different senses. It is just this vagueness that made me think of going back to Plato and Aristotle when, over the last years, I got involved in the debate on questions of medical ethics and bioethics in my country. I thought that Plato and Aristotle might bring some light, perspective, and clarity into the current discussion.

In Germany 'Quality of Life' became a catchword in the early seventies, when Willy Brandt liked to draw a distinction between private affluence and so-called 'public poverty'. Quality of Life, he urged, meant more than just a high standard of living for individual people; it implied equality of chances, especially in education, participation and codetermination in the factory or office, preservation of the natural environment and a policy intent on securing world-peace.

On the other hand, talk of 'Quality of Life' in medical ethics, becoming more frequent in the same period, was concerned rather with *individual* interests and perspectives: fast progress in medical diagnosis and therapy made the question urgent whether the goal of prolongation of human life should be set off against the quality of such life for the patient in the subjective perspective of patients. This approach was well in tune with the attempts to reduce the strong element of paternalism in the traditional relation of doctor and patient, to establish a model of doctor and patient as partners, and to give the patient an important role in the decision process concerning the suitable therapy.

In the discussions of doctors and experts of medical ethics, it has turned out to be difficult to define criteria of 'Quality of Life' which might combine in a

* The author and editor thank the publishers Vandenhoeck & Ruprecht and Th. v. Wallmoden (Wallstein-Verlag), both in Göttingen, for permission to publish here in English a revised version of texts originally published in G. Seifert: *Lebensqualität in unserer Zeit* (Veröffentlichungen der Joachim-Jungius Gesellschaft der Wissenschaften Hamburg, Nr. 69), Vandenhoeck & Ruprecht, Göttingen 1992, 33-46, and in G. Patzig, *Gesammelte Schriften III, Aufsätze zur antiken Philosophie*, Wallstein-Verlag, Göttingen 1996, 230-50.

reasonable way objective medical assessments of the present condition and the future condition of the patient after the intended therapeutic measures, e.g. operations or chemotherapy, with the subjective situation of the patient and his value-preferences. We have at present no basis yet for a reliable assessment of 'Quality of Life' which could serve as a practical guide for doctors in more complex situations. Because 'Quality of Life' in this way seems to be a vague and ambiguous concept, some experts have advised us to drop this concept from serious discussion altogether; I think, however, that we cannot do without this concept, at least not for our first orientation in this field. The lack of focus we find in the concept mirrors only the complexity of the problems which we are confronted with in this new field of enquiry.

The modern concept of 'Quality of Life', in its political and medical application, seems to be associated with a certain demanding attitude, in German 'Anspruchshaltung'. The World Health Organization defined, in 1947, health as 'a state of complete physical, mental and social well-being'. It has been rightly criticized for the definition of what should be regarded as *normal* by reference to the *optimal*. 'Quality of Life' is often defined by reference to such an optimum as a measure of approximation to this limit. But it is clear that people can more or less successfully integrate handicaps and even some degree of suffering into their daily life and in this way can have a satisfactory or even contented sort of existence.

It is obviously difficult to make this important factor operational for the devising of test-batteries for measuring 'Quality of Life' in a reliable way.

Neither the subjective variability nor the demanding attitude which are connected with the concept of 'Quality of Life' today are prominent in the *philosophical* discussions concerning the good life. Such well-being is rather regarded as an objective goal, which demands constant endeavour and concentration. To reach this goal may be not in everybody's capacity, though it might be possible in principle.

If one looks for relevant arguments in the history of philosophy, it is very natural to turn to those traditions in philosophical ethics that are regarded as 'eudaimonistic'. That means mainly, if not exclusively, the ethics of the Greeks and modern Utilitarianism. Only there are the moral norms regarded as necessary and in some cases sufficient for the achievement of εὐδαιμονία (whatever that may be). And only there are moral norms justified by this means-end relation. In other ethical theories we find no such strong connection between moral norms and human well-being. Christian moral philosophy, especially in its medieval forms, did not emphasize the connection of Christian virtues and well-being in this world; Kant's deontological ethics was strictly against the 'Schlangenwindungen der Glückseligkeitslehre' ('contortions of the ethics of happiness'). And Hegel's contempt for individual, normal, bourgeois happiness is even more notorious.

Let us then look at the classical concepts of what might be called 'flourishing human life' in Plato (no doubt strongly influenced by Socrates) and in Aristotle.

Plato, in the conceptual frame of his Two-World-Theory of corruptible empirical things on the one hand and eternal ideas on the other, has no difficulty in formulating rules of behaviour for human beings, which take care of their, as he customarily says, true or real interests. Man's body belongs to the transient world of empirical things, the soul is akin to the world of ideas and therefore immortal. To suffer injustice damages only our body, may endanger our corporeal life, but to act unjustly damages the soul. What is health to the body, that is justice to the soul. In book 4 of the *Republic*, Plato develops the famous analogy between the three different classes in his state (Tradesmen, Auxiliaries and Rulers) and the three different parts of the soul (roughly the centre of desires, the centre of decisions and the centre of deliberation).[1] With the help of this analogy Plato can represent justice in the individual as harmony of the parts of the soul, comparable to the concord of the classes in the state. So justice, being harmony, is again health of the soul, therefore, it is in everybody's interest to be just. This argument contains obvious gaps, logical weaknesses and implausible premises. But for our present purposes, we are more interested in Plato's obvious intention to make moral standards of behaviour attractive as something which it is in the true interest of individuals to observe.

That this is against common sense, was obvious to Plato, and in many of his dialogues he attacks the view that pleasure could be the ultimate goal of human action. In the early *Protagoras* Socrates develops a theory of rational life-planning which takes the pleasure-principle quite seriously: the art of living consists in reaching a clever balance of pleasure and pain, considering their relative intensity and their remote effects and side effects.[2]

That was one possible interpretation of Socrates' dictum 'Virtue is Knowledge'. But even here Plato recedes from popular hedonism by introducing *moral* emotions into this evaluation: brave soldiers accept dangers gladly, because they think disgrace is more painful than death. In the – later – dialogues *Gorgias*, *Phaedo*, *Republic* and *Philebus* Plato becomes a relentless fighter against the pleasure-principle, with often quite unfair arguments. At the end he accepts only a small group of harmless pleasures: looking at beautiful geometrical forms, pure colours, listening to harmonious melodies (not exciting ones) and reflecting on scientific theorems.[3] All other, more intense, pleasures are seriously problematic, because they may be impure, mixed with pain, or because they are intrinsically deceptive, e.g. pleasure on account of an information which may turn out to be untrue.

In the *Timaeus* we find the thought carried to the extreme that the end of human life and the only real happiness exists in adjusting the movements of our soul to the cosmic reason, the effects of which we can perceive in the ordered movements of the heavenly bodies. Plato sees the main function of our faculty of vision and the end in view of which it was implanted, in the observation of the celestial sphere and the progression of the stars and planets. For from these observations we form ideas of number and time and develop an inclination to investigate the universe: from this

---

[1]   Plato, *Rep.* 4 434d-445e.
[2]   Plato, *Prot.* 351d-357e.
[3]   Plato, *Phil.* 51a-53d.

contemplation of the universe came all philosophy 'than which no greater boon has ever come or shall come to mortal man as a gift from heaven'.[4]

The sense of hearing, also, has been given to man mainly to enable him to receive instruction in philosophy or science; another important gain is the therapeutic and moderating effect of the right kind of music on our souls. Plato does not forget to add, as you will expect, that the music which was popular at his time, could not have these good effects, since it was concerned solely with 'irrational pleasure', 'Rock and Pop', in fact. We hear nothing about the vital importance seeing and hearing have for the satisfaction of our basic needs, for finding food, for avoiding dangers and for human communication in general. With some contempt, Plato speaks of the 'trivial comforts of sight, the loss of which a non-philosopher would lament with idle moan'.[5]

Plato shows a similar severity when discussing a question which is, I think, quite comparable to our modern discussion concerning quality of life: the problem is whether extension of life by medical measures is desirable in cases of marked reduction of capabilities.

Nobody, Plato declares in the third book of the *Republic*,[6] can have a life worth living, who suffers from an invalidating illness. His example is that of a carpenter who has a chronic illness such that he cannot continue with his work. It would make no sense for him to prolong, with the help of doctors, his life which could be only a 'protracted dying'. Much better for him to die immediately and be free of all his cares. Living without his usual work would not be worth while for him. Plato represents this as the reasonable view for the carpenter *himself*. The point is not, as Karl Popper[7] and others have maintained, to relieve society of members who cannot contribute any more to the common good, which would bring Plato near to the terrible German version of euthanasia, propagated by Binding and Hoche in 1920,[8] and practised by the National-Socialist government from 1940 until the end of the war. But neither is Plato interested, as we would like him to be, to leave the decision, whether he wants to continue living or not, to the *person concerned*. Plato expresses the view that from an objective point of view such a life has no value for the person concerned – no matter what the person concerned may think. The carpenter who rejects medication and leaves it to destiny whether he will spontaneously recover or die in due course is, for Plato, absolutely right. If he decided differently, he would be *wrong*. Plato thinks doctors are justified, even under an obligation, to stop treatment in cases in which the prolongation of life is 'neither in

---

4   Plato, *Tim.* 47ab.
5   Plato, *Tim.* 47b.
6   Plato, *Rep.* 3 406be.
7   K.R. Popper, *The Open Society and its Enemies*, Vol. I, *Plato*, London: Routledge (1945) [4]1962, 138f.
8   K. Binding and A. Hoche, *Die Freigabe der Vernichtung lebenswerten Lebens*, Leipzig: (1920) [2]1922.

the interest of the patient nor the community'.[9] Plato thinks the value continued life would have *for the patient* should be the main factor in the decision to continue or discontinue therapy for a given patient, which is plausible. But he also believes that one can decide here according to objective criteria, and that this decision could be made by a third person, e.g. a doctor, even against the wishes of the patient, which is not acceptable.

Let me take this opportunity to discuss very shortly a fundamental confusion about the concept of the 'Value of Life' which hampers the current discussion, at least in my own country, and especially the debate on Peter Singer's book *Practical Ethics*.[10] Many people think we should, in order to radically discourage notions of a 'life not worth living' (German: 'lebensunwertes Leben') in the sense of Binding and Hoche,[11] not even tolerate the idea that there may be *differences in value* between the life of different persons. The value of every human life should be regarded as infinite.

This view seems to me entirely unrealistic: it is, I think, obvious that for the person whose life it is, for some of his companions or relations, or for the community in general, the life of an individual can be of greater or lesser value. But these differences in value must be entirely irrelevant for the question e.g. whether we should try to save an endangered life. Here only the subjective assessment of the person concerned matters. If the person concerned cannot (not yet, no more or not at all) make his wishes known, doctors and relatives must try to decide as he most likely would himself decide. It is not their own idea about how they would feel, were they in his place, nor considerations of social costs which can be of importance. This is, in most respects, also the view of Singer; but in the case of severely handicapped new-born children Singer admits that the interests of the parents and the eventual financial burdens for the community might as well be of importance for the decision to let the baby live or die. This last suggestion I would reject.

Coming from Plato to Aristotle, we find that Aristotle's views about what might be called 'Quality of Life' are more realistic or, at least, nearer to our own views on this topic. Perhaps I am, in saying so, still a bit too dogmatic. Maybe I should just say that I personally feel more at home with Aristotle's approach than with Plato's attitude.

Aristotle has written three books on ethics. One of them, the *Nicomachean Ethics*, is undoubtedly authentic; the second, the *Eudemian Ethics*, was formerly suspect, but is nowadays almost universally regarded as genuine; the third, the shortest, paradoxically called *Magna Moralia*, of very doubtful origin, but containing at least in part Aristotelian teaching. In all of them, the concept of εὐδαιμονια plays a central role. This is the nearest we come in Greek philosophy to 'Quality of Life'. Ethics, for Aristotle, is the branch of philosophy which shows how we can

---

[9] Plato, *Rep.* III, 407e.
[10] P. Singer, *Practical Ethics*, Cambridge: Cambridge University Press, 1980.
[11] Above, n.8.

reach εὐδαιμονία and how to preserve this state once it is reached. εὐδαιμονία is a state in which all true needs and desires of a human being are fulfilled. It is a state which could not be made more perfect by an addition of further positive elements. At the beginning of the *Nicomachean Ethics*,[12] Aristotle regards it as obvious that all men see in εὐδαιμονία the highest possible good. It is, in fact, analytic: we call εὐδαιμονία what we think the very best we can reach out for. εὐδαιμονία is identical with εὖ ζῆν ('the good life') or εὖ πράττειν ('being well'). But opinions differ widely, what *kind* of life would give content to this formula.

We see from this that Aristotle does not pay any attention to the original meaning of εὐδαιμονία in Greek. Originally it means a situation in which a man receives favour from a divine power (his personal, or any other, δαίμων). The expression εὐδαιμονία was, already in Aristotle's time, secularized, as the explanation by 'flourishing life' or 'well-being' shows. Accordingly, Aristotle turns to current notions when looking for possible candidates for the role of εὐδαιμονία: popular favourites are pleasure, wealth and τιμή ('honour', today we would prefer to say 'social acceptance' or 'recognition'). The attitudes of people are, as Aristotle remarks, influenced by their actual situation: the sick think health the highest good, the poor wealth.[13]

These three candidates are then examined and found wanting: pleasure is something we share with the animals, therefore it cannot be the highest goal for man; social recognition depends not mainly upon ourselves but more on others, and is, therefore, unstable. Recognition is, further, welcome just because it strengthens our believe in our own ἀρετή (virtue or moral excellence), but, if so, virtue will be the real end. In this case, however, a man could be εὐδαίμων who lives without doing anything, but with high moral standards intact; or a good man who was persecuted by ill fortune, which would be absurd. Wealth likewise fails as a candidate because it is valuable as means to ends, which ends must then rank higher than wealth.

Aristotle's next step is to introduce a criterion for the highest good for man by making use of the concept of *function*. If all occupations as that of a flute-player or sculptor have their specific task and function, it seems reasonable to look for the function or task of humans as such. Man is the only living being that can think and act rationally. Therefore, his special task or function is the development and application of this singular faculty, and human life flourishes in the expression of this natural disposition, which might be truly called 'self-realization'. (This is, by the way, about the only sense of the term 'self-realization' I can easily understand.)

Aristotle, according to some critics, has committed here a fallacy of the 'is-ought'-type: from the *fact* that man is unique among the animals in having speech and reason, it does not follow that he is *obliged* to live according to reason. But we have here, it seems, the much less vulnerable assertion that actualization of

---

[12] Aristotle, *Nic. Eth.* 1 1095a10-20.
[13] Aristotle, *Nic. Eth.* 1 1095a22-5.

a disposition which is characteristic for a species or an individual may give them a special satisfaction.

Since the human soul is, according to Aristotle, the seat of reason or λόγος, he defines εὐδαιμονία as follows: 'The highest goal for man turns out to be the activity of the soul in accordance with (its specific) excellence.'[14] Aristotle adds immediately that there may be more than one such excellence, and that in such a case 'the best and most perfect excellence should be relevant here'. This is clearly a reference to a thesis which has been prepared already by the mention of *vita contemplativa* in 1 1096a4-5, and will be given full expression in the tenth book of the *Nicomachean Ethics*: human εὐδαιμονία consists in undisturbed intellectual activity, theoretical contemplation. This is, or at least seems to be, in contrast with many passages in all the other books of the Nicomachean Ethics according to which the active life, successful actualization of *practical* reason (φρόνησις), is a way or even *the* way to reach εὐδαιμονία. I shall later on say something on this much-discussed tension or even inconsistency in the Aristotelian theory of the good life.

This state of activity of the soul according to its appropriate excellence is not an elated feeling lasting possibly just for a moment; for 'one swallow does not make springtime nor a single sunny day.'[15] A short span of time is not sufficient for εὐδαιμονία, rather a full lifetime is required. No one can be εὐδαίμων, says Aristotle, just by himself: man is a social being; therefore his εὐδαιμονία is bound up in various ways with that of other persons: his parents, children, spouses, friends and fellow-citizens, not, however, beyond a reasonable limit.

We see from this, among other things, that Aristotle's εὐδαιμονία is not a subjective state, a special feeling, as the traditional translation 'happiness' or, in German, 'Glückseligkeit' might suggest. Quality of Life is something which can be assessed objectively, and is so assessed by others. It is part of the concept of εὐδαιμονία that a person who may be judged really to flourish should have good reasons to believe that this state will last into the future. These good reasons cannot, of course, human affairs being what they are, constitute a *guarantee* that the good life will last. 'There are many reversals and all kinds of chance in life, and even the most prosperous may fall into great misfortunes in old age, as we are told of Priam in the Trojan Cycle; and no one would call flourishing the life of a man who has experienced such chances and has perished miserably.'[16]

Shall we then, with Solon, say that only those may be called 'happy' who have already died with their εὐδαιμονία intact – 'all's well that ends well'? That would be, for Aristotle, unacceptable, since εὐδαιμονία is, as we have seen, *activity*, and equivalent to εὖ ζῆν, flourishing *life*. If Solon and Aristotle were both right, the living could *not yet* be happy, the dead *no more*; so reliable εὐδαιμονία would be

---

[14] Aristotle, *Nic. Eth.* 1 1098a15-16: τὸ ἀνθρώπινον ἀγαθὸν ψυχῆς ἐνέργεια γίνεται κατ' ἀρετήν.

[15] Aristotle, *Nic. Eth.* 1 1098a18-20.

[16] Aristotle, *Nic. Eth.* 1 1100a5-9.

nonexistent. Aristotle insists that there is such εὐδαιμονία, but with the fragility we find in all human affairs. εὐδαιμονία which is founded on moral excellence is the most stable form of happiness we know, because its main element, virtue, is something like a second nature, durable and reliable. The good man can cope much better with blows of ill fortune, as the competent general will achieve even with battered troops more than his incompetent colleague with fresh forces would.[17]

Referring to Solon's counsel to call nobody happy before he died,[18] Aristotle discusses a question strange at first sight: can people who have died, nevertheless be affected in their happiness subsequently? That might e.g. be the case if hopes they had for their children come to nothing, or projects they have lived for fail utterly. To this question Aristotle gives an answer which is again, on first sight, strange: a gradual one, where we would expect a general one: one should not think that the dead oscillate between happiness and the opposite state under the impact of events. But what happens e.g. to the immediate descendants could not be irrelevant to the happiness of the parents.[19]

Does Aristotle, then, believe in an afterlife of the individual person? All evidence would be against this. The air of paradox dissolves if we remember that according to Aristotle εὐδαιμονία is a state based on *objective* foundations, the presence of which may be ascertained by impartial observers. If the εὐδαιμονία of a person implies, in some measure, the εὐδαιμονία of his or her relatives, and if it also implies the reasonable expectation that the favourable conditions will continue, a witness observing the ruin of a family's prosperity may come to the conclusion that the confidence, necessary for the deceased person's εὐδαιμονία, was ill-founded already during his lifetime. I suppose that Aristotle has been stimulated in his considerations by Plato's detailed analysis of 'false pleasures' in the *Philebus*.[20]

Aristotle differs from Plato in accepting external goods, in some measure, as necessary conditions for εὐδαιμονία. 'It is impossible or at least difficult to act nobly without the necessary equipment. For in many actions we use friends and money or political influence as instruments and the lack of some things makes human happiness paltry, as good birth, good children and good looks.'[21]

Aristotle is also, much more so than Plato, convinced that a share of pleasure is indispensable for the good life. He criticizes philosophers, such as Socrates, who thought that one could be happy even under torture, if only one was morally righteous.[22]

---

[17]   Aristotle, *Nic. Eth.* 1 1100b35-1101a6.

[18]   Aristotle, *Nic. Eth.* 1 1100a10-18, *Eud. Eth.* 2.1 1219b6-8.

[19]   Aristotle, *Nic. Eth.* 1 1100a18-30.

[20]   Cf. J. Cooper, *Reason and Human Good in Aristotle*, Cambridge: Cambridge University Press, 1975, 89f. and 168-80, and D. Frede, 'Rumpelstiltskin's Pleasures', *Phronesis* 30 (1985) 151ff.

[21]   Aristotle, *Nic. Eth.* 1 1099a32-b6. Similar lists of goods: *Eud. Eth.* 8.3 1248b 27-30, *Rhet.* 1.5 1360b19-1362a14.

[22]   Aristotle, *Nic. Eth.* 7 1153b19-21.

These concessions of Aristotle, that external goods and pleasure are indispensable for the flourishing life, may seem to imply that they are *the elements* of this life or among the elements of it. In this view, Aristotle would be not far from the modern attempts to build up 'Quality of Life' as a sum total from different elements from different dimensions, to be gathered from questionnaires and test-batteries. That would be mistaken: for Aristotle, external goods are *instruments* which men need for leading a good life and not elements of it, and pleasure is, according to Aristotle's teaching,[23] which I think philosophically relevant even today, not a *goal* of human action but a side-effect of successful natural activities.

The basis of εὐδαιμονία remains the activity of soul in accordance with its appropriate excellence or, in more old-fashioned terms, the exercise of virtue. Let us recollect shortly what that amounts to: there are two kinds of excellence or virtue of the soul: moral and intellectual.[24] Moral virtues are concerned with a mean (μεσότης) in the choice of actions.[25] This has been misunderstood such that our *actions* should be somehow moderate: give not too much nor too little for charity; accept reasonable dangers in war etc. That sounds rather like well-tempered comfortableness, the 'aurea mediocritas' of Horace.[26]

But Aristotle has in mind something entirely different: from repeated right action we develop by habit a stable disposition (ἕξις) towards our emotions, which shapes these emotions and enables us to act appropriately in (almost) all situations. In this way, we can develop a quiet self-confidence, free from arrogance and humility, a realistic attitude towards dangers, equally different from timidity and bravado, and a mature sexual orientation: neither repression by the super-Ego, nor domination by the Id, but expression of the Ego. (I think in fact that Freud's theory is, in this respect, near enough to Aristotle's.)

Aristotle's model of moral development presumes that we are able, partly by education, partly by our own exertions, to get used to actions such as practical reason would recommend. This habituation will change, gradually, our emotional constitution. We later on take pleasure in doing what initially we manage to do only with difficulty. Kant has special admiration for the person who acts according to the moral law against strong inclinations to act otherwise. Aristotle prefers the person to whom correct action has become second nature, who actually enjoys doing the right thing. In this controversy, if it is one, I would rather opt for Aristotle's side. And here we have another reason why Aristotle thinks moral activity is closely bound up with εὐδαιμονία.

But, as I have remarked already, there is a tension in Aristotle's text. In most books of the *Nicomachean Ethics* εὐδαιμονία seems to be the actualization of all the virtues, such that each virtue requires all the others for perfect development. In the

---

[23] Aristotle, *Nic. Eth.* 10.1-5.
[24] Aristotle, *Nic. Eth.* 2 1103a14-25.
[25] Aristotle, *Nic. Eth.* 2 1106b14-1107a6.
[26] Hor. *Od.* 2, 10.5.

tenth book, however, when Aristotle in chapter 6 takes up again the discussion of εὐδαιμονία, he introduces an entirely new line of thought: if reason (νοῦς) is either itself divine or only the most divine element in us, *the acting of reason according to its specific excellence will be perfect εὐδαιμονία.*[27] Aristotle offers arguments why contemplation is better than all other activities: it is the best, because its objects are the most valuable, it is especially pleasant (for philosophers); it is self-sufficient, because for the exercise of all the other virtues we need partners, but we can think by ourselves; and it is loved for its own sake, not for any results we may derive from it. So we have a clear ranking in the field of εὐδαιμονία: 'For man, then, the life according to reason is best and most pleasant, since reason is man more than anything else. It is therefore also the happiest life (εὐδαιμονέστατος). The second rank must go to the life according to the other kind of virtue (κατὰ τὴν ἄλλην ἀρετήν).'[28]

Dirlmeier, in his commentary,[29] has tried to play down the 'second rank' (δευτέρως): it does not, he says, express a ranking, a difference *in value,* but greater or lesser affinity to God, who is himself pure reason. But this does not really help us in the face of the clash between books 1 and 10 of our text.

Another, clear cut and more plausible, solution comes from John Cooper in his excellent book *Reason and Human Good in Aristotle.*[30] In our passage from book 10 Aristotle describes, according to Cooper, a special εὐδαιμονία reserved for philosophers, who are on this account excused, too, if they will not join in the rough and tumble of economic and political πρᾶξις. (Most philosophers, in their weaker moments, have in fact, I think, a tendency to think that only philosophers can lead a life that is truly human! I must confess I belong to this majority.)

But John Cooper has, over time, changed his position: in his later 'Reconsiderations' from 1987[31] he characterizes his old view: 'If Aristotle had been intending eventually to prevent two separate life ideals, – a less ideal but more widely suitable life devoted largely to moral virtue, and a more ideal contemplative life suited only for philosophers and not involving common morality at all –, surely he ought to have made this clear in a preliminary way already in the first book and to have presupposed it at many places as he proceeded through the intervening discussion.'

Cooper revises this position of his 1975 book by harmonizing these two Aristotelian positions: if Aristotle says[32] 'The good for man turns out to be activity of the soul in accordance with excellence, and if there are more than one virtue, then in accordance with the best and most complete', he cannot, according to Cooper,

---

27 Aristotle, *Nic. Eth.* 10 1177a12-21.
28 Aristotle, *Nic. Eth.* 10 1178a6-9.
29 F. Dirlmeier, *Aristoteles Nikomachische Ethik*, übersetzt und kommentiert, Deutsche Aristoteles Ausgabe Bd. 6, Berlin: Akademie-Verlag, 1956, 593.
30 Above, n. 20, at 167-80.
31 J. Cooper, 'Contemplation and Happiness. A Reconsideration', *Synthèse* 72 (1987) 187-216, especially 194.
32 Aristotle, *Nic. Eth.* 1 1098a15-17.

mean that one of these excellences, namely the best, could be sufficient for εὐδαιμονία. He can only mean that this special excellence must in any case be *included* in perfect εὐδαιμονία. In the same spirit Cooper explains our passage from Book 10 1177a12-21, that the activity of reason, the excellence most characteristic for man, is perfect εὐδαιμονία: according to Cooper this means only that contemplation makes human εὐδαιμονία perfect by *completing* the life of moral virtue. But Aristotle says, squarely, that contemplation is perfect εὐδαιμονία. He does *not* say that it is a necessary part in all perfect εὐδαιμονία. The last sentence of Book 10, chapter 8, or to be more precise, the penultimate (last but one) sentence of the chapter (1178b28-31), Cooper takes in his new, harmonizing spirit: 'εὐδαιμονία extends, then, just so far as contemplation does, and those to whom contemplation more fully belongs have also more of εὐδαιμονία; not just contingently but in virtue of the nature of theory, for theory has value in itself.'

By reference to Aristotle's earlier remarks on the εὐδαιμονία of gods[33] that the gods have activity, but need no productive nor moral activities, so that there remains for them only contemplation, Cooper wants to support his new 'inclusive' interpretation of *vita contemplativa* as full εὐδαιμονία, embracing *vita activa*. But he leaves out of account the sentence that actually concludes the chapter, immediately after the passage Cooper has quoted: ὥστ᾽ εἴη ἂν ἡ εὐδαιμονία θεωρία τις, 'It follows that εὐδαιμονία is a form of theoretical activity.'[34]

I conclude, with regrets, that we had better follow the Cooper of 1975 rather than the Cooper of 1987. The latter has, at most, shown what kind of synthesis Aristotle could have had in mind, even if he did not work it out in detail: the talk of κυρίως and δευτέρως (*Nic. Eth.* 10 1176a26-9) might have suggested to Aristotle a 'πρὸς ἕν' structure, as we have it in the field of οὐσία in the *Metaphysics*: there πρώτη οὐσία is form, δευτέρα οὐσία is enmattered form, and even ὕλη is a kind of οὐσία, by being potentially οὐσία. But to transfer this πρὸς ἕν structure ('focal meaning', in Owen's terminology)[35] from ontology to ethics, we would need an argument showing e.g. that second-grade εὐδαιμονία, moral activity according to practical virtue, *presupposes* theoretical reflection in the sense of pure contemplation. But nothing of such an argument do we find in Aristotle's text. We seem, then, to have the choice between a *clear inconsistency* in Aristotle (Cooper 1975) or an *obscure consistency* (Cooper 1987). Also in Aristotle's interest, I would opt for the former. Obscurity, I think, is, in philosophy, much worse than inconsistency.

But not only for philological reasons am I hesitant to accept Cooper's new, harmonizing, interpretation. From a systematic point of view also I would not like to say that contemplation is an essential, even most important part in all human

---

[33] Aristotle, *Nic. Eth.* 10 1178b8-22.
[34] Aristotle, *Nic. Eth.* 10 1178b32; see also 10 1179a30-2.
[35] In his classic paper 'Logic and Metaphysics in some earlier Works of Aristotle', in I. Düring and G.E.L. Owen, eds., *Aristotle and Plato in the Mid-Fourth Century*, Göteborg: Elanders, 1960, 163-90.

εὐδαιμονία. It might be understandable that Aristotle saw a difficulty in identifying perfect εὐδαιμονία with competent and morally blameless conduct in our roles as individuals and citizens. He may have thought that some *creative* activity was required in addition, which corresponds to our talents and inclinations and is regarded by us as intrinsically worthwhile and meaningful.

So, for a born philosopher, philosophizing may be the keystone of *his* εὐδαιμονία. But different people have different goals; the doctor may find his εὐδαιμονία in the successful treatment of his patients, the artist in producing significant works of art, and a mother may have her εὐδαιμονία perfected by raising a family competently and cheerfully. It is the idea of ranking human capabilities and activities, with philosophical contemplation at the top, which seems to be at the root of Aristotle's troubles. For all such ranking is without a rational basis. Maybe Aristotle was too much impressed by the idea, that contemplation is unique among human activities in being self-sufficient, needing neither equipment nor partners.[36] But then it is very easily disturbed, and we must accept the fact that all human εὐδαιμονία is dependent on favourable conditions. Aristotle's reasoning, then, if we have reconstructed it correctly, rests on premises which we can appreciate, but which we have good reason not to accept.

To sum up: we have looked at two important Greek approaches to what we are nowadays used to call 'Quality of Life'. We have found grave difficulties in both of them. But in spite of this I think that the level of reflection and the attempts which we find in Greek philosophy to construct a systematic connection between the different spheres of value are philosophically more interesting than most of what we can find in the present-day discussion on the topic of 'Quality of Life'. There is much we can still learn here from Plato and Aristotle, and if I should have succeeded in making this contention somewhat plausible to you, I would be εὐδαίμων in Aristotle's sense, if only for one evening.

SELECTED FURTHER READINGS

Broadie, Sarah. *Ethics with Aristotle*, New York: Oxford University Press, 1991.
Holzhey, Helmut. 'Lebensqualität'. In J. Ritter and K. Gründer, eds., *Historisches Wörterbuch der Philosophie*, Basel: Schwabe 1989, vol. 5, 141ff.
Kraut, Richard. *Aristotle on the Human Good*, Princeton: Princeton University Press, 1989.

---

[36] Aristotle, *Nic. Eth.* 10 1177a27-b1.

Chapter Four

Do we need new Editions of Ancient Philosophy?*

Jacques Brunschwig

I

Aware that I had devoted a part of my life to preparing a new edition of Aristotle's *Topics*, and that I am still working on it now, one of my friends, an intelligent and cultured person but in no way a specialist in this sort of thing, recently led me, by his questions, to ask myself about the point of this enterprise.

'From what I know so far,' he said to me, 'I don't understand you very well. I like ancient authors; I did a small amount of Greek when I was young; sometimes I read or re-read a bit of Homer, Sophocles, Plato or Marcus Aurelius, in translation of course, and I always find pleasure and profit in it. In the bookshops which I use, I have noticed that these great works are regularly the subject of fresh translations. I am not surprised; it is natural to want to make them accessible to the greatest number of people, regardless of their language and time. In this way these fundamental texts can continue to speak to different nations simultaneously and to successive generations. New translations, some more rigorous and literal, others more elegant and literary, can reveal aspects of them which have not been noticed till now, bring them more in tune with contemporary taste, and, to use a modern image, strip away the old coats of paint in which they were covered. A good Hellenist today, with even a modest equipment of rational interpretative principles – or even of attractively irrational ones – is well able to provide unexpected viewpoints and felicitous novelties to the reader of his translations. This is especially so, to be sure, with literary, poetic or dramatic works; but Plato, not to mention anyone else, is a great writer as well as an outstanding philosopher. Certainly one could also suppose that some authors of the second rank, up till now translated only rarely or badly, also deserve to emerge from the shadows; but you have told me that for some time people have been bravely working

---

* The second part of this lecture was subsequently delivered (in French) at a conference in Montreal in September 1996 on 'Le texte de l'*Organon* d'Aristote', the proceedings of which are being edited by R. Bodéüs.

on them too. And what I say in no way diminishes, in my view, the legitimacy of these new garments in which the most famous figures are periodically re-clad.'

'On the other hand,' my friend continued, 'I am more perplexed when I look at the proliferation of commentaries and interpretations of which ancient texts continue to be the subject. Let us speak just of the philosophers, since this is your specialism; and let us take the example of Plato, the most distinguished among them. Some time ago you showed me a bibliography which catalogues, every five years, all the books and articles devoted to him; in each issue of this dauntless publication, they are counted in the hundreds. You also told me about a recent colloquium, where a dozen Plato specialists met. Their plan was to study together fifteen lines which are among the best known of the *Republic*. No-one agreed with anyone else on the correct way to understand the passage; everyone thought that his own was the right one. What lesson should the rest of us laymen draw from this apparently discouraging experience? I grant that on the general interpretation of Plato there are almost as many opinions as there are interpreters. But if the conflict of interpretations extends to the level of fifteen lines, the temptation to scepticism awaits us. Or should one rather think that Plato wrote in such a way that there is no end to seeking a truth that he did not want to impart to us just like that?

'So you and your colleagues may write commentaries on Plato and those like him till the end of time, if you feel the need. But is it also necessary to re-edit their texts? That is yet another question. I imagine that the twelve interpreters of the fifteen lines of the *Republic* had before them a text which was the same for them all; their disagreements were not about the words, but about what they meant. I am well aware that Plato's own autograph texts have not survived; you have explained to me that his text has been transmitted to us by numerous manuscript copies, much later than his death, preserved in our great libraries. These are not photocopies; each one inevitably contains, compared with its model, divergences which are sometimes unintentional and sometimes deliberate. Starting from this evidence, to which must be added, as you have told me, the so-called "indirect tradition" (that is the ancient translations and commentaries), modern scholars have to construct what is called a critical edition, like the one you are working on; and I think I understand more or less what a critical apparatus is, without thereby knowing how to use one. But this work is concerned – isn't it? – with material which has been completely catalogued, and it follows methodological rules most of which have been fixed for a long time, since the great period of philology and textual criticism was the nineteenth century, and especially the nineteenth century in Germany. It is understandable, then, that texts are being re-edited today that have not yet had the benefit of these methods. But *Plato*? *Aristotle*? Have you not for a long time now had the use of editions of their works in which the text, established according to the principles of textual criticism, no longer really raises any problems?

'Let us take the case of your beloved *Topics*, a treatise by the great Aristotle, to be sure, but one of which you yourself say that it is not the most important of those he has left us. Yet when you started to work on your edition, there were already four critical editions of truly professional quality, the work of excellent philologists with great knowledge of Aristotle's work. One was included in a complete edition of his works (Bekker, 1830), another in a complete edition of his logical treatises (Waitz, 1844-1846); the two more recent ones include only the *Topics* and its appendix, the *Sophistical Refutations* (Strache and Wallies, 1923; Ross, 1958). Is this increasing concentration on the *Topics* not sufficient in itself to show that the editors have, as time passed, worked more slowly and with more attention? Moreover, in the same period there have also appeared numerous translations, four in English, three in Italian, two in German and one in French, and the notes to these, which are often copious, often involve questions concerning the establishing of the text. After all this work, is there any sense any more in adding a new critical edition to the pile of those that exist already? Perhaps in yours you have corrected, or believe that you have corrected, a small error of your predecessors here or there, an unhappy choice between the variants presented by the manuscripts, a pointless or questionable conjecture, or whatever. But I ask you whether it has never occurred to you to think, during your long sessions of work in libraries and in your study, that the game perhaps isn't worth the candle.'

'Friend', I replied to this speech, 'your questions clearly touch me in a sensitive spot. They deserve replies which are both thorough and different to suit different cases. If you agree, I will reply to you in two stages. In the first, I will reply to you directly, and I will try to justify my work in general terms. But as it is always a good idea to illustrate general points by specific examples, and since these cannot be provided without going into technical details, allow me, as a second stage, to speak to my learned colleagues in particular. I am sure that you will forgive me for this, for you are certainly clever enough to understand what I want to achieve by doing this.

'Sometimes there are completely objective reasons why the text of a critical edition can rightly differ from its predecessors; for example, the discovery of a document that was previously entirely unknown. It is rare, but it happens. In dealing with a treatise like the *Topics* one could scarcely expect such a discovery; the direct and indirect sources are today more or less completely catalogued. But it is precisely the bulk and quantity of the documents whose existence is known that makes it possible to find some which previous editors have not thought of using; I have myself used two manuscripts which fit this description, whose early date attracted my attention, and which, without producing overwhelming revelations, it is true, nevertheless proved to be interesting in more than one respect.

'However, it is in re-reading the witnesses already used by my predecessors that I have most often found reasons to disagree with them, or with some of them (for on more than one occasion I have disagreed with the more recent ones only in order to side with the earlier ones). There is a first and very simple reason for this; it is that, in the great majority of cases, I have had the opportunity to re-read the manuscripts themselves, in their evocative physical presence (what is called "autopsy" in the jargon of the trade). One cannot imagine the number of details (such as erasures, over-writings, corrections in the copyist's own hand or in a different hand) which cannot be seen when one works on the convenient substitute provided today by the photographic copy; and these details are often richly informative. But this is not all; even when the previous editors have "collated" (that is to say, recorded) the different readings of the manuscripts from the manuscripts themselves, they themselves or their collaborators may have made errors either in deciphering the handwriting, or in copying their notes, or in reading the proofs of their own printed critical apparatus. It is not a sign of arrogance to say that these errors can be discovered and corrected, for I am quite sure that I have made some of the same sort myself. It will be the task of my successors to correct them in the future.

'The evidence of the indirect tradition, too, belongs in that class of documents of which one can say that their existence was known and their contents had been used, but which are such that one can find ways of using them which are more complete and more detailed almost without limit. In the case of the *Topics*, the principal texts to consult are the massive commentary by Alexander of Aphrodisias and the Latin translation of Boethius, evidence all the more valuable because it is older than the oldest surviving manuscripts of the text of Aristotle. Excellent editions have been published, by Wallies (1891) and Minio-Paluello (1969) respectively. The reason why making use of these documents is a task of almost infinite complexity is itself very simple; they have themselves been preserved in a number of manuscripts; so the editions of them that have been published are themselves critical editions. Consequently, in comparing a passage of Aristotle and the corresponding passage of Alexander, for example, numerous permutations can confront us; the unanimous reading of the manuscripts of Aristotle may only be found in some of those of Alexander; the reading of some manuscripts of Aristotle may be found in all those of Alexander, but also in only some of the latter. It should also be added that, even supposing an ideal case where all the manuscripts of Aristotle gave the same reading as all those of Alexander, it would still not be certain how this agreement should be interpreted; it could indicate that the text of Aristotle used by Alexander had this reading, but also that it had been introduced into the text of Aristotle, at one stage or another in its transmission, precisely in order to make this correspond with Alexander's commentary on it.

'Moreover, reading the commentary in Wallies' edition sometimes reveals previously unnoticed details concerning the manuscripts of Aristotle. For example, Alexander himself from time to time notes variants between the text of the copy which he normally follows and other manuscripts which he has been able to consult. It also happens that, contrary to his custom, he passes over an expression or a paragraph without commenting on it; one can therefore suppose that these were missing from his copy. When one or more of the manuscripts of Aristotle have an omission at the corresponding place, this hypothesis becomes a near certainty.

'I hope, my friend, that these details will not cause you to lose sight of my objective in listing them. I want to give you a strong sense of what might be called the precarious nature of ancient texts; in reality, nothing is completely firm, and the editor, as a sort of Archimedes, does not easily find a fixed fulcrum for his lever. In this respect the typographical presentation of a critical edition, with the sharp distinction which it creates between "the text" and "the apparatus", is deceptive; in spite of oneself one is subconsciously tempted to consider the upper part of the page as *the* text of Aristotle, and its lower part as a muddled collection of erroneous distortions which this text has undergone in the course of centuries. In fact, the two halves of the page are the result of decisions which the editor has made, in each line and often several times in the line, to divide and arrange the materials provided by the tradition. Some of these, sent to the top, become "the text", that is, what he suggests his reader should read as the text; the others, sent to the bottom, become the "variants", that is, what the editor suggests should be read as mere accidental deviations from the text. But each of these decisions is his responsibility.

'Perhaps the editor's dream would be to free himself from this responsibility, by applying to his task methodological rules which would tell him the "right choice" mechanically. I do not mean to make the absurd claim that these rules do not exist; textual criticism may not be an exact science, but its principles are sufficient to give a definite shape to the editor's task. But these principles, which are eminently rational when considered in general terms, turn out to be very difficult to apply when the time comes to put them to work to solve a particular problem. To take just one example among many possible ones, let us consider the principle described as *lectio difficilior*. That is the label given to the reading which is more difficult and more unlikely than another, or to that which is the most difficult and the most improbable of all. It is sound methodology to favour this reading, because, if one supposes that it is the genuine one, it is easy to understand its giving rise to its rivals (by unconscious simplification or deliberate normalisation), but not so easy to understand how the latter might have been, in one place or another, replaced by the former. But the problem is that there are several points of view – of grammar, sense, style, argument, history, philosophy, and so on – from which a reading can be "more difficult" than another; so a given reading can be "more difficult" than another from one point of view, "more easy" than it from another point of view. Straight away the editor is given back his frightening freedom.

'The multiplicity of points of view which it is appropriate to take into account, in a particular case such as I have just indicated, seems to me to show well the still more problematic multiplicity of criteria which the editor must satisfy in each of his decisions. He cannot hope to establish his text by relying only on criteria of a purely literal and palaeographical type, which he might suppose were suitable to indicate choices which would be virtually automatic, a greater degree of freedom being granted to the translator and the commentator. In that case one could suppose, in the limiting case, that the best editor of a text would be one who did not know the language in which it is written (in the same way as it is said that the best corrector of printer's proofs is the one who reads them backwards). I do not mean to say here that it is the letter that kills and the spirit that gives life; in reality, both the letter and the spirit give life to each other.

'One more example, which shows that sometimes there is the opportunity to make several completely independent criteria work together, and that applying them together makes it possible to introduce something new into the generally accepted text. In analysing the internal logic of a passage in book 3 of the *Topics,* I was led a long time ago to conjecture that a word of four letters was missing. Although the conjecture was modest, it was also quite daring, for, without this word, an Aristotelian technical term in the passage would be understood in its classical sense, while with this word, it would have to be accepted that the technical term in question was used with an unusual sense. But at the same time I noticed that in one of the manuscripts I was using, an erasure had obliterated a space corresponding, more or less, to the same number of letters, at the exact place where I wanted to introduce the word whose presence seemed to me necessary for the logic of the passage. One could understand why the text had been corrected in antiquity, and how this erroneous correction could be corrected; the pieces of the puzzle fitted together in a marvellous way. Without the support which they gave to each other, I would probably not have had either the idea or the courage to alter the established text.

'A piece of good luck of this sort certainly does not occur every day, and one must recognize that it has not caused the earth to revolve in the opposite direction. But it has acquired for me, I confess, a paradigmatic status which is perhaps indeed excessive. It seems to me to teach us that it is possible not only to work on textual problems already recognized by previous editors, but also to discover new ones, which have not been identified, and which have all the ingredients for their solution present in our evidence, provided that one pursues sufficiently far, and if possible together, the detailed examination of the evidence and the logical analysis of the text.

'Thus you can understand, my friend, that what has interested me in my work, even apart from its official aim of producing a new edition of a particular text, is also to observe, in ancient manuscripts and modern editions, what I would like to call the adventures of the meaning, indissolubly linked with the adventures of the text. To see how and why a text is transformed, distorted and corrupted with the passage of time; to see whether and how we have the necessary data and tools to reverse, in some way, the progress of this corruption, and thus to have an opportunity to save a few small pieces of the meaning which had become lost on the way (even if very few people notice them, and even fewer people find them of any interest) – here are some apparently modest ambitions; perhaps a little less modest than they seem to be?

'And now that I have attempted to reply to you, my friend, allow me to present to a different audience the more technical sequel to these thoughts.'

II

The text of the *Organon* raises problems for students of its transmission, its reception, the translations and the ancient commentaries; it also raises problems for its editors, and has done so for long enough to make one think that the task of publishing new critical editions of it is not entirely without point. A long time ago I published a critical edition of the first four books of the *Topics*,[1] and the joke is on me that I have till now left it without a sequel. But it is not that I have been

---

[1]   Paris: Les Belles Lettres (Collection des Universités de France), 1967.

overcome by incurable despair concerning this subject. That is why I would like to devote the second part of this lecture – at the risk of not being very faithful to the tradition of the Keeling Lectures – to some observations, quite disjointed indeed, taken from the work which I have been able to do on books 6 and 7 of this treatise. They involve passages in which I think one can improve the text, at any rate in comparison with the most recent editions, and in some cases in comparison with all previous editions, if one uses the resources both of the direct and of the indirect traditions carefully. These observations will I hope also cast a little light on the processes – sometimes deliberate, sometimes not – by which the text is distorted both in the ancient manuscripts and in modern editions.

I will quickly note that in this work I have used seven manuscripts, first the two which make up what has traditionally been called the first family:

A = Vaticanus Urbinas 35 (slightly earlier than 901)
B = Venetus Marcianus 201 (954)

Then, three manuscripts which belong more or less clearly to a second family:

D = Parisinus 1843 (13th century)
u = Basileensis 54 (F.II.21) (12th century)
M = Neo-Eboracensis Pierpont Morgan Library 758 (11th century)

And finally two manuscripts which seem to me to occupy a special position:

C = Parisinus Coislinianus 330 (11th century)
V = Vaticanus Barberinianus 87 (10th century)

These manuscripts have already been used by my predecessors, with the exception of **M** and **V**; their antiquity however recommends that they be consulted, and using them confirms their interest.

I have naturally also used the two principal witnesses in the indirect tradition:

Alex = the commentary on the Topics of Alexander of Aphrodisias (2nd-3rd century)
Λ = the Latin translation of Boethius (5th-6th century)

I will now proceed to the observations that I would like to put forward. For convenience the texts follow Ross' edition;[2] my proposals appear in the *apparatus criticus*. Clearly in the finished edition the arrangement will be different.

---

[2]   *Aristotelis Topica et Sophistici Elenchi*, Oxford, Clarendon Press, 1958. I also cite the editions of Bekker (Berlin, 1831), Waitz (*Aristotelis Organon graece*, Leipzig 1844-1846), Strache and Wallies (*Aristotelis Topica cum libro de Sophisticis Elenchis*, Leipzig: Teubner, 1923). I indicate these editions together by the abbreviation "edd.".

1. 6.3 140b27-141a6

Πάλιν εἰ ταὐτὸν πλεονάκις εἴρηκεν, οἷον τὴν ἐπιθυμίαν
ὄρεξιν ἡδέος εἰπών· πᾶσα γὰρ ἐπιθυμία ἡδέος ἐστίν, ὥστε καὶ
τὸ ταὐτὸν τῇ ἐπιθυμίᾳ ἡδέος ἔσται. γίνεται οὖν ὅρος τῆς ἐπι-
30 θυμίας ὄρεξις ἡδέος ἡδέος· οὐδὲν γὰρ διαφέρει ἐπιθυμίαν εἰ-
πεῖν ἢ ὄρεξιν ἡδέος, ὥσθ' ἑκάτερον αὐτῶν ἡδέος ἔσται. ἢ τοῦτο
μὲν οὐδὲν ἄτοπον· καὶ γὰρ ὁ ἄνθρωπος δίπουν ἐστίν, ὥστε καὶ
τὸ ταὐτὸν τῷ ἀνθρώπῳ δίπουν ἔσται, ἔστι δὲ ταὐτὸν τῷ ἀνθρώπῳ ζῷον πεζὸν δίπουν, ὥστε ζῷον πεζὸν δίπουν δίπουν ἔσται,
35 ἀλλ' οὐ διὰ τοῦτο ἄτοπόν τι συμβαίνει· οὐ γὰρ κατὰ ζῴου
πεζοῦ τὸ δίπουν κατηγορεῖται (οὕτω μὲν γὰρ δὶς ἂν περὶ τοῦ
αὐτοῦ τὸ δίπουν κατηγοροῖτο), ἀλλὰ περὶ ζῴου πεζοῦ δί-
1 ποδος τὸ δίπουν λέγεται, ὥστε ἅπαξ μόνον τὸ δίπουν κατηγορεῖται. ὁμοίως δὲ καὶ ἐπὶ τῆς ἐπιθυμίας· οὐ γὰρ κατὰ τῆς
ὀρέξεως τὸ ἡδέος εἶναι κατηγορεῖται ἀλλὰ κατὰ τοῦ σύμπαντος, ὥστε ἅπαξ καὶ ἐνταῦθα ἡ κατηγορία γίνεται. οὐκ
5 ἔστι δὲ τὸ δὶς φθέγξασθαι ταὐτὸν ὄνομα τῶν ἀτόπων, ἀλλὰ
τὸ πλεονάκις περί τινος τὸ αὐτὸ κατηγορῆσαι.

29-30 ὅρος τῆς ἐπιθυμίας ὄρεξις ἡδέος ἡδέος C² edd.: ὁ ὅρος τῆς ἐπιθυμίας ὄρεξις ἡδέος
A²uΛ: ὁ ὅρος τῆς ἐπιθυμίας ὄρεξις ὄρεξις ἡδέος fort. Cᵃᶜ: ὁ ὅρος τῆς ἐπιθυμίας ὄρεξις
ἡδέος ἡδέος DVM: ἡ ὄρεξις ὄρεξις ἡδέος AB: ἡ ὄρεξις ἡδέος ἡδέος ego

Book 6 is devoted to the dialectical discussion of definitions. Certain definitions are to be rejected because they have a formal defect; they are not formulated
καλῶς. One of these formal defects is that of saying more than is needed (139b15);
one way of saying more than is needed is to say the same thing several times
(140b27). Paradoxically, taking this context into account has led to a distortion of
the text by copyists and editors.

Ross' text (140b27-31) translates as follows: 'See also whether [the
respondent] has said the same thing several times, in saying for example that
desire (ἐπιθυμία) is appetition for the pleasant (ὄρεξις ἡδέος); for all desire is for the
pleasant [sc. has the pleasant for its object], with the result that what is identical to
desire is for the pleasant. So, the definition of desire becomes "appetition for the
pleasant for the pleasant"; for there is no difference between saying "desire" and
saying "appetition for the pleasant", with the result that each of the two is "for the
pleasant".'

There is, clearly enough, something that does not fit in the argument reconstructed like this. The respondent proposes to define desire as 'appetition for the
pleasant'. Basically, he needs to be shown that this definition contains, or implies, a
redundancy. Now in fact, in lines 28-9 and 30-31, he is shown something quite
different; namely, what would happen if, in the statement 'all desire is for the pleasant' (which is *not* itself a definition of desire) one was to substitute for the definiendum, 'desire', the suggested definition, 'appetition for the pleasant'. Clearly one
would get the following statement: 'all appetition for the pleasant is for the

pleasant', which involves redundancy, at least in appearance, but is *not* a transformation of the definition of desire as 'appetition for the pleasant' originally given, and which cannot therefore be used to show that this definition itself involves redundancy.

It is therefore apparent that the source of the problem is the reference to the 'definition of desire', ὅρος τῆς ἐπιθυμίας, in lines 29-30. This reference is only attested, with or without the article, in the MSS other than A and B. A corrector or glossator must have thought that the argument ought to show that the proposed definition involves redundancy, and that it was therefore necessary to show that the redundancy was in the definition itself; he did not understand that Aristotle simply wanted to show that a statement in which the definiendum was replaced by the proposed definition would involve redundancy.

One should therefore follow A and B, and delete ὅρος τῆς ἐπιθυμίας. Unfortunately, one cannot adopt just as it is the text which these two MSS give in what follows, namely ἡ ὄρεξις ὄρεξις ἡδέος. But only a slight change, one authorized moreover by the second family, is needed to replace the repetition of ὄρεξις by a repetition of ἡδέος, and in this way to get the required sense; if, in the statement 'desire is for the pleasant', one replaces the definiendum 'desire' by what is identical to it according to the proposed definition, namely 'appetition for the pleasant', one gets the statement 'appetition for the pleasant is for the pleasant'. The text which should be given in an edition is therefore ἡ ὄρεξις ἡδέος ἡδέος.

This correction is fully confirmed in the text that follows (140b31-141a6). In this long self-critical commentary, which is extremely interesting in itself, Aristotle shows that the statement which he has just been speaking of involves nothing absurd after all. One can establish precisely which the statement is that he has in mind, thanks to the comparison he introduces. If one says 'the two-footed land animal is two-footed', one certainly says 'two-footed' twice, but without any redundant predication and so without absurdity, because the first occurrence of 'two-footed' is *not* predicated of 'the land animal', while the second is predicated of 'the two-footed land animal' (140b32-141a2). In exactly the same way (141a2-6), 'for the pleasant' (τὸ ἡδέος εἶναι) is not predicated of appetition (κατὰ τῆς ὀρέξεως) but of the whole (τοῦ σύμπαντος). This explanation is perfectly comprehensible if one considers that the statement to which it relates is indeed ἡ ὄρεξις ἡδέος ἡδέος; the first instance of ἡδέος is not in fact predicated of ἡ ὄρεξις, while the second is indeed predicated of the 'whole' constituted by the expression ἡ ὄρεξις ἡδέος.

The expression ἡ ὄρεξις ἡδέος ἡδέος also appears in a passage of *On Sophistical Refutations*, 13 173a38-40. In this chapter, where Aristotle is showing how the sophist can involve his partner in 'parroting',[3] there appears the following sample of dialogue, in which the leader in the game is a sophist: '(a) Desire is for the

---

[3]   Following Louis-André Dorion's precise and elegant translation of ἀδολεσχεῖν (*Aristote, Les Réfutations sophistiques*, Paris: Vrin/Presses de l'Université Laval, 1995, 154).

pleasant, isn't it? (b) Now this [*sc.* desire] is [identical to] appetition for the pleasant; (c) so desire is appetition for the pleasant for the pleasant.' One may wonder whether this parallel confirms or weakens the suggestion that has just been made relating to the text of the *Topics*. In the sophism set out by Aristotle, premiss (a) is predicative, while premiss (b) is a definition; the sophism consists in the very fact that instead of drawing the legitimate conclusion, which would be predicative ('appetition for the pleasant is for the pleasant'), and which only apparently involves 'parroting', the sophist draws the conclusion which is implicitly a definition, 'desire is [identical to] appetition for the pleasant for the pleasant'. This conclusion could not be rescued from absurdity by the points which Aristotle makes in the second part of the passage from the *Topics*; it would not indeed be possible to say that only one of the instances of ἡδέος is predicated, because in reality neither of the two is. One can therefore consider the sophism in *De sophisticis elenchis* as a possible source of the dialectical process analysed in the *Topics*, but nothing more; in the *Topics*, the predicative premiss ('all desire is for the pleasant') and the premiss which is a definition ('desire is [the same thing as] appetition for the pleasant') produce a predicative conclusion which one can rescue from its apparent absurdity; each of the two, the desire (definiendum) and the appetition for the pleasant (definiens) is 'for the pleasant'.

2. 6.8 146b9-12.

> ἢ εἰ πρός τι εἰρημένον μὴ πρὸς τὸ τέλος ἀπο-
> 10 δέδοται· τέλος δ' ἐν ἑκάστῳ τὸ βέλτιστον ἢ οὗ χάριν τἆλλα.
> ῥητέον δὴ ἢ τὸ βέλτιστον ἢ τὸ ἔσχατον, οἷον τὴν ἐπιθυμίαν οὐχ
> ἡδέος ἀλλ᾽ ἡδονῆς· ταύτης γὰρ χάριν καὶ τὸ ἡδὺ αἱρούμεθα.

11 ἢ τὸ βέλτιστον ἢ τὸ ἔσχατον CDuVML edd.: τὸ βέλτιστον ἢ τὸ ἔσχατον AB Alex. recte

The context of this short passage is the discussion of definitions of relative terms. These definitions are defective when they do not mention the correlative of the defined term, and also when they mention a correlative which is not the ultimate correlative, the τέλος, of the term defined. Aristotle goes on to explain that the τέλος in each case is what is best (τὸ βέλτιστον) or that with a view to which the other things are sought (οὗ χάριν τἆλλα). In the following sentence (146b11) the two families of MSS disagree on a minute detail: A and B, supported by Alexander, give ῥητέον δὴ τὸ βέλτιστον ἢ τὸ ἔσχατον; the other MSS, followed by all the modern editors, give ῥητέον δὴ ᾗ τὸ βέλτιστον ἢ τὸ ἔσχατον.

However, the reading of A and B is to be preferred, first of all for formal reasons. The expression τὸ βέλτιστον ἢ τὸ ἔσχατον has the same structure as the one which immediately precedes it, τὸ βέλτιστον ἢ οὗ χάριν τἆλλα; the conjunction ἢ does not introduce a disjunction between the two parts of the expression, rather an equivalence ('what is best, or in other words that with a view to which the other things are sought'). Moreover, if the strongly disjunctive version in the second family, ἢ τὸ βέλτιστον ἢ τὸ ἔσχατον, were correct, one would expect to find two examples, each intended to illustrate one of the disjuncts; but Aristotle only gives one (146b11-12).

This example is the following: 'one must say that desire is not desire for the pleasant, but for pleasure; for it is with a view to pleasure that we seek what is pleasant'. The origin of the disjunctive version is immediately apparent. If one accepts the reading of A and B, pleasure is not only τὸ ἔσχατον but also τὸ βέλτιστον. A well-intentioned reader must have found this thought shocking, and in order to absolve Aristotle from it very ingeniously introduced an extra word, a single word and a single letter, ἤ. Thanks to this modest addition, pleasure is still τὸ ἔσχατον, because lines 11-12 could scarcely be taken to say anything else; but it is no longer τὸ βέλτιστον.

The previous example shows that correctors of the *Topics* worried about Aristotle's being coherent; the present one, that they also worried about his morals ...

3. 6.12 149a29-37.

Εἰ δὲ τῆς διαφορᾶς τὸν ὅρον ἀποδέδωκε, σκοπεῖν εἰ καὶ
30 ἄλλου τινὸς κοινὸς ὁ ἀποδοθεὶς ὁρισμός. οἷον ὅταν τὸν περιττὸν
ἀριθμὸν ἀριθμὸν μέσον ἔχοντα εἴπῃ, ἐπιδιοριστέον τὸ πῶς μέσον ἔχοντα. ὁ μὲν γὰρ ἀριθμὸς κοινὸς ἐν ἀμφοτέροις τοῖς
λόγοις ὑπάρχει, τοῦ δὲ περιττοῦ μετείληπται ὁ λόγος· ἔχει
δὲ καὶ γραμμὴ καὶ σῶμα μέσον, οὐ περιττὰ ὄντα. ὥστ' οὐκ
35 ἂν εἴη ὁρισμὸς οὗτος τοῦ περιττοῦ. εἰ δὲ πολλαχῶς λέγεται
τὸ μέσον ἔχον, διοριστέον τὸ πῶς μέσον ἔχον. ὥστ' ἢ ἐπιτίμησις ἔσται, ἢ συλλογισμὸς ὅτι οὐχ ὥρισται.

31-2 ἐπιδιοριστέον τὸ πῶς μέσον ἔχοντα ABu: non habent CDVMΛ non legisse vid.
Alex.: delendum censeo

The context here is the discussion of possible errors in defining the differentia. Here there is a major difference between the two families of MSS. ἐπιδιοριστέον τὸ πῶς μέσον ἔχοντα is given by ABu, followed by all the modern editors; these words are absent from the other MSS and from Boethius' translation, and Alexander does not seem to have read them.

To see what should be done, I first translate the whole passage, putting the clause at issue in italics.

If the respondent has given the definition of a differentia, see if the definition he has given is also shared with something else. For example, when he says that odd number is a number which has a middle, *one should define more exactly, in addition, in what way it has a middle*. 'Number' is indeed common to the two expressions [*sc.* 'odd number' and 'number which has a middle'], and it is 'odd' that has been replaced by its definition. But a line and a solid also have a middle, without being odd, so that this [*sc.* 'which has a middle'] cannot be the definition of 'odd'. Now, if 'has a middle' is said in many ways, one should define the way in which [odd number] has a middle. Consequently, either there will be something to criticise, or one will have shown that a definition has not been given.

It is clear enough that there are two distinct stages in this argument. In the first (149a29-35) Aristotle shows that μέσον ἔχον cannot be the definition of περιττόν, because there are things, such as a line or a solid, which have a middle without being odd. In this first stage, there is no question of μέσον ἔχον being said in many ways, except in the clause at issue, and it would not help if there were. The second stage (149a35-6) is precisely prompted by a possible reply of the respondent; if his defence is to say that a line and a solid do indeed have a middle, but in a different sense from that in which an odd number has a middle, one can criticize him for not having defined at the outset in what specific sense an odd number has a middle.

The concluding sentence confirms this analysis; it takes up the two stages of the argument in chiastic order. If μέσον ἔχον is said in many ways, and if the respondent has not said in what sense he is taking it, there is the basis for a criticism (ἐπιτίμησις); if μέσον ἔχον is not said in many ways, the counter-examples of the line and the solid are sufficient to demonstrate (συλλογισμός) that this expression is not an appropriate differentia for defining odd number correctly (οὐχ ὥρισται).

It is clear, therefore, that the clause at issue, ἐπιδιοριστέον τὸ πῶς μέσον ἔχοντα (149a31-2) is a clumsy anticipation of διοριστέον τὸ πῶς μέσον ἔχον (149a36), perhaps prompted by the need to have a main clause for the subordinate one introduced by ὅταν (a30).[4] This anticipation destroys the argument's proceeding in two stages; it should be removed from the text. For once, the second family has preserved the correct reading.

4. 6.12 149b24-30.

Ἐνίοτε δ' ὁρίζονται οὐ τὸ πρᾶγμα ἀλλὰ τὸ πρᾶγμα
25 εὖ ἔχον ἢ τετελεσμένον. τοιοῦτος δ' ὁ τοῦ ῥήτορος καὶ ὁ τοῦ
κλέπτου ὅρος, εἴπερ ἐστὶ ῥήτωρ μὲν ὁ δυνάμενος τὸ ἐν ἑκάστῳ πιθανὸν θεωρεῖν καὶ μηδὲν παραλείπων, κλέπτης δ' ὁ
λάθρᾳ λαμβάνων· δῆλον γὰρ ὅτι τοιοῦτος ὢν ἑκάτερος ὁ μὲν
ἀγαθὸς ῥήτωρ ὁ δ' ἀγαθὸς κλέπτης ἔσται. οὐ γὰρ ὁ λάθρᾳ
30 λαμβάνων ἀλλ' ὁ βουλόμενος λάθρᾳ λαμβάνειν κλέπτης ἐστίν.

26 δυνάμενος cod.: non habet Alex. ‖ 27 θεωρεῖν codd.: θεωρῶν Alex. ‖ παραλείπων Cu Alex.: παραλείπειν [-λιπεῖν B] ABDVΛ.

---

4   Punctuating lightly after ὁρισμός is sufficient to get rid of this difficulty.

This is an especially interesting case, in which in my opinion the correct text has only been preserved by Alexander, and where the MSS variants allow one to follow, as if in a geological section, the successive corruptions.

First I translate the text as Ross gives it.

> Sometimes people define not the thing, but the thing in a good or in a perfect condition. Like this are the definitions of the orator and of the thief, if indeed an orator is the one who is able (δυνάμενος) to see what is plausible in each case and who does not neglect anything (μηδὲν παραλείπων), and if indeed a thief is the one who gets hold of (λαμβάνων) things in secret. For it is clear that in being like this they will be, in the one case a good orator, in the other a good thief; for it is not the one who gets hold of the things in secret who is a thief, but the one who wants (βουλόμενος) to get hold of things in secret.

There is clearly something that does not fit in this passage. To show this, let us start with the case of the thief. There is a clear opposition between the good definition of the thief, 'the one who *wants* to get hold of things in secret', and the definition of the good thief, 'the one who gets hold of things in secret [successfully]'. The latter is not a good definition of the thief. A bad thief wants to get hold of things; he does not succeed, but he is still a thief.

On the basis of this example, one would expect to find, in parallel, a good definition of the orator, as the one who *wants* to do certain things, and a definition of the good orator, as the one who *succeeds* in doing these same things. But this is not we find in Ross' text; here the definition of the good orator is 'the one who is *able* to see what is plausible in each case and who does not neglect anything.' To be sure, it would be possible to construct an opposition between the ability to do something and the wish to do it; Aristotle proceeds in this way in another passage of the *Topics* (4.5 126a30-b3) where he shows that the sophist, the slanderer and the thief should be defined by their προαίρεσις and not by their δύναμις, because δύναμις always has a positive value, even when it is an ability to do what is bad. In this passage of book 4 he says explicitly that a thief is not the one who is *able* to get hold of someone else's possessions in secret, but the one who *deliberately chooses* to do it. But this contrast between *wanting* and *being able* is quite different from that which is indicated in our passage from book 6, which is a contrast between *wanting* and *succeeding*.

The solution to the problem is in Alexander's commentary (484.8-25). In Alexander, the definition that is criticized as being that of the good orator rather than of the orator is not, as in Ross, ὁ <u>δυνάμενος</u> τὸ ἐν ἑκάστῳ πιθανὸν <u>θεωρεῖν</u> καὶ μηδὲν παραλείπων, but ὁ τὸ ἐν ἑκάστῳ πιθανὸν θεωρῶν καὶ μηδὲν παραλείπων, 'the one who sees what is plausible in each case and does not neglect anything'. This definition is exactly parallel to that of the good thief, ὁ λάθρᾳ λαμβάνων, 'the one who *gets hold of* things in secret'.

Starting from the text preserved by Alexander, one can reconstruct what has happened, stage by stage.

Stage one: a reasonably intelligent corrector was surprised not to see the good orator defined in terms of his δύναμις; doubtless he remembered the definition of rhetoric as '*ability* (δύναμις) to see (θεωρῆσαι) what could be plausible in each case' (*Rhet.* 1.2 1355b25). He therefore replaced the participle θεωρῶν by δυνάμενος θεωρεῖν. But he gave away his crime by forgetting to make the parallel change to the participle παραλείπων. His text therefore suffered from a sort of syntactic imbalance between the two expressions joined by καί, ὁ δυνάμενος ... θεωρεῖν and μηδὲν παραλείπων. Nevertheless, this awkward text survives in the MSS C and u, followed by Ross, and already by Strache and Wallies in the Teubner.

Stage two: a second corrector, conscious of this imbalance, replaced the participle παραλείπων by the infinitive παραλείπειν, which made it possible to make it co-ordinate with θεωρεῖν, and to make the two infinitives θεωρεῖν and παραλείπειν depend on δυνάμενος. This text, made regular by two successive corrections, is found in the MSS A and B, among others, even though these are the oldest of the surviving MSS; it was adopted by Bekker and Waitz. A salutary warning, nevertheless: *vetustiores, non meliores*, or at any rate *non semper meliores*.

5. 7.1 151b33-6.

> ὁμοίως δὲ καὶ ἐπὶ τῶν ἀντικειμένων· εἰ γὰρ τάδε
> ταὐτά, καὶ τὰ ἀντικείμενα τούτοις ταὐτὰ καθ' ὁποιανοῦν τῶν
> 35 λεγομένων ἀντιθέσεων· οὐδὲν γὰρ διαφέρει τὸ τούτῳ ἢ τούτῳ
> ἀντικείμενον λαβεῖν, ἐπειδὴ ταὐτόν ἐστιν.

35 τούτῳ ... τούτῳ ABCuVM: τοῦτο ... τοῦτο DΛ recte ‖ post ἢ add. τὸ CVM ‖
36 ταὐτόν AB: ταὐτά A¹CDuVMΛ

In this first chapter of book 7, Aristotle examines dialectical methods of solving problems of identity, more precisely numerical identity (151b29-30) and difference. One can discuss these problems starting from co-ordinate terms, σύστοιχα (for example, if justice is identical to courage, the just person is identical to the courageous person), or starting from inflections, πτώσεις (if justice is identical to courage, 'justly' is the same thing as 'courageously'). One can also make use of opposites, ἀντικείμενα. On this point, Aristotle says 'if this [**A**] and this [**B**] are identical, their opposites are also identical, according to any whatsoever of what are called oppositions (τῶν λεγομένων ἀντιθέσεων).' By this he clearly understands the distinction between four sorts of opposites (contraries, contradictories, relatives, possession and privation) which he has already listed several times in the *Topics* (2.2 109b18, 2.8 113b15).

In Ross' text, what follows (151b35-6) says this: 'For it makes no difference whether we take the opposite of the one [**A**] or of the other [**B**], because they are identical.' This text makes no sense. If we want to establish identity between justice and courage, Aristotle would be advising us that it makes no difference whether we consider injustice or cowardice, on the grounds that they are identical. But one cannot presume their identity without committing a *petitio principii* with regard to the identity of their respective opposites, justice and courage. Moreover, it is impossible to see how considering just one of the opposites, the opposite of [A] *or* the opposite of [B], could serve to establish a relationship between [A] *and* [B].

To this inappropriate text we should prefer the variant preserved by MS D and by Boethius' translation: in place of τὸ τούτῳ ἢ τούτῳ ἀντικείμενον λαβεῖν we should read τὸ τοῦτο ἢ τοῦτο ἀντικείμενον λαβεῖν. The sense is then perfectly clear: 'For it makes no difference whether we take one opposite or the other [i.e. an opposite of this or that type, among the four types that are regularly distinguished], provided that it is the same [i.e. provided that we take the same type of opposite for both the terms compared and not, for example, the contrary of [A] and the contradictory of [B]].'

The corruption of the text in a large number of MSS is undoubtedly explained by the strangeness of the expression τὸ τοῦτο ἢ τοῦτο ἀντικείμενον λαβεῖν: at first glance, τὸ seems to be go with ἀντικείμενον, not with λαβεῖν, and as τὸ τοῦτο ἀντικείμενον does not mean anything, τοῦτο must twice have been corrected into τούτῳ. Subsequently this correction prompted others; first the addition of a second article before the second τούτῳ, in order to reinforce the new construction (MSS CVM); then, the replacing of ταὐτόν by ταὐτά, in an attempt to adapt the clause introduced by ἐπειδὴ to its new context. This is how an initial corruption often spreads like wildfire.

6. 7.1 152a5-18 and 25-30.

5   σκοπεῖν δὲ καὶ ὧν θάτερον μάλιστα λέγεται ὁτιοῦν, εἰ
    καὶ θάτερον τῶν αὐτῶν τούτων κατὰ τὸ αὐτὸ μάλιστα λέγε-
    ται, καθάπερ Ξενοκράτης τὸν εὐδαίμονα βίον καὶ τὸν σπου-
    δαῖον ἀποδείκνυσι τὸν αὐτόν, ἐπειδὴ πάντων τῶν βίων αἱρε-
    τώτατος ὁ σπουδαῖος καὶ ὁ εὐδαίμων· ἓν γὰρ τὸ αἱρετώτα-
10 τον καὶ μέγιστον. ὁμοίως δὲ καὶ ἐπὶ τῶν ἄλλων τῶν τοιούτων.
    δεῖ δ' ἑκάτερον ἓν ἀριθμῷ εἶναι τὸ λεγόμενον μέγιστον ἢ αἱ-
    ρετώτατον· εἰ δὲ μή, οὐκ ἔσται δεδειγμένον ὅτι ταὐτόν. οὐ
    γὰρ ἀναγκαῖον, εἰ ἀνδρειότατοι τῶν Ἑλλήνων Πελοποννήσιοι
    καὶ Λακεδαιμόνιοι, τοὺς αὐτοὺς εἶναι Πελοποννησίους Λακε-
15 δαιμονίοις, ἐπειδὴ οὐχ εἷς ἀριθμῷ Πελοποννήσιος καὶ Λακε-
    δαιμόνιος, ἀλλὰ περιέχεσθαι μὲν τὸν ἕτερον ὑπὸ τοῦ ἑτέρου
    ἀναγκαῖον, καθάπερ οἱ Λακεδαιμόνιοι ὑπὸ τῶν Πελοποννη-
    σίων ...
25   δῆλον οὖν ὅτι ἓν ἀριθμῷ δεῖ εἶναι τὸ βέλτιστον καὶ
    μέγιστον λεγόμενον, εἰ μέλλει ὅτι ταὐτὸν ἀποδείκνυσθαι. διὸ
    καὶ Ξενοκράτης οὐκ ἀποδείκνυσιν· οὐ γὰρ εἷς ἀριθμῷ ὁ εὐδαί-
    μων καὶ ὁ σπουδαῖος βίος, ὥστ' οὐκ ἀναγκαῖον τὸν αὐτὸν εἶ-

ναι, διότι ἄμφω αἱρετώτατοι, ἀλλὰ τὸν ἕτερον ὑπὸ τὸν
30 ἕτερον.

15 καὶ CDuVM Alex. Λ Strache and Wallies Ross: οὐδὲ AB Bekker Waitz recte ‖
28 καὶ CᵣᵃˢDuVM: οὐδ' AB recte

Still in the chapter devoted to problems of identity, Aristotle criticizes an argument of Xenocrates, which claims to establish the identity of the happy life and the virtuous life by saying that they are, both of them, the most choiceworthy of lives. For the argument to be valid, each of the terms compared must be numerically one (152a11-12); otherwise, their identity has not been demonstrated. One can see this from a more familiar example; if the Peloponnesians and the Spartans are the bravest of the Greeks, this does not necessarily imply that the Peloponnesians are identical to the Spartans. The clause which explains why this is so, introduced by ἐπειδὴ (152a15) has a slightly different text in the two families of MSS. In the second family, which Strache and Wallies and Ross follow here, we read ἐπειδὴ οὐχ εἷς ἀριθμῷ Πελοποννήσιος καὶ Λακεδαιμόνιος, 'since the Peloponnesian *and* the Spartan (understand: taken together) are not a numerically single and identical thing.' In the first family, followed by Bekker and by Waitz, we read ἐπειδὴ οὐχ εἷς ἀριθμῷ Πελοποννήσιος οὐδὲ Λακεδαιμόνιος, 'since neither the Peloponnesian nor the Spartan (understand: taken separately) are a numerically single thing.' It is clear that the reading of the first family is the correct one; what prevents us from concluding the identity of the Peloponnesians and the Spartans is that they constitute two sets of which the one is included in the other (152a16-18). If the two compared terms were *each* numerically one, their identity could easily be established, as one can see by imagining another example: Achilles and the only son of Peleus are the bravest of the Greeks; Achilles is numerically one; the only son of Peleus is numerically one; so Achilles and the only son of Peleus are one and the same person.

The MSS show the same variation at 152a28, where Aristotle returns to Xenocrates' argument. The second family has ὁ εὐδαίμων καὶ ὁ σπουδαῖος βίος, and the first ὁ εὐδαίμων οὐδ' ὁ σπουδαῖος βίος. Thus one can see with what clumsy, but real, carefulness the correctors of Aristotle worked; after correcting a given passage, they took care to carry out the same correction in parallel passages. Here too, in spite of their enthusiasm, we should go back to the reading of the first family.

7. 7.1 152b30-4.

30 Ἔτι ἐπεὶ πολλαχῶς τὸ ταὐτὸν λέγεται, σκοπεῖν εἰ καθ'
ἕτερόν τινα τρόπον ταὐτά ἐστιν· τὰ γὰρ εἴδει ἢ γένει
ταὐτὰ ἢ οὐκ ἀνάγκη ἢ οὐκ ἐνδέχεται ἀριθμῷ ταὐτὰ εἶναι·
ἐπισκοποῦμεν δὲ πότερον οὕτω ταὐτὰ ἢ οὐχ οὕτως.

30 post εἰ add. καὶ AᵃᶜB ‖ ἢ οὐκ ἀνάγκη ἢ οὐκ ἐνδέχεται codd. rec. edd.: ἢ οὐκ ἀνάγκη οὐκ ἐνδέχεται AB: οὐκ ἀνάγκη AᵖᶜDVΛ: οὐκ ἐνδέχεται CuM Alex. recte

My final two examples, this and the following one, are probably the most interesting from a philosophical point of view.

The first is still connected with the discussion of problems of identity. Aristotle has first been concerned with the principal type of identity, numerical identity.[5] He now moves on to consider the others, identity in species and identity in genus. In this connection he says 'since "identical" is said in many ways, see whether <the things being compared> are in fact identical according to some other type <of identity>.'[6]

But the important textual problem is in the explanatory clause which follows. Ross' text gives: 'For in the case of things which are identical in species or in genus, either it is not necessary (ἢ οὐκ ἀνάγκη) or it is not possible (ἢ οὐκ ἐνδέχεται) for them to be identical numerically.' The alternative is easily understood. Two things are identical in species if they belong to the same species (and similarly they are identical in genus if they belong to the same genus); but these expressions, as Alexander explains very well in his commentary (502.8-18) are ambiguous. If for example one says that two things are identical in species, this can be true in the case where they belong *at least* to the same species, which does *not rule out* their being numerically identical; but it can also be true in the case where they belong *at most* to the same species, which *rules out* their being numerically identical. In the first sense, which one may call the 'broad' sense, Plato and Aristotle are identical in species, without being numerically identical, but Plato and Aristocles[7] too are identical in species; they are the same individual, and so, *a fortiori*, they belong to the same species. Specific identity in the broad sense does not therefore imply numerical identity, but it does not rule it out either. In the second sense, which one may call the 'narrow' sense, Plato and Aristocles are *not* identical in species, precisely because they are one and the same individual, and so they do not belong *at most* to the same species. On the other hand, Plato and Aristotle *are* identical in species, and consequently they are two distinct individuals.[8]

Ross' text corresponds exactly to this distinction; if two things are identical in species in the broad sense, it is not necessary (οὐκ ἀνάγκη) for them to be numerically identical; if they are identical in species in the narrow sense, it is not possible (οὐκ ἐνδέχεται) for them to be numerically identical. But the question is whether Aristotle really alluded to this alternative here.

---

[5]   Cf. 151b28-30.

[6]   I think that the καί of the first family can here be retained after εἰ in line 30, in the sense of 'in fact'.

[7]   As is well known, Plato was originally named after his grandfather Aristocles; he was nicknamed 'Plato' by his gymnastics teacher (Diogenes Laertius 3.4).

[8]   This type of ambiguity, which is common in Aristotle's usage, deserves a systematic study. Another example of it is provided by the particular proposition: 'some S is P' can mean either that *at least* some S is P (which does not rule out that all S is P), or that *at most* some S is P (which rules out that all S is P).

There is an initial reason to doubt this. The *apparatus criticus* shows that οὐκ ἀνάγκη and οὐκ ἐνδέχεται, rather than being co-ordinated as in Ross's text, are simply placed next to each other in asyndeton in the MSS of the first family; moreover, some MSS of the second family have only οὐκ ἀνάγκη and others only οὐκ ἐνδέχεται. It is clear that one of these expressions has been added to or substituted for the other. Which should we keep? There is an initial, purely textual reason for thinking that we should keep οὐκ ἐνδέχεται; this is that it is only οὐκ ἀνάγκη that is preceded by ἢ in A and B.

This supposition becomes certainty when we read the final sentence (152b33): 'but we examine whether things are identical or not in this way (οὕτω, that is to say numerically).'[9] To decide whether two things are numerically identical or not, the only useful tool provided by identity in species and identity in genus is the case in which these types of identity *rule out* numerical identity, that is to say the case where they are taken in the narrow sense (οὐκ ἐνδέχεται); when on the other hand two things are identical in species or in genus in the broad sense, they can be numerically identical, but they can also not be (οὐκ ἀνάγκη), so that no conclusion can be drawn from such a situation. The only correct text is therefore the one which has only οὐκ ἐνδέχεται.

8. 7.3 153a11-22.

εἶθ' ὅτι δι' ἀκριβείας μὲν ἄλλης ἐστὶ πραγματείας
ἀποδοῦναι καὶ τί ἐστιν ὅρος καὶ πῶς ὁρίζεσθαι δεῖ, νῦν δ'
ὅσον ἱκανὸν πρὸς τὴν παροῦσαν χρείαν, ὥστε τοσοῦτον μόνον
λεκτέον ὅτι δυνατὸν γενέσθαι ὁρισμοῦ καὶ τοῦ τί ἦν εἶναι συλ-
15 λογισμόν. εἰ γάρ ἐστιν ὅρος λόγος ὁ τὸ τί ἦν εἶναι τῷ πρά-
γματι δηλῶν καὶ δεῖ τὰ ἐν τῷ ὅρῳ κατηγορούμενα ἐν
τῷ τί ἐστι τοῦ πράγματος μόνα κατηγορεῖσθαι, κατηγορεῖται δ' ἐν τῷ τί ἐστι τὰ γένη καὶ αἱ διαφοραί, φανερὸν ὡς
εἴ τις λάβοι ταῦτα ἃ μόνα ἐν τῷ τί ἐστι τοῦ πράγματος κατ-
20 ηγορεῖται, ὅτι ὁ ταῦτα ἔχων λόγος ὅρος ἐξ ἀνάγκης ἂν
εἴη· οὐ γὰρ ἐνδέχεται ἕτερον εἶναι ὅρον, ἐπειδὴ οὐδὲν ἕτερον
ἐν τῷ τί ἐστι τοῦ πράγματος κατηγορεῖται.

19 ταῦτα om. C suppl. C² ‖ ἃ om. ABuM Bekker Waitz recte ‖ μόνα Strache and Wallies Ross: μόνον codd. Λ Bekker Waitz recte ‖ 19-20 κατηγορεῖται DVΛ Strache and Wallies Ross: κατηγορεῖσθαι ABuM Bekker Waitz recte: κατεγορεισθαι δεῖ C

Examination of the text of this passage is significant, for it can help to solve a problem that is often discussed; did Aristotle change his mind, between the *Topics*

---

9   Aristotle is referring, implicitly but without question, to 151b28-30.

and the *Posterior Analytics*, on the question whether it is possible to deduce a definition (ὅρον συλλογίζεσθαι)? Did he accept this possibility in the *Topics*, and subsequently reject it in the *Posterior Analytics*? In the passage that concerns us, he begins by saying that it would be for another treatise to explain with complete precision what a definition is and how one should give a definition (153a11-12). For the present however, he adds without any other qualification or limitation, it is sufficient to say that it is possible to get a συλλογισμός of the definition and of the essence (153a12-15). Then he describes the method to follow, in a long and complex sentence (153a15-22); I will begin by summarizing its argument in a schematic form.

D is the definition of S if and only if (a) D is a *proprium* of S (that is to say: all that is S is D and all that is D is S) and (b) D is a set Σ of predicates {P₁, P₂, ... Pₙ} such that all are essential predicates (ἐν τῷ τί ἐστι) of S and they are the only essential predicates of S.

The complex sentence which describes this argument can be set out in following way:

First protasis (153a15-16): 'If the definition is the formula which gives the essence of the thing <to be defined> ...'
Second protasis (153a16-17) '... and if the predicates in the definition must be the only ones predicated essentially of the thing <to be defined> ...'
Third protasis (153a17-18) '... and if the genera and differentiae are predicated essentially ...'
Apodosis (153a18-21): '... then it is clear that ...'
Supplementary protasis, inserted in the apodosis, and with significant textual variants (153a19-20):
With the text of Strache and Wallies and of Ross, based partly on the MSS of the second family: εἴ τις λάβοι ταῦτα ἃ μόνα ἐν τῷ τί ἐστι τοῦ πράγματος κατηγορεῖται. The sense is then: 'if one were to take (λάβοι) the attributes which are the only ones that are predicated essentially of the thing ...'
With the text of Bekker and of Waitz, based on the MSS of the first family: εἴ τις λάβοι ταῦτα μόνον ἐν τῷ τί ἐστι τοῦ πράγματος κατηγορεῖσθαι. The sense is then: 'if one were to assume (λάβοι, with a necessarily different sense) that only these attributes are predicated essentially of the thing ...'

One can easily see why the version of Bekker and Waitz is the *lectio difficilior*, in principle always to be preferred: at a first reading, ταῦτα would appear to be the object of λάβοι, and the rest of the clause is then impossible to construe; hence the introduction of the relative ἃ and the replacing of κατηγορεῖσθαι by κατηγορεῖται.

The end of the passage (153a20-22) does not present any further difficulties; it gives the eventual apodosis and its justification: '[it is clear] that the formula which contains these predicates must necessarily be the definition; for it is not possible for there to be another definition, since nothing else is predicated essentially of the thing.'

What then is the significance of the variants in lines 19-20? At first sight it seems minimal; in fact it is not. With Ross' text the dialectician must 'take', λαβεῖν, the essential predicates of the *definiendum*, that is to say identify and assemble them, as if they were already there as objective data. With Bekker's text, he must 'assume', λαβεῖν, that such-and-such attributes (ταῦτα) make up the complete set of essential predicates of the *definiendum*. With Bekker's text one can understand much better how Aristotle came to consider that a συλλογισμός of the definition would necessarily involve a *petitio principii* (what is called λαμβάνειν ἐν ἀρχῇ, and often λαμβάνειν *tout court*). Here indeed is what he says on this matter in the *Posterior Analytics* (2.6 92a6-10):

> But can one demonstrate what something is essentially by arguing from a supposition (ἐξ ὑποθέσεως) and assuming (λαβόντα) that the essence of a thing is the *proprium* composed of its essential predicates, that only such-and-such attributes (ταδὶ μόνα) are in the essence, and that the totality of them is proper to the thing? For it is the essence of the thing. But is it not true that in this case too one has assumed (εἴληφε) the essence? For one must prove it by means of the middle term.

We should add, to explain the last sentence, that this middle term is precisely the set of the essential predicates, that is to say the very definition that one is claiming to demonstrate.

So it seems clear, not only that the *Topics* accepts an argument which is rejected in the *Posterior Analytics*. but also that the way Aristotle expresses it in the *Topics* enables one to understand why he comes to reject it in the *Posterior Analytics*.

Here I end my catalogue of textual problems. I hope they are sufficient to show that there is still, in this area, interesting work to do and innocent pleasure to take.

Chapter Five

Aristotle and the Atomists on Forms and Final Causes

David Furley

I

The lines of battle are sketched clearly enough in a couple of quotations:

> Anaxagoras says it is because Man has hands that he is the most intelligent of the animals. But the right account is that he got hands because he is the most intelligent. For hands are a tool; and nature, just like an intelligent human, allots each tool to one who can make use of it.
>
> (Aristotle, *On the Parts of Animals* 4.10 687a6-11)

The opposite view is expressed by Lucretius:

> This fault we urgently desire you to avoid, this error to shun with fearful care. Do not take the bright shining eyes to have been created in order that we may be able to see. Do not believe that the tops of calves and thighs supported on feet are able to be bent in order that we can advance our eager steps. Do not accept, again, that arms are fitted to strong shoulders, and hands provided as servants on either side, in order that we can make what will be of use for life. All such theories are back to front, the product of misdirected thinking. There was no seeing before the lights of the eyes were born, no mouthing of words before the tongue was made. Rather, the origin of the tongue long preceded speech; ears were made far earlier than sound was heard; there were in fact, as I hold, all the members, before there was their use.
>
> (Lucretius, *On the Nature of Things* 4.824-41)

The focus of this lecture is on Aristotle: 'Hands are a tool,' he says, 'and nature, just like an intelligent human, allots each tool to one who can make use of it.' What is the point of the simile, in which he compares nature to a thinking being, planning the creation of man with specific purposes in mind? Everyone knows that Aristotle held that the cosmos was not created by any Craftsman, like the purposive, planning God of Plato's *Timaeus*. So what exactly is the sense of comparing nature with a planning craftsman? If the processes of nature are craftsmanlike, just how do they work? What makes them differ from the natural motions of matter in the opponents' view?

Aristotle attacks a theory, or a group of similar theories (Democritus was the prime target), according to which the physical cosmos in which we live, and all its contents, originated at some point in time from some kind of disorderly condition – some state of matter that was the opposite of a cosmos. Its origin was a matter of chance, or sheer physical necessity – necessity being a technical term for the unplanned interactions of bits and pieces of matter. The first problem is simply that no complete or even nearly complete record of such a theory has survived from the period before Aristotle. We have a wonderful record of the revival of the theory, after a century of criticism, in the work of Epicurus and his greatest follower, Lucretius. But the original targets of Aristotle's criticisms have been reduced to muddled and distorted fragments.

My chief concern today is with explanations of biological structures. But almost the only information about Democritus' ideas on the origin of man and the other animals is that 'somehow' they grew spontaneously out of warmed up mud. The most direct criticism of such ideas is levelled not at Democritus, but at Empedocles, in some famous passages of Plato and Aristotle. For example, Aristotle happens to mention (*PA* 640a19) that according to Empedocles the division of the spine into vertebrae is due to its being twisted in the womb, and he adds that that cannot possibly be the right explanation.

II

Before continuing with Aristotle, however, it is necessary to put Plato's *Timaeus* into the foreground of the picture, for several reasons. According to Bekker's index, there are nearly fifty references to the *Timaeus* in Aristotle's works, not always giving the name of the dialogue and sometimes arguable, but still significant – fewer only than references to the *Republic* and the *Laws*. The *Timaeus* is Plato's Περὶ φύσεως and Aristotle takes it seriously as such. And that is to say that he starts with the image of the divine Craftsman, and his work in shaping the natural world.

To continue with the example of the spine, Plato presents a picture of how men and animals were made in the first place by the Craftsman god, the Demiurge. In outline, this particular story goes like this. The God's primary concern is to ensure the eternity of the species, and that means that the most important physical element in the structure of animals is the seed. The seed is located in the marrow, which stretches down from the brain through the rest of the body. The seed is protected by being encased in the hollow spine; but if the spine were an uninterrupted bony tube, there would be a danger (so Plato says) that the seed would be too confined, and perhaps spoilt by excessive heat or cold. The spine needs flexibility and the capability of variation for the good of the animal species.

This strange idea will serve as an example to make a simple point. The right way of explaining the structure of the spine, Plato argues, is not to tell a story of its being broken purposelessly in the course of its growth, but to focus attention on the good that its structure contributes to the life of the species. And Plato adds that this is due to the action of a creator god, who works always with a mind to achieving goals that are good in various ways.

As everyone knows, Aristotle criticizes his predecessors for failing to understand the need, in explanations of natural processes and structures, for inquiry into four kinds of causes – material, efficient, formal, and final – the last one answering the question ἕνεκα τίνος, 'for the sake of what goal or end?' He criticizes the Presocratics, including the Atomists, for supposing that the works of nature are caused by the material constituents of the universe and their properties – especially their motions. The crux of his criticisms is encapsulated in the last chapter of his *Meteorologica* (some think that the last book is not by Aristotle, but I believe it is). The basic material stuffs of plants and animals may come into being just because of cold and heat and the changes brought about by them; but the organs and limbs composed of these simpler elements and their motion – a head, a hand, a foot – could never be caused just by cold and heat and such causes, nor could a saw or a cup or a box be produced in that way. In the latter case, craftsmanship is the cause, in the former it is nature or some other cause.

If we accept Plato's divine Craftsman at face value, there is no philosophical difficulty in understanding how the final cause operates. The Craftsman has a goal, to make the best possible material copy of the immaterial Form. The analysis of his work follows the pattern of the work of any human artist. He has a certain form in mind as his goal, and because he has that in mind he works in this way rather than that. He desires to achieve the goal, and arrives by the processes of reason at the belief that such and such means will be best for achieving this goal.

The reasoning mind thus provides the paradigm for the operation of the final cause. The idioms 'in order that' and 'for the sake of' (or their Greek equivalents) were understood primarily from their use in the context of a reasoning mind. And I take it that that context is the standard one from which we too learn the use of these idioms.

Aristotle's analysis of intentional action in *On the Motion of Animals* raises no problems at this level. He lists the causes of intentional motion as being reasoning, φαντασία, choice, wish, and appetite, and shows how these basically boil down to thought and desire. Except in the case of involuntary motions, there is no causal link between the external object, the goal or end, except through the desire and the belief of the animal, which are the direct moving causes.

He makes a similar point in the *Nicomachean Ethics*, in his discussion of praise and blame in book 3. He suggests that someone might offer an excuse for some misdemeanour by claiming that pleasant and good things are so attractive that one can't prevent oneself from going after them. 'But it's absurd,' he answers, 'to blame external objects, rather than oneself as being too easily caught by such attractions' (1110b14). It is the agent who is responsible for the action, not the external object.

III

Aristotle drops the Craftsman from his cosmology. That means that the analogy between cosmology and art or craft can no longer be used, unless some other basis can be found for it. Notoriously, Aristotle often writes as though there were no trouble here at all: he simply substitutes 'Nature' for the Craftsman, and continues with the language of human agency in talking about the structure of the physical world. 'Nature does nothing in vain'. Nature acts like a prudent householder. Nature is analogous to art or craft, except that art works on material that is outside itself, nature works from the inside.

Such statements – and there are dozens of them in Aristotle's works – have in the past led interpreters to postulate a super-agent in Aristotle's cosmology, a unified figure called Nature who chooses the right course and steers everything in the physical world (or nearly everything) towards good ends. After all the criticism that has been aimed at this kind of interpretation, there is no need to add to it now. No doubt Aristotle uses a popularizing abbreviation, not to be taken literally: he is aiming to draw attention to the abundant testimony offered by inspection of natural processes, that they do characteristically move towards advantageous ends – that they move ἕνεκά τινος, for the sake of something, for the sake of some good.

It has become almost orthodox now to claim that Nature is to be interpreted not as a unified figure, but as the collection of individual natures – the nature of this and that natural object, this plant, this animal, this human being. The notion that nature works for ends is interpreted as a summary of the vast numbers of cases collected by Aristotle, especially in the *Parts of Animals*, of tissues, parts of the body, and functions that contribute to the goal of enabling the animal to live its life in its normal environment.

The problem with such interpretations, I believe, is this. Aristotle speaks of four *causes* (αἴτια), and one of them is the final cause.

> Since the aim of our investigation is knowledge, and we think we have knowledge of a thing only when we can answer the question about it 'On account of what? (διὰ τί)' and that is to grasp the primary cause (αἰτία), it is clear that we must do this with regard to coming to be, passing away, and all natural change, so that, knowing their sources (ἀρχαί) we may try to bring all particular objects of inquiry back to them.

He lists what we know as the material cause, the formal cause, and the efficient cause, and then this:

> And again, a thing may be the cause as end (τέλος). That is what something is 'for the sake of', as health might be what walking is for the sake of.
>
> (*Phys.* 2.3, 194b17-35)[1]

---

[1]   Translation adapted from W. Charlton, *Aristotle: Physics books I and II*, Oxford: Clarendon Press, 1970, 28-9.

The difficulties of thinking of the τέλος as a cause of the action leading up to it are obvious. Chronologically the τέλος is a state of affairs that is later than the action: how can a cause be later than its effect? Again, how can the τέλος be a cause of the processes leading up to it if the being that undertakes the processes is unconscious of the advantage of reaching the τέλος? How can the pumping of the heart be caused by the beneficial distribution of blood through the body (rather than the other way round)? Some choose just to accept the facts and Aristotle's analysis of them, and talk of 'the unconscious teleology of nature'. When challenged with the objection that the τέλος is not functioning as a cause of the process, they substitute the word 'explanation' for 'cause' as a translation of αἰτία or αἴτιον. Or building on Aristotle's statement just quoted that we think we understand something when we know the 'διὰ τί', the *because* of it, some speak of Aristotle's four 'becauses' instead of 'four causes.'

I want to offer some reasons for thinking that these manoeuvres will not do. But it may be objected at this point that I am making a blatant mistake in thinking that Aristotle's idea of a cause must be roughly the same as our own. So as a first move I want to look back briefly at earlier and non-philosophical contexts in which Aristotle's cause-words appear.

IV

What lies at the core of the word αἴτιον and its cognates – the word Aristotle uses for 'cause' – is the idea of responsibility. The Attic orators, Hippocrates, and Thucydides are the most convenient sources for this comparison, because they are all particularly interested in αἴτια. We find, briefly, the following.

Hippocrates, in the essay *On Ancient Medicine* (19) offers a definition of cause: 'Those things should be deemed causes of each ailment which are such that in their presence it must necessarily come about in this manner, and when they change to another combination it ceases.'

The orators, especially, attach the adjective αἴτιος to people, in the sense 'responsible for' – usually responsible for something culpable, sometimes for something meritorious. Often the person's responsibility is defined by a participial phrase: (an invented example) 'he is to blame for the damage his sheep did to my property, having let his fence fall into disrepair.'

Thucydides sometimes shifts this use from the adjective αἴτιος in agreement with the subject to the neuter form, to make a noun: 'the cause (αἴτιον) of sending the ships was the people of Chios, not knowing what was going on' (8.9.3). 'The cause of all these things was government that was greedy and ambitious' (3.82.7).

Both in the orators and in Thucydides it is not only people who qualify as causes. 'The war was the cause of a whole lot of things' (Lysias 7.6). 'The cause was not so much shortage of men as shortage of money' (Thucydides 1.11).

I want to stress (and many more examples could be brought into play if necessary) the following. The early examples tend to pick out people or states of affairs as causes, and to specify some property belonging to them as that which makes them causes of the effect in question. Sometimes their possession of this property is put in the form of a proposition: 'the cause was that he (Pericles), being powerful in esteem and opinion and obviously quite incorruptible, commanded a willing people' (Thuc. 2.65.8).

Although some agent, in a very broad sense, is picked out as the cause, it is common to specify something about the agent that makes him or it the cause. It is not necessarily something done by the agent that plays this role. It may be something neglected. Or it may be just some property of the agent, although in that case the Hippocratic definition shows that there should be some change in the property or in its relations such as to make it into a cause.

I want to argue just three points about Aristotle's theory of the working of the final cause in nature. First, I want to claim that he understood final causes as being real *causes*, in a sense that I will try to make clear. Secondly, I will try to present an explanation of how final causes *can* be real causes, and put up some evidence that Aristotle thought of them in this way. This is not a new explanation that I have invented, but the one that I consider to be the best one, and perhaps the only one that works. Thirdly, I want to extend the application of this explanation beyond the limits usually accepted by its proponents.

V

It may be helpful to have an example from the biological works:

> In birds, it is what is called the beak that is the mouth; this is what they have instead of lips and teeth. It differs according to its uses and services. The birds called 'crook- taloned' all have a crook-shaped beak, because they feed on flesh and eat no grain or fruit; a beak of this sort is by nature more forceful and better at mastering prey. Their offensive weapon is in this and in their claws, and so they also have exceptionally curved claws. Each of the others also has a beak that is useful for their life-style. In woodpeckers, for instance, it is strong and hard, also in crows and crow-like birds; in small birds it is delicate, for picking up seeds and catching tiny creatures. Herb-eaters and those that live by marshes, such as those that are swimmers and web-footed, have various kinds of serviceable beak, some of them being flat, because with such a beak it is easy to dig – just like the pig, which is also a root-eater, to take an example from the quadrupeds.
>
> (*PA* 3.1 662a33-b14)

Aristotle claims that the raptors have crook-shaped beaks *because* they feed on flesh; Empedocles (and the Atomists) would claim that they feed on flesh *because* they have that kind of beak. Aristotle must answer the question: how can the usefulness of the beak for a particular goal be a *cause* of the shape of the beak? remembering that there is no creator god and no other agent of the process sensitive to the goodness of this kind of beak for this kind of bird.

Evolutionary biologists are in a position to answer this question by appealing to the survival value of this type of beak for raptors. Those birds which had beaks of the most suitable shape in given conditions had an advantage that enabled them, rather than their weaker competitors, to survive and reproduce in these conditions, and so to pass on this advantageous feature to succeeding generations.

Aristotle, however, was not an evolutionist; he held that biological species are eternal, and eternally the same. On the face of it, two possible lines of interpretation suggest themselves, both of them wrong, in my view. The first is that his teleology is after all no more than an 'as if' teleology. We can understand the link between a certain way of life and certain physiological or anatomical features, such as curved beaks, if we continue to think of the creatures of nature as if they were the creatures of Plato's designing Craftsman. Alternatively, without invoking an imaginary Craftsman, we could establish by observation that the creatures of nature exhibit a vast range of well adapted features of this kind. So we could explain a particular feature in a particular species by claiming that once you had perceived its usefulness it is only what you would expect to find, given the fact that adaptedness is to be found everywhere.

The weakness of interpretations of this kind, as it seems to me, is that they do not give the τέλος, the end to be achieved, the role of *cause*. Aristotle has shown, perhaps, that the curved beak is only what you would expect to find, given that nature behaves like a Craftsman or just that the creatures of nature habitually possess the parts and the tissues that are useful for their way of life. And you might well count this as an explanation of the curved beak. But Aristotle has not yet shown that the way of life is the cause of the curved beak, in the sense that it is this way of life that is responsible for this hawk's having a beak of this shape. Moreover, he has certainly not shown *how* the goal manages to act as a cause of the processes that lead up to it.

Recently there have been attempts at a new kind of analysis of the final cause in Aristotle's biology – an analysis that succeeds in giving the τέλος or goal the status of real cause, in a sense that Aristotle and we could agree to, and emphasizes the crucial fact that the τέλος is a good for the creature in question. It originated, I think, from Andrew Woodfield's book, *Teleology*, and has been adopted, in more or less the same form, by David Balme in the last of his many attacks on the problem, Jonathan Lear, and Terry Irwin, perhaps others too.[2]

The species survives, obviously enough, by means of the reproductive process. What makes any particular feature a *good* for an animal is its contribution to the animal's success in making a living for itself in its characteristic environment, and

---

[2]　A. Woodfield, *Teleology*. Cambridge: Cambridge University Press, 1976; D.M. Balme, 'Teleology and necessity', in A. Gotthelf and J.G. Lennox, eds., *Philosophical Issues in Aristotle's Biology*, Cambridge: Cambridge University Press, 1987, 275-85; J. Lear, *Aristotle: the Desire to Understand*, Cambridge: Cambridge University Press, 1988; T. Irwin, *Aristotle's First Principles*, New York: Oxford University Press, 1988, 102-16.

engendering offspring possessed of this same good feature. Aristotle worked out a detailed theory of reproduction in his *Generation of Animals*. The seed of the male is imprinted, so to speak, with the form characteristic of the species, and it passes on to the embryo the potentiality for developing that same form in the actuality of adulthood.

We have a pattern to which Aristotle draws attention in the *Physics*: three varieties of cause often 'come together in one' (συνέρχεται εἰς ἓν πολλάκις): the seed is the efficient cause of the growth of the next generation; the seed is also a bearer of the active specific form – the formal cause; and the specific form is also the final cause (that for the sake of which) of the reproductive process. Aristotle puts this point in almost telegraphic form:

> The three come together into one often: for the 'what it is' [i.e. the form] and 'that for the sake of which' [i.e. the final cause] are one, and that from which the motion starts primarily [i.e. the efficient cause] is the same in form as these: for Man begets Man.
>
> (*Phys.* 2.7, 198a24-27)

Let us return to the example of the raptors and their well-adapted beaks. If we ask why this particular hawk has a curved beak, we may give a teleological answer: 'in order to get a living by catching fieldmice and tearing their flesh.' We are not committed to saying that this particular specimen grew such a beak *with a view* to future acts of catching and tearing. Any given specimen has this equipment because its sire had it, survived by its means, and passed it on through the reproductive process. It is *because* the parental bird got a living by catching and eating little animals and had a beak well adapted to this end, that his offspring has a beak of this kind. In this way Aristotle could defend the claim with which we began: it is because man is the most intelligent animal that he has hands. It is not the case that *this* man's forthcoming intelligent actions are the cause of his getting hands. But if we collapse the generations together, so to speak (if we 'fudge the chronology,' to adopt Woodfield's expression), we can claim that the intelligent actions of the species man are the cause of the hands of the species.

There is a kind of reciprocity. It is true, as Anaxagoras said, that man has the capability of performing intelligent actions *because* he has hands. But what is the cause of his having hands? Aristotle asks. He has hands *because* his ancestors had hands and survived by their means.

If this is acceptable, we now know how the final cause acts as a cause of the formation of biological structures. It is because (first) the final cause is identical to the form of the animal, as Aristotle remarks in the opening sentence of the *Generation of Animals*: the goal of the growth of the embryo is just to reproduce the form that was imparted to the embryo by the parent (the male parent, in Aristotle's view); and (second) this formal/final cause is an aspect of the efficient cause of the growth of the embryo: as Aristotle said in the *Physics*: 'The three come together into one.'

But this needs a further distinction. The formal/final cause does not tell the whole causal story of the generation of animals. The material cause plays its part too. Given that there is to be a new member of the species, there must be present the right materials as well as the potentiality for reproduction of the form. The potentiality for growth is embedded in materials of a certain kind, and these materials have properties of their own, including active properties such as rising and falling, heating and cooling; these properties are unquestionably efficient causes, in Aristotle's terminology. This accounts for a puzzle that has sometimes led interpreters away from the kind of explanation of Aristotle's theory that I have been outlining. As we would expect if this kind of explanation is right, Aristotle often groups together the formal, final and efficient causes and contrasts them with the material cause. But often, too, he pairs off the efficient cause with the material cause, and contrasts them with the others. But the efficient cause, the cause 'from which comes the principle of motion or change', is complex. The fact that it is often paired with the material cause is no obstacle to its coincidence with the formal and final cause in other contexts.

VI

At this point it may be useful to sum up the position for which I am arguing.

In the first place, I claim that Aristotle's analysis of four kinds of αἴτια, four kinds of cause, is intended to indicate ontological connections, not epistemological or heuristic methods. When he maintains that A is an αἴτιον of B, he is claiming that A is in some way responsible for B – responsible for B's existence or for the occurrence of B, depending on what sort of an item B is.

This language is primarily used in circumstances where we have an agent bringing about some state of affairs or creating some object, and in the case of the final cause we can most easily understand the language if the agent is conscious of the goodness or usefulness of the goal that is aimed at. The physical world is described by Plato in the *Timaeus* as being the product of such an agent. But in Aristotle's ontology there is no divine Craftsman and no universal, personified Nature. There is a real problem, then, in finding an interpretation of Aristotle that gives the goal or end the role of cause in the relevant cases.

If we are to give the τέλος a causal role that will square with Aristotle's conception of an αἴτιον, we are bound to reject the kind of interpretation that makes teleology into a metaphor, just a handy way of describing the observed facts that biological processes tend towards particular ends and that the part of living beings seem to be organized for the good of the whole creature.

What is observed is that the goods aimed at in the living world are the survival of individual specimens in their appropriate lifestyle, their proper niche in the ecology, and the reproduction, the continued generation of new bearers of the appropriate form. As Aristotle puts it in a famous but tiresomely metaphorical passage in *On Generation and Corruption* (2.10, 336b27-35):[3]

> In all things, as we affirm, Nature always strives after the better. Now being ... is better than not-being; but not all things can possess being, since they are too far removed from the principle. God therefore adopted the remaining alternative, and fulfilled the perfection of the universe by making coming-to-be uninterrupted; for the greatest possible coherence would thus be secured to being, because that coming-to-be should itself come-to-be perpetually is the closest approximation to eternal being.

I have tried to defend a demythologized version of this passage, removing nature and God from the role of conscious and purposive agents. I believe this can be done if we recognize the identity of Form in parent and offspring. The Form that is to be reproduced acts as a cause in reproduction, not by pulling the growing embryo along from in front like some kind of magnet, but by serving as an aspect of the efficient cause of the embryo, in that the parent's form is, in a sense, the same as the form that is to be produced. 'Fudging the chronology,' as Woodfield expressed it, or overlooking the difference between numerical identity and formal identity.

VII

But I want to continue by widening the focus.

I began this lecture with a contrast between Aristotle and Lucretius, and I shall conclude it with a more extended contrast between Lucretius and an unknown admirer of Aristotle, possibly of about the same date as Lucretius. I mean the author of the brief essay *On the cosmos*, *De mundo*, addressed to Alexander ('O Alexander') and handed down in the manuscript tradition as part of the Aristotelian corpus. I think this author lived in the first century B.C. or thereabouts, although I should mention that there has recently been a revival (by Giovanni Reale) of the idea that he is Aristotle himself.

It is possible that we can get some insight into Aristotle's theory about the causes at work in the cosmos from these two works. Book 5 of Lucretius and chapters 5 and 6 of the *De mundo* share some subject matter in common, they are both addressed to an audience that is philosophically fairly naive, and they are rather precisely opposed in their outlook.

The crux of the matter is to find the causes of the regularity and order in the world. Even the words themselves – the Greek word κόσμος and the Latin word *mundus* – draw attention to this feature of the world in their etymologies. There is a

---

[3]   Translation from J. Barnes, ed., *The complete works of Aristotle : the revised Oxford translation*, Princeton: Princeton University Press, 1984 with modifications.

regular cycle of seasons, year by year; the motions of the sun and the other heavenly bodies are a paradigm of orderly movement. All of life on earth depends, in one way or another, on this regularity, and living species are manifestly shaped in such a way that they can profit from it.

But how could regularity, order, and adaptiveness come from the random jostlings of innumerable atoms in illimitable space? That was the central problem of the atomic theory of Epicureanism. Lucretius starts book 5 with a long denunciation of theories of divine creationism, and the rest of the book is devoted to the proof that the world order was the product of nothing but atoms in motion in the void.

It is essential to the plausibility of Lucretius' account of the origin of the world that we keep in mind the laws of chance. Without this idea the whole atomic theory would collapse or need some new support. If we accept the arguments of the earlier books of Lucretius' poem, we know that atoms, with their various shapes and sizes, can produce all the varied compounds that we see in the world around us. But if they *can* produce these things, then we must accept that random conjunctions repeated an unlimited number of times *will* ultimately produce all of them (so Lucretius believed), including things as vast and complex as a world. Our world is indeed a remarkable and untypical set of atoms: but even such remarkable sets must be expected to turn up occasionally in an unlimited series of randomly formed sets.

That is the basis of the theory. It does not say, of course, that our world came into existence all at once, exactly as we see it now, out of a colliding set of atoms. The growth of the world is a gradual process, and it is described by Lucretius step by step. First is the formation of 'seeds', that is to say, groups of atoms that because of their shapes and the way they move have the power to adhere together and to retain others as they collide, gathering mass like a snowball. There is first a 'storm' (*tempestas*); a host of atoms meet in confused motion; and as the motion continues, atoms of similar shape and size are sorted into different regions, thus separating the sky, the earth, and the sea.

The argument has its high and low points. It is at its least convincing in its account of the motions of the heavenly bodies. Greek astronomy had reached a high level of mathematical precision long before Lucretius' time, and it was hardly enough to offer suggestions that the sun and moon are blown this way and that by currents of air. Lucretius could do little better by way of explaining the regularity of the natural cycles than to assert, hopefully, that similar causes always produce similar effects. We observe regularity, for example, in the blossoming of trees and the growth of beards, and we do not habitually invoke the action of gods or other unnatural causes to explain it. So with the motions of the heavenly bodies: their regularity can be attributed to nature and not to divinity. For the Epicurean programme, this was enough: the goal was to eliminate the action of the gods by showing that it was an unnecessary hypothesis.

The story of the development of living forms from the earth deserves special mention. After the elaborate teleological accounts of animal structure in Aristotle's biological works, the Epicureans had to find a plausible story to explain how these well-adapted creatures could appear spontaneously on earth where none had been before. The answer was provided by a theory of the selective survival of the fit. The earth produced, spontaneously, not only the ancestors of all the well-adapted creatures that we see around us, but also, at the same time, a host of ill-adapted monsters that could not make a living. Lucretius enjoys listing some of them:

> The androgyne, not one thing nor another,
> remote from both: the footless and the handless;
> the dumb without a mouth, the faceless blind;
> the stuck-together limb-locked holomorph –
> all such that could not act nor move at all
> to flee from harm or seek for sustenance.
> And many other prodigies earth made –
> in vain, since nature stopped them from increase:
> they could not pluck maturity's sweet flower,
> not capture food, nor mate in Venus' way.
>   (5.839-48)

Thus all inefficient creatures perished.

Lucretius continues with a marvellously imaginative description, step by step, of the progress of human civilization from primitive men who lived in the woods and ate whatever they could pick up or catch, to sophisticated peoples who created cities, agriculture, music – and war. In each stage his concern is to show how necessity, coupled with human ingenuity, can reasonably be supposed to have produced the next step in the sequence, up to our own times. There are, of course, moral dimensions in the story he tells, but we are not concerned with them now.

To turn now to the *De mundo*. In chapter 5, the author's aim is to insist on the eternity of the world order. You might think, he says, that since the cosmos is made of components with opposite qualities, it must necessarily be unstable, but that is wrong. It is like a city, a πόλις: 'the most wonderful thing about the harmonious working of a city-community is this: that out of plurality and diversity it achieves a homogeneous unity capable of admitting every variation of nature and degree' (an optimistic picture, perhaps). He goes on:

> But perhaps nature actually has a liking for opposites: perhaps it is from them that she creates harmony, and not from similar things. ... The complex of the Universe (ἡ τῶν ὅλων σύστασις), I mean heaven and earth and the whole cosmos, by means of a mixture of the most opposite elements has been organized in a single harmony: dry mixed with wet, hot with cold, light with heavy, straight with curved – the whole of earth and sea, the aether, the sun, the moon and the whole heaven are ordered by the single power (δύναμις) that interpenetrates all things: from things unmixed and diverse, air and earth and fire and water, it has fashioned the whole cosmos and embraced it all in the surface of a single sphere, forcing the most opposite elements in the cosmos to come to terms, and from them achieving preservation (σωτηρία) for the whole.

There is a touch of Stoic vocabulary in this, but the main theme is wholly Aristote-lian, and the key word is 'preservation' (σωτηρία), repeated several times in the chapter. This is the good aimed at, the final cause of the interaction of the elements as described in this chapter. The author finds good in everything: 'this earth keeps its never-aging nature unchanged, though it is racked by earthquakes, swamped by floods, and burnt in part by fires. All these things happen for the good of the earth, and give it preservation from age to age.' Earthquakes ventilate the earth, he suggests, hopefully; floods clean it, winds purify it, fires soften things that are frozen and frost moderates the force of the fires. And so on.

In chapter 6, the theme is not preservation, but order in diversity. In a series of elaborate similes, the author stresses three points at considerable length: there is a single ultimate cause of motion in the cosmos, each different kind of being in the cosmos responds to this cause in its own characteristic way, and the resultant product is good order. The most elaborate simile compares the cosmos with the organisation of the Persian empire in the fabulous days of its greatness. The King himself lived in a great and marvellous palace, surrounded by a vast hierarchy of bodyguards, revenue officials, generals, palace servants; and further afield, satraps, subordinate kings, couriers, scouts, signals-officers, etc. 'And such was the orderly arrangement of this, (he concludes) and particularly the system of signal-beacons that were ready to burn in succession from the uttermost limits of the Empire to Susa and Ecbatana, that the King knew the same day all that was news in Asia.'

Now let me finally get to the point that I want to extract from these brief summaries of parts of Lucretius' poem and the *De mundo*. In Lucretius we have a cosmology that insists on the origin of our world from a storm of atoms, through no agency but their own shapes, weights, sizes and motions. There is no Craftsman, no plan, no final cause. The world exhibits such permanence and orderliness as it has as a result of the natural motions of bits of matter, and it will come to an end at some time and vanish back into the stormy mass. Our popularizing Aristotelian on the other hand emphasizes permanence and orderliness above everything else. His world has no origin and will have no end. Throughout its existence in time and throughout its extension in space it has those qualities that enable it to survive. These qualities are not imposed by any external agent; they are immanent in the whole structure. Even the simile of the Great King of Persia makes no mention of his having created the structure, or even of his intervening in its operation – indeed, it makes a particular point of insisting that he does not intervene but sits in majesty in the palace, an unmoved mover of all the elements below him.

Now the contrast with the Lucretian cosmos, and the emphasis of the *De mundo*, both suggest that the teleological analysis of the Aristotelian cosmos should extend through the whole structure. This is a point that will be regarded as thoroughly controversial in the present climate of opinion. It will be conceded (with a certain amount of embarrassment) that Aristotle's description of the heavens is teleological in a very simple way: the starry spheres are alive, they have souls, and they eternally perform circular motions in intentional imitation of the eternity of the supreme god. In the lower cosmos, biological structures and processes are unquestionably given final causes by Aristotle – that has been the main focus of the earlier part of this lecture. But there seems to me to be something unsatisfactory in leaving out of the teleological picture the rest of the working of the cosmos – I am thinking particularly of the relations between biological species, and the relations between the parts of the sublunary cosmos.

Speaking of the σωτηρία, the preservation of animal kinds, David Balme wrote the following in one of his last and most influential articles:

> Just as the very existence of a species requires no deeper cause than the survival of those animals that best fit into a niche, so the preservation of a species requires only the survival of the fit ... the real problem is what ensures the reproduction of the individual.[4]

This represents a common tendency, I believe. We may ask what are the causes of the continued existence of the species that we see around us, but not why there are the species that there are. David Balme has himself done much to undermine the notion that Aristotle thought of filling in all the links in a great chain of being, and the notion that he aimed at a comprehensive and systematic classification of animals. The prevailing idea is that in the Aristotelian cosmos it is just a fact, for which no teleological explanation is to be sought, that we have the four elements situated where they are and interchanging through the seasons as they do; and that we have all the biological species that we see around us. However, David Sedley has reminded us[5] of the evidence in Aristotle's text for a much wider application of the teleological view: the repeated phrase 'nature does nothing pointless', the insistence on the balance of the elements and their opposed qualities, the argument about seasonal rainfall and the growth of crops (which I wrote about a while ago),[6] the comparison in *Metaphysics* Λ 10 between the cosmos and a well-ordered army, and the famous claim in the *Politics* (1.8) that plants are for the sake of animals, and animals are for the sake of men. I would add one argument from *On the Heaven* (2.3) that I find attractive. At this point, Aristotle claims to have shown that

the activity of god is eternal life,
eternal life entails eternal motion,
eternal motion entails circular motion,
therefore there must be a body that moves eternally in a circle;
therefore, finally, there must be a centre that is at rest.

---

[4] D.M. Balme, 'Teleology and necessity', above n.2, at 280.

[5] D.N. Sedley, 'Is Aristotle's teleology anthropocentric?', *Phronesis* 36 (1991) 179-96.

[6] D.J. Furley, 'The rainfall example in *Physics* 2.8', in A. Gotthelf, ed., *Aristotle on Nature and Living Things: Philosophical and Historical Studies presented to David M. Balme* ..., Pittsburgh: Mathesis, 1986, 177-82, reprinted in D.J. Furley, *Cosmic Problems*, Cambridge: Cambridge University Press, 1989, 115-20.

This is the earth. There is a final cause, therefore, of the position of the earth: it is there in order that the heavens may circle around it. In *On Generation and Corruption* he goes on to show that the other elements must be there in order to balance the qualities of earth and of each other. Balance is necessary for eternity.

What about the relations between living species? I have quoted from Balme the notion that each living species has a niche, in which it manages to survive by uninterrupted reproduction. But niche itself is a normative word: it is the *right* place for this species. David Sedley has proposed, in the article I have already mentioned, that the sublunary cosmos, including other living species, is for the sake of man, in the way that became familiar in the post-Aristotelian generation, in Stoic cosmology. There is some evidence for this, but frankly, not a lot.

However, whether the anthropocentric view is true for Aristotle or not, the question that I have been asking about individual species of living things arises again: how can the balance of the sublunary elements, or the relations between biological species, or meteorological phenomena be *caused* by their benefit to the structure as a whole? Perhaps it can be done by a manoeuvre with the chronology similar to the one I have suggested for the internal teleology of biological species. The structures and processes in question have in the past served to keep the cosmos in existence because they contribute to its good order. Their past behaviour is a cause of their present behaviour. It could not be so if they were disruptive; by being ordered as they were, they are responsible for the continuance of the order.

The eternity of the cosmic order is what is most characteristic of Aristotelian cosmology, and the author of the *De mundo* is right to make this the climax of his rhetorical essay. The worlds of the atomists had beginnings and ends; the world of the Platonists, Neoplatonists, and later the Christians had a beginning. The world order of the Stoics went through a repetitive cycle of beginnings and ends.

Chapter Six

An Aristotelian Theory of the Emotions*

John M. Cooper

I

Aristotle's ethics and political theory are constructed round a closely knit family of psychological concepts: those of happiness (εὐδαιμονία), virtue (ἀρετή), practical wisdom (φρόνησις), action (πρᾶξις), state or habit (ἕξις), desire (ὄρεξις), pleasure and pain (ἡδονή and λύπη), choice or decision (προαίρεσις) – and the emotions or passions (the πάθη). In his ethical treatises Aristotle elaborates theoretical accounts of all the members of this family but two: desire and emotion – and since two of the three types of desire that he recognizes (appetites and spirited desires) are cross-classified by him as emotional states, the emotions are even more isolated in that anomalous position than that may make it sound. The most we get in any of the ethical treatises is an illustrative list, the longest of which (in *Nicomachean Ethics* 2.5) reads as follows: appetite, anger, fear, confidence, envy, joy, feelings of friendliness, hatred, yearning (that is, for an absent or lost person that one is

*   Cooper, John M. *Reason and Emotion*, 406-423. Copyright © 1999 by Princeton University Press. Reprinted by permission of Princeton University Press.

    This essay is a lightly edited version of my 1992-93 S.V. Keeling Memorial Lecture, delivered at University College, London, in May 1993. The lecture, in turn, was based on my paper 'Rhetoric, Dialectic, and the Passions.' The first version of that paper was prepared for delivery at an international Symposium on Philosophical Issues in Aristotle's Rhetoric sponsored by the Philosophical Society of Finland, Helsinki, August 1991. Subsequently I read revised versions at departmental colloquia at Dartmouth and Pomona colleges. I would like to thank the organizers of the Helsinki symposium, and especially Juha Sihvola, for their hospitality, and the other participants, both local and from abroad, for stimulating and helpful discussion of many interesting issues in the *Rhetoric*, including the ones treated in this essay. The essay as published owes a great deal to criticisms and suggestions made in discussion on all three of these occasions, but I am especially grateful to Alexander Nehamas for his detailed and perceptive written comments on the penultimate version. It was while I was a Fellow of the Center for Advanced Study in the Behavioral Sciences that I prepared the Keeling Lecture, and I am grateful to the Center and to the Andrew W. Mellon Foundation, which provided financial support for my fellowship, for their assistance.

attached to), eagerness to match another's accomplishments, and pity. Aristotle provides no general, analytical account of the emotions anywhere in any of the ethical writings. And we are in for disappointment if we look for this in his supposedly scientific account of psychological matters in the *De Anima*.

As is well known, Aristotle does however develop fairly detailed accounts of some eleven or twelve emotions – on a generous count, perhaps fifteen – in an unexpected place, the second book of the *Rhetoric*, his work on the art of public speaking. Can we turn there to find Aristotle's full theory of the emotions? Regrettably, an adequate answer must take account of a number of complexities – I will be elaborating some of these as I go along, and attempting to assess their significance. But, by way of preliminary orientation, let me give the short answer that I will be attempting to justify in the course of the essay. The discussion of the *Rhetoric*'s specifically limited set of emotions cannot be regarded as based upon or providing us with Aristotle's final, 'scientific' theory (as we would be entitled to regard any comparable theory in the ethical works or the *De Anima*). Rather, what we find there is, from the point of view of Aristotle's mature ethical and psychological theory, a preliminary, purely dialectical investigation that clarifies the phenomena in question and prepares the way for a philosophically more ambitious overall theory, but does no more than that. However, as we go through the particular emotions that he discusses, we can see certain patterns emerging that, although not found in his discussion of each emotion, plainly could be made the basis for a comprehensive general theory, and one that is of considerable interest, both philosophically and historically. Having done the work on the selected emotions dealt with in the *Rhetoric*, Aristotle had achieved certain systematic insights that he could have used as the basis for a positive philosophical theory of the nature of emotions. But he never got around to doing that; at least as far as we know, he did not.

Before turning to Aristotle's accounts of the emotions in Book 2 of the *Rhetoric*, I need to say something about how the emotions fit into his overall project in that work.

At the beginning of *Rhetoric* Book 1, Aristotle argues that there are precisely three 'technical' or artful ways that public speakers have of persuading their audiences. In the body of the work, including his discussion of the emotions, he aims to provide the information aspiring orators need in order to train themselves to wield these three instruments on the basis of real knowledge, and so lay claim to the possession of a true art of oratory. First, Aristotle says, public speakers need to appear to their hearers to be intelligent, good, and well-intentioned persons (that is, ones who have good character). Second, they need to induce in their audiences appropriately directed states of emotion that will influence their audiences' judgment on the matter under discussion in a way favourable to the orators and their cases. Third, they need to present reasons that the audience will find plausible and will cause them to judge as true whatever conclusions the orators are trying to promote (they need to *argue* well). It is mostly in connection with the first and especially the second of these objectives that Aristotle provides information about the emotions in Book 2. The orator needs to know how to represent himself to the audience as being moved by such emotions as will help to establish him as a good person in general, and well-intentioned toward the audience in particular; and he needs to know how to engender in them the emotions that will cause them to judge the matter as he wishes them to.

Throughout the *Rhetoric* Aristotle limits himself, in preparing and presenting his material on how to wield the three instruments of persuasion, to a dialectical survey of the relevant data from common sense and 'reputable opinion' (in Greek, the ἔνδοξα) that bear on the matters he takes up. He does indeed say that rhetoric is something like an offshoot of both dialectic *and* ethics (or politics), but it is clear that by referring to ethics as one parent of rhetoric he does not intend to say that rhetoric borrows opinions from an accomplished philosophical theory of ethical matters. He says quite plainly, so far as the premises of an oratorical argument go, that opinions must be drawn from what is reputable and plausible, and not from the results of a special science, not even from the philosophical theory of politics or ethics (1.4 1359b2-18, with 1.2 1358a21-6) – what here he actually calls political or ethical science (ἐπιστήμη). If rhetoric did that it would no longer be mere rhetoric, but would turn itself into the science or theory in question, actually establishing its conclusions, rather than merely getting people to believe them on grounds persuasive to them. And it seems that this restriction to ἔνδοξα applies across the board: in selecting the materials from which to represent his own character in a favourable light and in engendering in the audience helpful emotions, as well, the orator will depend upon a dialectical knowledge of reputable opinions about the emotions, and not a 'scientific' knowledge derived from a fully justified philosophical theory of them. Accordingly, when Aristotle in Book 2 offers to the orator information about the emotions that he is to use in engendering or preventing emotions in his hearers, this is an exercise in dialectic. He is collecting and sorting through, for the aspiring orator's benefit, the established and reputable opinions about what the various relevant emotions are, and about various relevant points about them.

Where the instilling of emotions is concerned, it is easy to see, however, that the dialectical appeal to such opinions will be different from what it is in the case of the other two instruments of persuasion. A systematic, dialectical study of the various ἔνδοξα – the recognized and highly reputed opinions – about what is good and bad for communities, right and wrong, legal and illegal, worthy of praise and the reverse, is obviously a very good way of preparing oneself to construct arguments on these matters before a classical Greek audience, whether in a deliberative, judicial, or ceremonial context. These are precisely the opinions that the audience can be expected to regard highly themselves, and so to be swayed by, if the opinions can be marshalled in such a way as to support logically the point of view for which the orator is speaking, or at any rate to seem to the audience to do so (see 1356a35-6). Likewise, in attempting to represent himself to the judges as intelligent and perceptive about practical matters, and as a serious person of good general character, he needs to be guided by the recognized and reputed indicators of these characteristics. For, again, it is likely that his audience will be disposed to regard a person as having good character if he displays just those indicators in his speech, and avoids displaying the contrary ones. Here what matters is to know what one's hearers will think favours a certain conclusion that one desires them to reach.[1]

When one comes to the orator's wielding of the remaining 'way of persuading,' by inducing the appropriate emotional state of mind in his audience, the story must necessarily be more complicated. For here it is evidently not enough to know what the audience will think people are like who are prone to become angry or afraid, or to feel pity, or to have vindictive or friendly feelings, and so on. Nor is it enough to know toward what sorts of persons the audience thinks that people typically feel these feelings, or under what circumstances and occasions.[2] (These are the three subtopics into which Aristotle divides his treatments of the emotions in Book 2 [see 2.1 1378a23-8].) The orator's purpose is actually to make his hearers feel in some of these ways, and prevent them from feeling in other ways, toward specific persons on given occasions and circumstances (toward his client in a judicial case, for example), and to use these feelings to direct or influence their judgment. Plainly, whatever the grounds are for proceeding dialectically here, it ought not to be simply because doing so gives one the ability to influence the audience's opinions about who is or isn't in a given state of feeling toward a given other person! If what he needs to do is actually to make them angry, it hardly matters whether they also think they are.

It seems clear that Aristotle's restriction of the orator to dialectical knowledge of the emotions rests upon his general view that qualification for expertise in oratory must rest only upon that kind of knowledge. But from his own

---

[1]   Here and throughout this discussion of ἔνδοξα I restrict my attention to the aims and practices of the individual Aristotelian artistic orator. His function is to do the best the circumstances permit to find things to say that his hearers will take as bases for believing whatever it is he is arguing for; his art does not consist in discovering the truth and attempting to persuade them of that. Two considerations should be borne in mind, however, lest my discussion give the impression that for Aristotle the art of rhetoric is completely value- and truth-neutral. First, as we will see more fully below, Aristotle thinks that the ἔνδοξα the orator appeals to in marshalling his argument and representing his character bear a strong positive relation to the truth – they somehow reflect, and so indicate, the truth. Second, his remarks at 1.1 (1355a20-4, 29-33) about the usefulness of the art of rhetoric indicate that, at least in judicial and deliberative oratory, where there are speakers on both sides, the joint function of the artistic orators who speak on any question is to help the hearers to reach the best, most truthful decision possible on the matter at hand. By listening to excellently prepared speeches on all sides of the question, a mass of people are placed in the best position such a mass can be in to decide correctly: they have before them all the relevant truth-indicators, each as favourably presented as possible.

[2]   See 2.1 1378a23-8, where Aristotle gives this threefold division of the material to be treated in preparing the orator for his task – except, of course, that there he says he will investigate how people *are* when they are angry, etc., not how any audience will think they are.

philosophical point of view what makes it acceptable to him to restrict the orator in this way is that he himself believes that ethical theory (what he calls here ethical or political science, which does aim at establishing the facts about what the emotions really are, and so on), itself starts from, and is responsible to, the very ἔνδοξα that dialectic and rhetoric are specially directed to acquire effective control over. So, if in learning about the various passions – their surrounding psychology, their objects and occasions – the 'artistic' orator turns to the recognized and reputable opinions about these matters, and not somehow directly to the phenomena themselves, he is at least behaving no differently from the way Aristotle's full-fledged moral and political philosopher behaves, in beginning his own investigations of these matters.[3] If what results is less than what Aristotle thinks a fully independent philosophical theory might ideally be able to achieve, he himself thinks there is good reason to accept the accounts he will provide as approximately true. As we proceed we will see for ourselves that what Aristotle offers his aspiring orators, and us modern readers too, is well grounded in an appropriately thoughtful study of the emotions themselves, and not merely what people say about them.

II

As I have said, Aristotle distinguishes and devotes at least some direct attention to the defining characteristics of fifteen emotions. He gives separate, formal treatment to twelve, in the following order: feeling angry (ὀργή), feeling mildly (πραότης), feeling friendly (φιλία, i.e., τὸ φιλεῖν), feeling hatred (μῖσος), feeling afraid (φόβος), feeling confident in the face of danger (θαρρεῖν), feeling disgraced (αἰσχύνη), feeling kindly (χάριν ἔχειν), pity (ἔλεος), righteous indignation (νεμεσᾶν), envy (φθόνος), and feeling eagerness to match the accomplishments of others (ζῆλος). Actually, it is not perfectly clear whether Aristotle means to say that πραότης (feeling mildly) is a state of feeling on its own, or only the absence of angry feelings when they would be expected or justified; his definition of πράυνσις, becoming calm or mild, explicitly makes it simply a settling down and quieting of anger (1380a8).[4] But I take this to be a lapse, and suppose he does mean to treat

---

[3] On this see John M. Cooper, *Reason and Emotion*, Princeton: Princeton University Press, 1999, chapter 12 pp. 288-9; and chapter 18, pp. 398-9.

[4] By contrast, in his treatments of the other two 'negation' feelings on his list, hatred and confidence, it seems fairly clear that he regards them as positive states of feeling on their own, not merely the absence of the feelings with which they are contrasted – friendly feelings and fear, respectively. But he gives no formal definition of μῖσος at all, and the closest he comes to a definition for θάρσος (1383a17-18) is partial at best, so we are left to draw this inference from his descriptions of the circumstances, etc., for these feelings. One should note, however, that at one place Aristotle equates those experiencing confidence simply with those who are ἀπαθεῖς under certain circumstances (1383a28): he means, of course, free of the πάθος of fear, but this is certainly a careless remark at

feeling mildly as a separate emotion. Two further feelings are named more or less incidentally and accorded briefer, but still not insubstantial treatment: *Schadenfreude* (an accompaniment of envy [1386b34-1387a3 and 1388a23-5]), and feeling disdainful, an accompaniment of eagerness to match others' accomplishments (1388b22-8). A third, unnamed feeling, which stands to righteous indignation as *Schadenfreude* does to envy – it is pleasurable feeling at the punishment or other come-down of those who deserve it – also comes in for brief treatment (1386b25-33 and 1387b14-20).

In studying these chapters it is important to bear in mind that Aristotle means to discuss throughout states of feeling – passions or emotions, conditions in which one's mind or consciousness is affected, moved, or stirred up. This applies equally to φιλία and χάρις (feeling friendly and kindly) despite some awkwardness of expression, as it does to anger, fear, and the other more obvious cases of such feelings. I begin, then, with some remarks on Aristotle's discussions in 2.4 and 2.7 of these two feelings.

Awkwardly, Aristotle defines χάρις (what I am translating as 'kindly feelings') in 2.7 in terms of action not feeling: it is 'helping someone in need, not in return for anything[5] nor for the good of the one helping, but for that of the one helped.' Formally, then, the person who 'has χάρις' is the one who acts in this helping way; the definition apparently makes no reference to the emotion that might lead to such action. Or does it? Perhaps one should take Aristotle's reference to helping actions as indicating, elliptically, the emotion that leads to them (akin to friendly feelings, I suppose: a warm feeling of attachment to someone, with a desire to do that person good for her or his own sake). But of course what Aristotle should primarily be telling aspiring orators about is a feeling that they need either to engender in or remove from their audience's mind. And in what follows in 2.7 (1385a30-1385b11) he seems to limit himself to discussing the means of showing an audience that someone has shown *them* χάρις or failed to do so. Nevertheless, the connection to an emotion of the audience's is perhaps implicit even here, as is suggested at two places (1380a27 and 1380b32) in 2.3, where Aristotle says we don't (can't) get angry at people who are apparently mistreating us, if they have treated us excessively kindly in the past. His point is that, just as fear of someone conflicts with and prevents simultaneous anger at them (1380a31-3), so the emotion of kindly feeling (that results from one's recognizing kind treatment from a person in the past) conflicts with and prevents simultaneous anger against them for a present apparent insult or unjustified belittlement. So his point in talking in 2.7 about who has and who has not behaved kindly to the audience in the past is to provide the

---

best if he thinks of confidence as one *among* the πάθη, as it seems clear that, officially, he does.
[5]   That is, not so as to get anything in return: acting to return a favour already received is not being ruled out here, as Cope, *The Rhetoric of Aristotle*, wrongly feared the language might suggest.

orator with a means of engendering, out of naturally arising gratitude, or preventing, feelings of kindness in the audience – for example, toward persons in court or toward the people of other cities whose petitions might be before an assembly or council for decision.

I turn now to 2.4, on friendly feelings and hatred. This chapter is anomalous in several ways. In every chapter except this one Aristotle overtly organizes his discussion in accordance with a tripartite pattern for discussing the emotions that he lays down at the end of 2.1 (1378a23-30). After giving his definition of the specific state of feeling, he goes on to discuss (not always in the same order) (a) what personal conditions or circumstances, especially what psychological conditions (what other feelings or beliefs, in general what frames of mind), make people apt to experience the feeling (πῶς ἔχοντες or διακείμενοι), (b) what sorts of people they do or do not feel the feeling toward (τίσιν or πρὸς τίνας), and (c) what the occasions are of their having, or not having, the feeling for that kind of person (ἐπὶ ποίοις or διὰ ποῖα). His allegiance to this programme is quite striking in each chapter, even where he understandably lumps together the discussion of the second and third points. We get this tripartite structure presented in every chapter, in virtually the same language each time.[6]

This language and this structure for the discussion are totally absent from the chapter on friendly feeling and hatred. It is true that the chapter begins with a promise first to define friendly feelings[7] and then to say who people feel that way (τίνας) toward and why (διὰ τί). But there is no separate mention anywhere in the chapter of the very important first point, the frames of mind that tend to promote our feeling that way. And the language here (and subsequently in the chapter where he addresses the third point, the occasions of friendly feeling) is not paralleled in any of the other chapters (see ποιητικὰ φιλίας, 1381b35, ποιητικὰ ἔχθρας, 1382a1-2). Finally, the whole discussion, although genuinely illuminating and

---

[6] See 2.2 1379a9-10, 1379b27-8; 2.3 1380a5-7; 2.5 1382b27-9, 1383a14-15; 2.6 1383b12-13; 2.7 1385a16-17, 30-31; 2.8 1385b11-12, 1386a3-4, 16-17; 2.9 1387a5-8; 2.10 1387b21-4, 1388a23-4; 2.11 1388a29-30, 1388b24-7.

[7] He writes: τὴν φιλίαν καὶ τὸ φιλεῖν ὁρισάμενοι λέγωμεν, 1380b34. I believe the καὶ here is likely to be epexegetic; that is, I think it likely that φιλίαν has the sense here that Aristotle gives to it at *Nic. Eth.* 2.5 1105b22 and *Topics* 4.5 126a12, where the contexts put it beyond doubt that it means not 'friendship' (an established personal relationship, or a settled state of character of some sort) but an occurrent feeling, or type of feeling. In effect, φιλία substitutes in these contexts for φίλησις as the noun for τὸ φιλεῖν. Hence in the first sentence of *Rhetoric* 2.4 Aristotle is not promising to give us two definitions, one of friendship and one of friendly feeling, but only the one definition, of friendly feeling, that he immediately provides. (This is the only formal definition, with the usual ἔστω, anywhere in the chapter.) When he adds (1381a1-2) a statement about what makes someone a friend of someone else, this is not a backward way of fulfilling a promise to define friendship, but the needed introduction of the notion of a friend – the sort of person who regularly experiences friendly feeling – on which so much of what follows is going to be based.

insightful, has fewer signposts and is more of a miscellany than any other discussion in this part of the treatise.

As a consequence, we face special difficulties in interpreting what Aristotle says about these emotions in this chapter. I mentioned just now that he begins by giving a definition of friendly feelings, τὸ φιλεῖν. This is exactly as we should expect: in the *Nicomachean Ethics* (8.5 1157b28-9) he ranks friendly feeling (φίλησις) as an emotion or feeling, in contrast to friendship (φιλία), which he says is a settled state involving decision. The definition itself in the *Rhetoric* is very close to the account given in the *Nicomachean Ethics* of goodwill (8.2 1155b31-2), which helps to make the connection that Aristotle promised at the beginning of Book 2 (*Rhet.* 2.1 1378a19-20) between the discussion of the emotions and instruction in how to present yourself in speaking as having the interests of your audience at heart (i.e., as he says, having goodwill for them).[8] The definition of τὸ φιλεῖν runs as follows: 'Let us suppose having friendly feelings to be wishing someone what you think are good things, for his sake and not for your own, and being ready, as far as you can, to act accordingly.'[9]

However, he goes on immediately[10] to speak instead of friendship, or rather what it is to be friends with someone – the established relationship in which two

---

8   I take it that Aristotle's language at 1378a19-20 (περὶ δ' εὐνοίας καὶ φιλίας ἐν τοῖς περὶ τὰ πάθη λεκτέον), linking the two terms together in this way, indicates that we are to go to the chapter on friendly feeling to find out how to represent this aspect of our own characters. Alternatively, one might think he is directing us to the entire subsequent discussion – so that, for example, one might pick up pointers from 2.7 on kindly feelings and 2.8 on pity to use in presenting oneself as 'well-disposed' to the audience by making oneself appear to feel pity or kindness for them or theirs. In view of the special linkage at 1378a19-20 between εὔνοια and φιλία, however, I think this alternative interpretation is not likely to be correct.

9   The Greek for 'wish' here is βούλεσθαι. In Aristotle's technical philosophy of mind, a 'wish' is a rational kind of desire, one deriving from our capacity to reason about what is good or bad for us, whereas what he is talking about here is supposed to be a πάθος, a nonrational feeling. (βούλησις never appears in any of Aristotle's lists of πάθη, in the *Rhetoric* or elsewhere – as both of the other two sorts of ὄρεξις do, at one place or another.) It is worth noting, also, that earlier in the *Rhetoric* (1.10 1369a1-4) Aristotle presents his division of desires into rational and nonrational, with 'wish' serving as the name for the former kind, as grounded in ἔνδοξα. How can Aristotle think that friendly feeling is based in wishing and yet that it is a πάθος, something essentially nonrational? Perhaps we should take his use of the word *wish* in some broader way in 2.4, one that permits it to cover at least some nonrational desirings; see 2.12 1389a8 where he seems to use 'wishes' to refer in a general way to the desires of young people, which he characterizes before and afterward as appetitive, sharp but not persistent.

10   I do not believe Kassel is right to put 1381a1-2, φίλος ... ἀντιφιλούμενος in brackets as a later addition, possibly by Aristotle himself, to the text. The δ' after φίλος is perfectly in order, as marking the additional remark about friends that this sentence introduces, and the sequence of thought runs a lot better with the sentence than without it.

persons are disposed to feel friendly toward one another at appropriate times. This shift of focus continues virtually throughout the chapter, to such an extent that people sometimes take the chapter to be about not mere friendly feelings, but friendship itself. But that is a mistake. Aristotle's introduction into a discussion of friendly feelings of talk about friends and friendship is quite understandable, from two points of view. First of all, one purpose of the discussion is to provide an orator with material from which to represent himself in speaking as moved by genuine concern for his audience's interests, and he will succeed especially well in this endeavour if he can get them to think of him as actually a friend of theirs – someone who is habitually moved by such feelings in relation to them. Moreover, knowing who is ordinarily taken to be someone's friend could give an orator excellent means of getting an audience to feel friendly feelings toward himself or those for whom he may be a spokesman: describing someone as their friend is a likely way to induce the audience to respond with friendly feelings. We must, then, guard carefully against the mistake of thinking that Aristotle's advice to the orator is aimed at helping him to make his audience actually become his own or his client's friends, rather than merely to make them have friendly and well-disposed feelings. The latter task is difficult enough: if taken seriously the former would actually be impossible in the time available!

III

In introducing the topic of the emotions at the beginning of Book 2, Aristotle characterizes emotions generally as follows (1378a20-23): they are things 'that change people so as to alter their judgments and are accompanied by λύπη (conventionally translated 'pain') and ἡδονή (conventionally translated 'pleasure') – for example anger, pity, fear, and the like, and their opposites.' The association of the emotions with λύπη and ἡδονή occurs so standardly in Aristotle[11] that one is apt to accept it here, too, without much thought – as if he meant nothing more than that when we experience these things we always have a mild like or dislike for the way we are then feeling, and/or that we tend to experience some pleasures or pains in consequence of feeling an emotion. I think it will repay us, however, to stop and ask carefully what Aristotle can or does mean by this. To begin with, we should notice that six of the ten emotions for which he gives formal definitions are defined as instances of λύπη (λύπη τις): fear, the feeling of being disgraced, pity, righteous indignation, envy, and eagerness to match others' accomplishments are all defined this way. A seventh (anger) is defined as a certain desire accompanied by λύπη

[11] See *Nic. Eth.* 2.5 1105b23; *Eudemian Ethics* 2.2 1220b13-14 (with the potentially significant addition of αἰσθητική before ἡδονή); *Magna Moralia* 1.7 1186a13-14. It appears that in some way Aristotle is following Plato in this: see *Philebus* 47E1-48A2, and what follows there (to 50E4).

(μετὰ λύπης). So he makes λύπη a central, essential feature of many of the emotions: it is even the genus of six of them. Curiously, he does not mention either λύπη or ἡδονή in his formal definitions of kindly and friendly feelings (which I quoted earlier); one would think the parallel with these other emotions would have led him to define them in terms of ἡδονή. Nor does he explicitly mention pleasure in his definition of confidence in the face of danger (τὸ θαρρεῖν) – although when he says that confidence essentially involves 'the impression (φαντασία) of what keeps us safe as being near, of what is fearsome as being nonexistent or far off' (1383a17-18),[12] one might think that indicates that pleasure *is* essential to it. 'The pleasant' is counted by him as one sort of apparent good, namely what impresses one as good quite independently of what one *thinks* is good,[13] and safety here would count as such an apparent good. And in discussing *Schadenfreude* and the unnamed accompaniment of righteous indignation (to neither of which does he give a formal definition), he mentions pleasure (χαίρειν, ἥδεσθαι) in such a way as to suggest that he thinks it is their genus, just as the genus of envy and righteous indignation is said to be λύπη.[14]

There is, then, ample evidence that Aristotle actually defines those emotions that he thinks involve λύπη in terms of it, and weaker evidence that he is correspondingly inclined toward defining the emotions that involve pleasure in terms of ἡδονή.[15] What does he intend here by λύπη and ἡδονή? Let us take λύπη first. Elsewhere Aristotle uses the term (together with its verb) quite variously, to cover both bodily pain and all kinds and degrees of negative mental response and attitude, ranging from mild dislike to deep distress.[16] In nonphilosophical Greek

---

[12]   Aristotle does not offer a formal definition of τὸ θαρρεῖν. He only says that what it is can be gathered easily from the definition already provided of fear, of which it is the opposite (1383a14-15), and then adds this remark about the impression of what keeps us safe. Perhaps one is licensed to infer from this (mimicking the definition of fear) that confidence actually is ἡδονή τις ἐκ φαντασίας τῶν σωτηρίων ὡς ἐγγὺς ὄντων, τῶν δὲ φοβερῶν ὡς ἢ μὴ ὄντων ἢ πόρρω ὄντων. But Aristotle does not explicitly say this.

[13]   See *EE* 2.10 1227b3-4, 7.2 1235b25-9.

[14]   See *Rhet.* 1386b26-32, 1387a1-3.

[15]   I have been led in examining this evidence to suppose that the general association of the πάθη with λύπη and ἡδονή announced at 1378a21-2 anticipates these definitions in terms of these two opposites. This does not preclude, as Aristotle makes explicit in the case of anger (see 1378b1-9), that in an emotion that was based in λύπη there should be involved (ἕπεσθαι) also some pleasure; but these pleasures will be, as they are for anger, secondary ones, ones that depend upon special further features of the state of mind of the person feeling the emotion. These secondary pleasures are not part of the definition of the emotion. On anger, see further below.

[16]   For bodily pain, see for example *De Anima* 2.2 413b23 (the pain of worms), *EE* 3.1 1229a34-41 (the pains that can kill you), and *EE* 7.8 1241b9 (the pains of childbirth); for bodily pain plus physical disgust, *Nic. Eth.* 7.7 1150a9-10 (the pains of touch, and of taste); the dislike of doing sums or writing, *Nic. Eth.* 10.5 1175b17-20; the distress caused a proud man if he is not given some honour or if he is put under the rule of some

λύπη usually indicates a pretty strong state of feeling, some real distress, and it has a special application to people when they are grieving.[17] It is in something close to this ordinary usage that Aristotle uses the word in this context in the *Rhetoric*. He speaks of pity, righteous indignation, and envy each as being a pain characterized by turmoil (λύπη ταραχώδης, 1386b18-19; and see 1386b22-5), although he mentions only pain and not turmoil in their formal definitions (1385b13-16, 1386b10-12, 1387b22-4). And he actually defines both fear and the feeling of being disgraced as 'pain and turmoil' (λύπη τις καὶ ταραχή, 1382a21, 1383b14) about something.[18] If, as I just did, one translates λύπη here as 'pain,' one must understand this as meaning 'distress,' 'feeling upset,' something that in these more extreme instances can be accompanied and qualified by psychic turmoil. Aristotle's words for pleasure have a similarly various usage elsewhere, covering everything from some bodily sensations to mental attitudes varying from simple liking and gladness to elation and vivid enjoyment.[19] Given the contrast with feelings of distress about something brought about by the pairing of ἡδονή and λύπη in this context, it would seem reasonable, perhaps mandatory, to take ἡδονή here as connoting some sort of positive mental excitement – the active relishing of something, and not merely being pleased or glad about it, or just liking it in some way or other.

So the terms λύπη and ἡδονή in Aristotle's definitions of the emotions, explicit or implied, serve much the same function that is covered in Stoic accounts by such picturesque terms as throbbing (πτοία), contraction and expansion (συστολή and διάχυσις), being uplifted and cast down (ἔπαρσις and πτῶσις), depression (ταπείνωσις), and gnawing (δῆξις). λύπη and ἡδονή indicate, with less descriptive ingenuity than the Stoics' terms do, the character of the emotions as psychic disturbances in which we are set psychically in movement, made to experience some strong affect.

Accordingly, the emotions as Aristotle represents them in *Rhetoric* Book 2 are feelings either of being distressed and upset about something, or of being excited about and relishing something. In both cases they are taken to be intrusive feelings, ones that occupy the mind and direct the attention (so that, as Aristotle says, they

---

unworthy person, *EE* 3.5 1232b12.

[17] At *MM* 1.7 1186a16 we find λυπηθῆναι given alongside ὀργισθῆναι and ἐλεῆσαι as examples of emotions: there λυπηθῆναι presumably has the sense of 'grieving,' rather than generic 'distress,' so as to be coordinate with these other two emotions, which are of course quite specific ones.

[18] Thus of the emotions based in λύπη Aristotle omits to associate ταραχή only with anger and eagerness to match the accomplishments of others (ζῆλος).

[19] For bodily pleasures, i.e., pleasurable sensations, see *Nic. Eth.* 2.3 1104b5-6, 7.13 1153b33-4, and *EE* 1.4 1215b5; the pleasure of eating sweets in the theatre, indulged especially when the play is bad, *Nic. Eth.* 10.5 1175b10-16; the refined pleasure in well-turned and becoming jokes taken and given by the tactful person, *Nic. Eth.* 4.8 1128a25-8; the wondrous pleasures philosophy is said to give, *Nic. Eth.* 10.7 1177a25.

can 'change people so as to alter their judgments'). Anger, fear, the feeling of being disgraced, pity, righteous indignation, envy, and the eagerness to match other people's accomplishments are feelings of distress at one or another apparent circumstance currently within one's attention that one takes to be a bad thing. Confidence in the face of danger, *Schadenfreude*, and the unnamed accompaniment of indignation that gives a person pleasure at the punishment or other comedown of those meriting it, are all instances of relishing what impresses one as being a good thing.

It is worth emphasizing that in his discussion of each of these ten emotions, with the exception of the last two, Aristotle is quite firm and explicit that the emotion arises from one's having the impression or appearance (φαντασία) that something good or bad has happened, is happening, or is about to happen. Indeed, for seven of them – anger, fear, the feeling of disgrace, pity, envy, righteous indignation, and the eagerness to match another's accomplishments – he includes this impression in the formal definition; and for confidence it is included in the nearest thing to a definition that he provides (1383a17-18, discussed earlier). Similarly, one finds references to such appearances also in his account of feeling mildly (1380a10 and 35), as one would expect if that is the emotion opposed to anger. The omission in the case of *Schadenfreude* and the unnamed accompaniment of righteous indignation should not cause surprise, given the extreme brevity of his treatment of them; but we are entitled to infer a role for such impressions in the generation of these emotions from their relationship to envy and indignation, respectively (as we also can for disdain from its relationship to 'eagerness'): all these latter emotions are said to depend upon one's impressions of things. It seems likely that Aristotle is using φαντασία here to indicate the sort of nonepistemic appearance to which he draws attention once in *De Anima* 3.3 (428b2-4), according to which something may appear to, or strike one, in some way (say, as being insulting or belittling) even if one knows there is no good reason for one to take it so. If so, Aristotle is alert to the crucial fact about the emotions, that one can experience them simply on the basis of how, despite what one knows or believes to be the case, things strike one – how things look to one when, for one reason or another, one is disposed to feel the emotion. It is not merely when you know or think that someone has mistreated you that you may become angry. Being unable to control an emotion is, partly, taking as a ground of it something that you know was not one at all.

Thus it is fairly clear that, for a majority of the emotions he deals with, Aristotle regards them as involving essentially a feeling of distress or pleasure caused by the way things currently in his or her attention strike the person in question. About hatred, and, as we have seen, friendly and kindly feelings, Aristotle is less forthcoming in identifying precisely what the feeling is, whether one of distress or of relishment. But on Aristotle's emerging general view one would expect friendly and kindly feelings, at least, to be cases of pleasurable excitement, just as confidence, *Schadenfreude*, and the unnamed accompaniment of indignation are. Nor with hatred and friendly and kindly feelings does he make a point of including in his account a reference to things appearing in some particular way. That is partly because for these emotions he makes no allusion at all in the definition itself to the emotion's objects and occasions.[20] For it is because he does that in the other cases that he finds the opportunity to insert the reference to such appearances.

On Aristotle's view, what, however, is the nature of the affect involved in hatred? Here I confess myself puzzled. He does not say anything to link hatred positively to either pleasure or distress, and it does not seem plausible to identify it as essentially a feeling of pleasurable excitement of any kind (however much, like anger, it might involve pleasurable thoughts about what you will do to the one you feel that way toward if you get the chance). On the other hand, Aristotle denies that it involves being distressed at all (2.4 1382a13). So it is quite unclear how he envisages hatred as based in the one or the other sort of feeling, as his general conception of the emotions seems to require. He is led to say that it does not involve a feeling of distress as a consequence of his correct, and very interesting, observation (1382a8-12) that anger makes you want to subject the person you are angry at to pain (physical or mental), in return for the distress he or she has caused you in belittling or insulting you and so making you angry, whereas hatred makes you want the person hated to be badly off, even to cease existing (1382a15). He seems to think that because in hatred there is no special desire to inflict pain (to affect how the hated one feels), but only to ruin him (to affect how he is), hatred ought not to involve any underlying feeling of distress either. That does not, however, seem a good reason: Aristotle recognizes that the feelings of disgrace and eagerness to match others' accomplishments both involve a distressed state of mind, but neither aims at causing distress in another; nor, it seems, does either of these feelings (seem to Aristotle to) derive in any way from imagining distress as felt by another person, as perhaps pity does. And, of course, there is no danger of failing to keep anger and hatred distinct if both are based in feelings of distress; the same is true of envy and pity, for example, on Aristotle's account, and they are nonetheless kept perfectly distinct by other features of the two definitions. But perhaps in saying that hatred does not involve a distressed state of mind, as anger does, Aristotle is thinking of the impersonality of hatred: you can hate whole classes of people, not merely individuals, as he points out (1382a4-7), and you need not have been personally affected in any way by a person you nonetheless hate (1382a2-3). It might seem to Aristotle that distress must have some local or immediate external cause of a kind that would therefore be lacking in hatred. Hatred is, in any event, an especially complex emotion: it seems much more a settled state, although subject to increased or lessened intensity, than many of the other emotions are, and it seems that unlike many of them there is no plausible

---

[20] At 1381b12 one reads that 'we hate people if we merely think (ὑπολαμβάνομεν)' they are thoroughly wicked. This might be taken to assign a role in hatred for full belief where in the other emotions an impression is said to be sufficient. But that would probably be to place too much weight on a somewhat incidental remark.

ground for thinking that other animals experience it. In fact, one might make the case that hatred rests upon a fully reasoned judgment, and not the mere appearance or impression, that the hated person is bad and detestable – so that it could seem to be an emotion of the reason itself, and not of the other parts of the soul as Aristotle conceives them.[21] So it may be to Aristotle's credit that he shows himself not comfortable imposing upon hatred his general account, according to which each emotion involves essentially either pleasurable excitement or a distressed state of mind.[22] Still, one remains puzzled.

IV

I come now to some special features of Aristotle's treatment of anger. Aristotle defines anger as 'a desire (ὄρεξις), accompanied by distress, for what appears to one to be punishment for what appears to one to be belittlement by people for whom it was not proper to belittle oneself or someone close to one.'[23] Of the several

---

[21] To make this case one would want to take seriously Aristotle's reference (see n. 20) to belief in (not an appearance of) the wickedness of the hated person. Even if hatred is an 'emotional' state of reason, however, that would provide no good grounds on which to deny that it involves distress or pleasure: on Aristotle's understanding of these latter phenomena, they can be experienced in the thinking of reasoned thoughts, as readily as in nonrational sorts of activity.

[22] In any event, the opinion that hatred does not involve a distressed state of mind appears a well-entrenched one with Aristotle. He repeats it, again by contrast with anger, in a very different context in *Politics* 5.10 1312b33-4 (anger and hatred are, together with contempt, the leading causes of the overthrow of tyrannies). His description of hatred there makes one almost think he is talking about no emotion or passion at all, but a fully reasoned, dispassionate rejection and dislike. (I have benefited from discussion with Myles Burnyeat about the issues raised in this paragraph.)

[23] 2.4 1378a31-3: I translate the text of Kassel taking τῶν ... μὴ προσηκόντων, as he suggests (following the construction at 1379b12), to refer to the perpetrators of the insult. It is odd that Aristotle only specifies within this appended explanatory phrase that the objects of the insult are the person himself or someone close to him, but there seems no reasonable alternative to so taking the text, as transmitted.

It is surely evident that the two occurrences of forms of φαίνεσθαι here are to be taken as references to how the angry person takes things (how they strike him, how they appear to him to be), if only because of the parallel here to the similar, and unmistakable, references to such appearings that occur regularly also in the case of other emotions analysed in this part of the *Rhet.* (fear, 1382a21, etc.; confidence, 1383a17; αἰσχύνη, 1384a23, etc.; pity, 1385b13, etc.; righteous indignation, 1387a9; envy, 1387b11; ζῆλος, 1388a30; and see also 1380a10, on feeling mildly, the feeling opposed to anger). And note the free variation between ὑπόληψις ὀλιγωρίας and φαινομένη ὀλιγωρία in the texts of the *Topics* cited in note 24 of this essay. The badly mistaken tradition of translating the forms of φαίνεσθαι in the Rhetoric's definition of anger by 'conspicuous' or the like (one finds this both in Roberts's Oxford translation and in Dufour's in the

definitions, or partial definitions, of anger that one finds elsewhere in his works, this is closest to that which, with slight variations, occurs several times in the Topics[24] – as suits the dialectical character of the definitions in the *Rhetoric*. Interestingly, anger is the only emotion he examines in these chapters that he defines formally as an instance of desire, that is ὄρεξις (which is Aristotle's usual word for desire in general) – although it is worth noting that, in contrasting hatred and anger, he says that hatred is a desire (ἔφεσις) for what is bad (for the person hated) (1382a8). That friendly feeling is also an instance of desire is perhaps implicit in his definition of it as 'wishing someone what you think are good things ...' (1380b35-1381a1), since 'wishing' is regularly treated by Aristotle as one of the three basic forms of desire. Presumably kindly feeling, too, involves a similar wish.[25] Both before beginning his detailed survey (at 2.1 1378a4) and immediately afterward (at 2.12 1388b33), Aristotle does indeed mention appetitive desire (ἐπιθυμία) as itself being one of the emotions, but he does not devote a chapter or part of a chapter to it.[26] Appetite comes in for prominent and highly interesting

---

Budé) seems to go back to Cope-Sandys (ad loc.). I doubt if it would even have occurred to anyone to take the Greek so, if it were not for the (odd-looking) first occurrence of φαινομένης here with τιμωρίας: it certainly does seem attractive to suppose that anger involves a desire for conspicuous punishment for the insult, and that rendering seems more appropriate to the facts about anger than 'apparent' or 'what one takes to be.' But it does not do well for the belittlement itself: anger does not require a conspicuous lack of regard, just one that one notices or takes to be there. One may suspect the text, as Spengel, followed by W.D. Ross in the OCT, did in overboldly bracketing φαινομένης; but in any event there seems no doubt at all that, if Aristotle did write it, he meant by it not 'conspicuous' but 'apparent,' 'what impresses one as being.'

24 See *Top*. 4.6 127b30-1, καὶ ἡ λύπη καὶ ἡ ὑπόληψις τῆς ὀλιγωρίας ἐν τῷ τί ἐστι; 6.13 151a15-16, λύπη μεθ' ὑπολήψεως τοῦ ὀλιγωρεῖσθαι; 8.1 156a32-3, ἡ ὀργὴ ὄρεξις εἶναι τιμωρίας διὰ φαινομένην ὀλιγωρίαν. It is worth noting that in the first two of these definitions, but not the third, the angry person's view that he has been belittled is cast in terms of belief, as opinion rationally arrived at (ὑπόληψις), rather than merely an impression or appearance. The *Rhetoric* seems more self-consciously decisive in favour of the latter type of definition, not only in the case of anger but in that of other emotions as well.

25 But, as we have seen, Aristotle's formal definition of friendly feeling speaks rather of what the person with this feeling is moved to do (to help someone in need) than the feeling itself and its characteristics. I have already mentioned (n. 9) the difficulties Aristotle causes himself by defining friendly feeling, supposedly an emotion and so something nonrational, as based in a 'wish'.

26 In taking up anger and appetite as causes of potentially condemnable actions at 1.10 1369b14-16, he refers the reader forward to his discussion of the emotions in Book 2 to find out about anger, but goes on right there to speak about appetite (at the end of 1.10 and in 1.11). The omission of a discussion in Book 2 of appetite therefore seems to have been well planned. The fact that in Book 1.10-11 he explains what ἐπιθυμία is, by way of telling us what pleasure is and what gives pleasure to different people, may explain why he omits to discuss ἐπιθυμία as a πάθος in 2.2-11; in effect, he had already said in

discussion at two places in the treatment of other emotions, anger (1379a10-22) – we will have a look at this passage shortly – and kindly feelings (1385a22-30), but it is not subjected there or anywhere in this part of the work to analysis as an emotion all on its own. So anger really does stand out from the other emotions as Aristotle treats them here: only it is defined in part as an ὄρεξις (desire) for anything.

From what we have already seen, it is clear enough what makes anger not only a desire but an emotion, according to Aristotle. Because it is accompanied by λύπη, anger is a distressful, agitated desire for revenge; the angry person is upset about having been treated with apparent disregard and belittlement. In other words, it is not a cool and 'rational' desire, a desire judiciously considered, to inflict pain or other punishment. In *Rhetoric* 1.10 1369a1-4, Aristotle uses 'anger' (ὀργή) itself as the name of one of the three types of desire that he there distinguishes (the other two being wish and appetite). That would imply that the type of desire to which anger belongs, according to the *Rhetoric* definition, was by its nature agitated and distressful. In other writings, however, Aristotle regularly distinguishes between anger and 'spirited' desire (θυμός), using the latter as the name for his second type of desire and treating anger as a special case of it, the case where the desire is extremely agitated and distressed.[27] It is perhaps understandable that in such a dialectical discussion as that provided by the *Rhetoric* such refinements are neglected. But when they are taken into account, anger on Aristotle's view turns out to be (*a*) an especially agitated and distressful instance of 'spirited' desire, (*b*) aroused by and directed specifically at what strikes the angry person to have been inappropriate and unjustified belittlement of himself or someone close to him, (*c*) aiming at inflicting a compensating pain on the belittler – as a means of demonstrating that he is not an inferior and trivial person, but a person whose power to inflict pain in return shows that he must be respected and paid heed to. Thus, in his account of anger, Aristotle combines three distinct elements that are indeed found elsewhere in his discussion but are nowhere else so clearly integrated: the angry person is in an agitated state of mind, caused by the way certain events or circumstances have struck him (whether or not he also believes that that is how they are), which is also a desire to respond in a well-motivated way to those events or circumstances as they appear to him.

As I mentioned above, anger has a special relationship, according to Aristotle, to the other type of nonrational desires, the appetites. The passage where he brings this out is worth quoting in full (1379a10-22):

1.10-11 what he thought needed to be said about it, and saw no need to go further. However, he nowhere gives or openly implies this explanation, so I put it forward only as a conjecture.

[27] On θυμός see, for example, *De an.* 2.3 414b2 and *MM* 1.12 1187b37; for ὀργή as a special case of θυμός-desire, see *De an.* 1.1 403a30 and *Top.* 8.1 156a32, with *Top.* 4.5 126a8-10 and 2.7 113b1.

As for our own frame of mind: we become angry when we are distressed. For a person who is feeling distressed is bent on something. So if anyone blocks him directly or indirectly in whatever it may be, for example a thirsty man in his drink, or if anyone acts contrary to him or does not act to support him, or makes trouble for him when he is in this state of mind, he becomes angry at them all. Hence people who are ill, or poor, or in love, or thirsty – in general, experiencing some appetitive desire and not getting what they want – are prone to anger and easily stirred up, especially against those who belittle their present condition. Thus a sick man is made angry when belittled in regard to his illness, a poor man in regard to his poverty, a man fighting a war in regard to the war, a man in love in regard to his love, and so with the others. Each of these people is carried along to his own anger by the emotion he is already feeling.[28]

The upset feeling that belongs to anger in all these cases is an offshoot of the upset feeling the person has been experiencing in having some aroused, but unsatisfied, appetite. It is as if a preexistent energy, the appetite, gets redirected when blocked or obstructed, and becomes or gives rise to this new feeling of distress, the anger.

It is only in connection with anger, and only in this passage, that Aristotle devotes full attention to the ways in which different emotions interact so as to cause or prepare the ground for one another. As I have mentioned in passing, he does allude two or three times elsewhere to the opposite effect, the prevention of one emotion by the presence of another: for example, he says that people do not have friendly feelings for those of whom they are afraid (1381b33), that fear for oneself prevents feeling pity for another (1385b32-4), and that people feel disgraced when something apparently dishonorable about themselves comes to light before persons whom they esteem or admire (1384a26-9). But it is only here that he points toward any general theory of the underlying psychology of the emotions through which one might attempt to explain such phenomena as these, and work out other interactions among the different emotional states.

In other respects, too, the discussion of the emotions in the *Rhetoric* offers a less than fully comprehensive theory. Aristotle limits himself to just fifteen states of mind, ones selected so as to cover the range of emotions that the orator needs to know about in order to compose his public addresses with full effectiveness – whether by representing himself as motivated by them, or by finding means to arouse them in his audience and direct them suitably for the purposes of his discourse. So Aristotle neglects, as not relevant for this purpose, a number of emotions that a more general, independently conceived treatment of the emotions would presumably give prominence to. Thus grief, pride (of family, ownership, accomplishment), (erotic) love, joy, and yearning for an absent or lost loved one (Greek πόθος) hardly come in for mention in the *Rhetoric* and are nowhere

---

[28]   I translate the text of Kassel, omitting the bracketed words in 1379a13 but disregarding the brackets in 1379a15-18.

accorded independent treatment.[29] The same is true even of regret, which one would think would be of special importance for an ancient orator to know about, especially in judicial contexts. Furthermore, as we saw especially clearly in the case of anger, Aristotle seems to recognize three central elements as constituting the emotions – they are agitated, *affected* states of mind, arising from the ways events or conditions *strike* the one affected, which are at the same time *desires* for a specific range of reactive behaviours or other changes in the situation as it appears to her or him to be. However, he does not draw special attention to this common structure, and he does not accord equal attention to each of the three elements in the case of every emotion he discusses. Thus he may seem to neglect unduly the element of desire in his accounts of fear, confidence, pity, and the feeling of disgrace, and the second element, that of being struck by an impression that things are a certain way, is barely indicated in his accounts of friendly and kindly feelings and hatred. Similarly, we have seen that he denies that hatred involves feelings of distress, and that seems to imply that the first element, an affected state of mind, is absent from this emotion; and the corresponding pleasurable affect is no part of his definition of friendly and kindly feelings. So one cannot say more than that there seems to underlie Aristotle's discussions of the emotions in *Rhetoric* Book 2 an emerging general theory along these lines. Having done the dialectical work of assembling the data about these fifteen emotions in the *Rhetoric*, he might have gone on to address similarly the remaining major emotions, and advanced to the construction of a general, independent theory that would surely have held great interest. I hope I have been able to show that, nonetheless, his accounts of the emotions in the *Rhetoric* are richly suggestive, and rewarding from the point of view of the history of philosophy and of philosophy of mind and moral psychology too.

SELECTED FURTHER READINGS

Frede, Dorothea. 'Mixed Feelings in Aristotle's Rhetoric.' In *Essays on Aristotle's 'Rhetoric,'* edited by A. Rorty, Berkeley: University of California Press, 1996, 258-85.

Rorty, Amélie Oksenberg. 'The Psychology of Aristotle's Rhetoric.' *Proceedings of the Boston Area Colloquium in Ancient Philosophy* 8 (1992) 39-79.

Sherman, Nancy. 'The Role of Emotions in Aristotelian Virtues.' *Proceedings of the Boston Area Colloquium in Ancient Philosophy* 9 (1993) 1-33.

Sihvola, Juha. 'Emotional Animals: Do Aristotelian Emotions Require Beliefs?' *Apeiron* 21 (1996) 106-44.

Striker, Gisela. 'Emotions in Context: Aristotle's Treatment of the Passions in the *Rhetoric* and His Moral Psychology.' In Rorty, *Essays on Aristotle's 'Rhetoric,'* 286-302.

---

[29]   The last two emotions are among the ones Aristotle lists in *Nic. Eth.* 2.5 1105b21-3.

Chapter Seven

Wittgenstein's Builders and Aristotle's Craftsmen*

David Charles

I. Introduction

Wittgenstein begins the *Investigations* with a quotation from Augustine, describing a child acquiring a first language:

> When they (my elders) named some object, and accordingly moved towards something, I saw this and I grasped that the thing was called by the sound they uttered when they meant to point it out. ... Thus, as I heard words repeatedly used in their proper places in various sentences, I gradually learned to understand what objects they signified; and after I had trained my mouth to form these signs, I used them to express my own desires. (*PI* §1)

As Wittgenstein notes (*PI* §32), Augustine writes as if the child already understood one language, and could describe the activities of his elders in terms he had already understood. Thus, it is as if the child 'already had a language, only not this one ...'. Augustine's description can be contrasted with another model, which Wittgenstein immediately introduces. Here the whole language of a tribe, including what is passed on to children, can be characterized completely as follows (*PI* §6):

> A is building with building stones: there are blocks, pillars, slabs and beams. B has to pass the stones, and that in the order in which A needs them. For this purpose they use a language consisting of the words 'block', 'pillar', 'slab', 'beam'. A calls them out; – B brings the stones which he has learned to bring at such and such a call. (*PI* §2)

In the builders' language, as in the one Augustine describes, individual words name objects. But the two builders, A and B, have precisely the same conceptual

---

* From *Wittgensteinian Themes: Essays in Honour of David Pears*, edited by David Charles and William Child, Oxford: Clarendon Press, 2001, 49-79. Reprinted by permission of Oxford University Press, with minor modifications and some additional references.

resources, the ones explicitly manifested in their practices. Neither relies on rich notions, such as naming, meaning, and signifying, which Augustine's child had already acquired. If these are to be introduced into the builders' language, their introduction must be intelligibly connected with their mastery of techniques of the type Wittgenstein describes.

There are two alternative pictures. In Augustine's account the child's mastery of certain basic concepts is presupposed. In Wittgenstein's, mastery of these concepts has to be situated in the context of a grasp of basic practices such as are exemplified by the builders. Augustine's account of language mastery takes it for granted that the child has access to a range of basic realist-sounding notions. But, according to Wittgenstein, we need to show what understanding of these notions (if any) can be gained by language users such as his builders. While Wittgenstein's route has the advantage of security, it brings with it the attendant disadvantages of hard work as opposed to theft.

Wittgenstein, in the early sections of the *Investigations*, considers accounts of meaning of the type he takes Augustine to have promoted. Here he describes the following pattern:

> Every word names something
> The meaning of a name is what it names
> The combinatorial power of words in elementary propositions is a reflection of the objects they name ... (and their powers).

In such theories, the world (and its objects) is fixed independently of us and puts its imprint on any language we are able to use to describe it. Thus, the structure of the world determines the concepts we possess, the meanings of our linguistic expressions. Further, our linguistic expressions are correctly used when and only when they reflect (or represent) independent reality. The truth of our sentences depends solely on how the world is. It is not determined by, or dependent on, our means for establishing or ratifying how the world is. This is why, for the Augustinian realist, our indicative sentences possess (what I shall call) realist, or ratification-independent, truth-conditions. They can possess truth-conditions of this sort because the meaning of the linguistic expressions they contain is determined by how the world is.

But, Wittgenstein asks, how can we take all this for granted? What is it for the world to imprint itself on us in the required way? It seems that the Augustinian realist simply assumes from the outset that our concepts, and linguistic expressions, are determined by how the world is and that (as a consequence) our sentences can enjoy realist truth conditions. But, Wittgenstein asks, how does this come about? What we need to know is how we can grasp the meaning of the relevant linguistic expressions (whether names or predicates). Without an answer to this question the Augustinian realist leaves it mysterious how the meanings of our terms are fixed, or how we can understand sentences with realist truth-conditions. For he simply assumes that the child comes to learn the language of his elders forearmed with a grasp of a language whose sentences already possess realist truth-conditions.

Wittgenstein's criticism is not confined simply to Augustine or to the theories Russell developed in the early years of the twentieth century. Consider the radical interpreter. She comes to meet her native, already equipped with her own linguistic notions. Her task is to map the native's language on to one which she already understands. In doing so, she aims to maximize agreement, to make the native come out speaking the truth by her lights. But, one can ask, how did she come to possess the notions she employs as the basis of her translation? How did she acquire her grasp of the meanings of her own expressions? She is often presented in a way which bears an uncanny resemblance to the child in Augustine's picture, who approaches his elders with a complete language already apparently at his disposal. Thus, she too seems, at the outset, to have already mastered the very notions whose grasp needs to be explained.

Wittgenstein prefers the more ambitious route, one in which our understanding of the relevant notions is to be explained by considering the everyday practices and techniques in which they are situated. It is through looking at these that we can see what is involved in understanding the relevant linguistic expressions. He is not, of course, seeking to explain our linguistic understanding from a starting point free of notions such as meaning and intentionality. Rather he is attempting to locate our grasp of the latter notions in a network of (meaning-involving) practices and techniques. I shall approach Wittgenstein's views by considering his criticisms of accounts of language which take for granted what (in his view) needs to be explained.

II. Wittgenstein on Technique and Language Mastery: A Short Description

Wittgenstein's opponent makes two claims. First, we grasp terms for objects and properties when they impact upon us. Thus, the meaning of these terms is fixed, when all goes well, by objects and properties in the world. We are justified in having such terms because they represent the world's objects and properties. Secondly, our sentences are true (or false) when the world contains (or fails to contain) objects related as we say they are related. Their truth-conditions depend on how the world is, not on our ability to ratify that this is the case. I shall describe one who makes both these claims as a 'Platonist'.[1]

For Wittgenstein, the first of these claims is quite mistaken. Rather than thinking of yellowness, gold, or the elm as 'impacting' on us, or of us as being

---

[1]   This characterization of 'Platonism' does not involve reference to Plato's Forms, abstract objects, inhabitants of another world, known only by an a priori route. Indeed, on this account, Aristotle, Plato's first major critic, would count as a 'Platonist'. The Platonist, so described, makes both claims and takes the first as the basis of the second.

'assimilated' to such objects, we should think rather of our concept mastery in terms of our mastering techniques which allow us to determine whether something is yellow, or gold, or elm-wood. What we do is master a technique, or set of techniques, on whose basis we can judge what is correct in particular cases.

Wittgenstein employs a variety of analogies to encourage us to think in this way. Sometimes he compares learning to apply a concept with learning to cook, sometimes with learning to build or mastering traffic rules. In learning to cook we do not at some point (miraculously) grasp the answers to all questions that could be asked about cooking. Rather, we master a technique, or set of techniques, armed with which we can work out or see what to do in a range of new and unforeseen situations. If we are good cooks, we will gain a technique sufficiently flexible to allow us to adapt to new cases and judge what is the appropriate thing to do when problem cases arise. At no point do we acquire answers to all the questions that we can expect to confront in the kitchen.

Some of Wittgenstein's most famous arguments are directed against the Platonist's account of concept mastery. Thus, he argues that we could not grasp a concept simply by being given a definition of the relevant term. For what makes that definition itself determinate or unambiguous?[2] Again, he asks, how could we grasp a concept of this type at one moment, as if foreseeing all actual and possible cases in an instant? What we need rather is an extendable technique which will enable us to judge what to do in cases not so far considered or envisaged. Mastery of a concept, like mastery of the art of cooking, involves grasping a technique which enables us to discriminate what is (for example) elm-wood or yellow in a variety of cases and circumstances. Indeed, mastery of the relevant techniques requires their practitioners actually to succeed in determining whether a range of cases are sufficiently similar to count as exemplifying the same property. Looking at one case cannot by itself make us masters of the relevant technique. For getting it right in a variety of cases is (partially) constitutive of what it is to master a technique. Without some such successes, one can at best be a potential master of the technique.

Underlying these and other remarks there is the following picture of what is involved in concept mastery. In the basic case, we find the teacher, the learner, and a set of objects. What is taught is a technique for discriminating between these objects. This is what the learner acquires in mastering the concept: the skill of picking out certain objects as the ones which fall under that concept. What is learned cannot be characterized without reference to the relevant technique, its successful application and the objects on which it is exercised.

This account has two basic features and one important consequence.

---

[2]   What makes the definition one of 'plus' rather than 'quus'? Saul Kripke focuses on this issue in his *Wittgenstein on Rules and Private Language*, Oxford: Blackwell, 1982. No doubt, a definition would be useful if one already understood the terms used in the definition.

(A) In acquiring a concept (such as that of yellow), the learner acquires a technique for discriminating yellow objects. Mastery of such techniques is partially constitutive of what it is to master the concept. (*Centrality of technique*)

(B) We cannot say what the relevant techniques are without reference to the objects on which we practise our techniques. We cannot say what it is to discriminate yellow objects without reference to the yellow objects thus discriminated. (*Externalism*)

The consequence is this: what is to count as yellow will itself be determined by what those with the relevant technique take to be yellow. It is their judgment that determines what is to count as yellow. Authority in such cases lies with the skilled practitioners, with what they find it natural to count as yellow (on the basis of their skill). There is no further or deeper question as to what is really yellow. For we have no access to a property of yellowness other than the one discriminated by the skilled masters of the relevant technique. In reality this is all we have to go on. We can make no sense of a notion of what is really yellow beyond that which our skilled judges (in favourable conditions, etc. ...) discriminate as yellow.

The Platonist, according to Wittgenstein, makes two closely related mistakes.

1. He regards meanings as fixed independently of our techniques in using them (as 'God-given' or determined solely by the impact of the world on us). In overlooking the importance of (A), the Platonist has simply 'magicked' himself into possessing concepts determined by the world, without explaining how this could come about.

2. As a consequence of his first mistake, the Platonist assumes that there are ratification-independent truths about what is yellow. But, if we focus on the techniques involved in determining what is yellow, we can see that his picture is an illusion. The correct extension of the relevant predicate 'yellow' is determined by agreement in judgment between skilled users of the term. The realist is led to assume that there are ratification-independent truths about colours through failing properly to consider the way in which such truths are determined. Once we pay due attention to this, we can see that his picture is mistaken.

According to Wittgenstein, if we focus on the relevant practices, both Platonist claims will seem ill-founded. We cannot regard meanings as fixed independently of the techniques we acquire in mastering the relevant concepts. Nor can we mark out or characterize the relevant objects or properties without reference to the techniques we employ in discriminating them. As Wittgenstein comments in *Zettel*: 'For the language-game with colours is characterized by what we can and cannot do' (*Z* 340). What we count as colours is grounded ineliminably in our trained discriminations (*Z* 419), the ones we master in acquiring the relevant techniques for using the word (*Z* 418). Our perceptual judgments, so far from merely registering what is given, reflect the application of our discriminatory skills. The resulting picture is not a form of idealism, if that is understood as requiring us to characterize the relevant techniques without reference to the objects on which they are exercised. The passages just cited in *Zettel* continue as follows: '"And what is red like?" – "Like *this*." Here the right paradigm must be pointed to' (*Z* 420). It is not that we begin with a set of skills that can be defined independently of objects or properties in the world and then project the deliverances of such skills on to the world. For there is no way fully to describe the relevant skills without reference to the objects or properties which they discriminate. Skills, as B above makes clear, cannot be acquired or exercised except on objects and properties beyond the subject. According to Wittgenstein, if one begins with the training perspective, there is no difference between realist and idealist save in 'battle cry' (*Z* 414).

His basic picture is both simple and powerful. All that is involved in the grasp of meanings are skills, which cannot be fully characterized without reference to certain objects and properties; but the objects and properties themselves cannot be characterized without reference to the skills involved in discriminating them. This picture seems to offer a way to bring peace in philosophy, peace as between realism and idealism. For, within its perspective, one cannot so much as raise the questions that lead to war. We have no access to a conception either of ratification-independent truths about objects and properties or of skills defined in isolation from objects and properties. Thus, both these realist and idealist options are empty. If we look carefully at the practices themselves, we will see that both are myths with which we beguile our intellects, fantasies forever removed from the reality of our everyday dealings with the world.[3]

---

[3] So understood, Wittgenstein is committed to regarding as empty the two Platonist claims, (A) and (B), introduced at the beginning of this section. For, if he is right, no sense can be made of the idea of objects, properties, or the world, conceived of as being what they are independently of our practices and techniques. Thus, there can be no ratification-independent truths of the type the Platonist envisaged. Wittgenstein's view, so understood, does not rest essentially on the (anti-realist) claim that, since human powers are limited, we cannot give determinate answers on issues that outrun our powers of discrimination. The Platonist conception, as stated, would be undermined even if our techniques were 'completely unbounded' or (*per impossibile*) we were possessed of godlike powers. For in neither case would we have access to objects and properties understood (in the Platonist way) as being what they are independently of practices or techniques. Indeed, Wittgenstein seems to think that some of our practices can be 'unbounded' (in the sense described) since we can learn how to 'go on' indefinitely, even when we cannot directly manifest what we have learned in action. In these cases, the learning 'points beyond itself'. (On this, see Peter Winch's 'Im Anfang war die Tat', in Irving Block (ed.), *Perspectives on the Philosophy of Wittgenstein*, Oxford: Blackwell, 1981, 168. For a somewhat different account of these issues, see Michael Dummett's *The Logical Basis of Metaphysics*, London: Duckworth, 1991, 316.

We have focused, so far, on the case of colours. But Wittgenstein's claims appear quite general. On the building site the workers will mark out certain types of wood or metal as relevant for their purposes. What counts as elm or ash will be determined by the skilled reactions of the builders involved, reactions dependent on what they can do with differing kinds of wood. Their judgment will be decisive in difficult or problematic cases. Here, too, it is not that one can characterize the type of wood independently of their trained reactions or their trained reactions independently of the objects on which they operate. All they have is a conception of their ability to act on objects and of the objects on which they act in this way.

For the builders, so conceived, there is just the fact that they can do some things and not others. Given their conception of objects, they cannot even ask whether the source of this impossibility comes from them or from the world. For they lack the notion of objects and properties, conceived of as possessing their own natures independently of their techniques and practices, the notion required to make sense of the question: does the source of the impossibility rest in us or in the objects themselves? Thus, when Wittgenstein asks (*Z* 357): 'Do the [colour and number] systems reside in our nature or in the nature of things?', he replies: 'How are we to put it? *Not* in the nature of numbers or colours.' The most they can do is point to their practices and to the objects those practices involve. There is no possibility of their being able coherently to formulate, let alone answer, questions about the relative importance, or order of dependence, as between us, and what we do, and an us-independent world on which we act. All attempts to do so are empty.[4]

---

4   Some will resist this interpretation of Wittgenstein, claiming that he sought to defend a non-empty form of realism which simultaneously gives due weight to our role as skilled practitioners. Surely, it will be said, he must have done justice to the commonsense idea that (for example) lions breed and cats catch mice, no matter what our practices as classifiers or discriminators may be. Is this datum not enough to vindicate a non-empty form of realism?

The exegetical options are complex, and are further discussed in W. Child, 'Pears's Wittgenstein: Rule-Following, Platonism, and Naturalism', in Charles and Child 2001 (above, n.*) 81-113, at 107-13. However, two interpretative points should be made. First, Wittgenstein's remark that idealism and realism differ merely in 'battle cry' is not an isolated one, but fits well with (a certain view of) his account of the autonomy of grammar and the internality of the point of our linguistic practices. Taken together, they appear to call into question the idea of our practices as answerable to an us-independent reality in the way the realist envisages. Secondly, if Wittgenstein did undertake the project envisaged by the objector, how (and where) did he do it? Its goal cannot be achieved simply by invoking the datum cited above. For all may agree that, given our practices, we can make sense of the idea of lions (as we now conceive them) breeding even if we had not existed or had thought differently about these matters. But this agree-ment does not, by itself, require us to accept either that lions form a kind marked out in reality independently of our practices or that our practices can be explained by the nature of such us-independent kinds. It is the latter claims that the realist must show to

III. Wittgenstein's Challenge: Possible Replies

Wittgenstein's account constitutes a powerful challenge to the realist: to show how a grasp of ratification-independent truth-conditions can emerge from our practices, as described in the previous section. There are several types of realist response to Wittgenstein's problematic.

1. One might challenge Wittgenstein's characterization of the basic teaching-learning situation, by arguing that it cannot be coherently described in the way he suggests. Thus, some may say that it cannot be properly characterized without reliance on more details about the external conditions on the building site, and the environment more generally, considerations beyond those grasped by the teacher and learner as Wittgenstein describes them. Thus, we might invoke (at the outset) the fact that the builders are operating in a world with us-independent natural kinds or colours.[5]

2. Alternatively, one might accept Wittgenstein's characterization of the concepts acquired (for example) on the building site, and seek to show that, consistently with the possession of just such concepts (and no more), one can nonetheless come to grasp ratification-independent truth-conditions. Thus, some have suggested that we can make sense of the notion of ratification-independent truth-conditions, even if our discriminatory skills and grasp on objects are precisely as Wittgenstein describes them.[6]

3. One might seek to show that there is more involved in our grasp of objects than Wittgenstein allows. It is not that our concepts are simply determined (in some miraculous way) by the fact that we live in one environment rather than another (as is suggested by proponents of option 1). But neither is it the case that our grasp is fully characterized merely by the types of skill attributed to the colour discriminators or builders above. Rather, according to the present suggestion, one can describe how, beginning from the situation Wittgenstein describes, one can achieve a grasp on objects with natures that are independent of us and our techniques. This would require us to see how realist

---

be non-empty parts of our everyday practices. Thus, if Wittgenstein was aiming to sustain this form of realism, he could have employed the Aristotelian master craftsman (as described below) to carry through his project.

5   I take this to be a form of extreme externalism, in which the mere fact that one is operat-ing in a world with certain features is sufficient to affect the correct description of one's practices, no matter that the practitioners themselves are not sensitive to such features in their teaching or learning of skills.

6   I take this to be the type of position advocated by, for example, John McDowell. An examination of McDowell's views on what is involved in the mastery of the relevant skills falls outside the scope of this chapter.

truth-conditions can emerge, by comprehensible steps, out of the primitive situation so far described. If it succeeds, such an account would show how we can (in a non-mysterious way) gain access to objects and properties, with their distinctive combinatorial capacities, which can provide a basic standard of correctness for what we do and say. The latter would not be simply grounded in our (world-involving) practices in the way described above.[7]

While each of these responses is worth detailed consideration, I shall focus in this chapter solely on the latter.

IV. Varieties of Practice, Varieties of Craftsmen

Wittgenstein's characterization of life on the building site does not seem fully to capture the range of skills and know-how employed in the building trade. In any event, his description of these skills appears limited when compared with that offered by another anti-Platonist philosopher, himself the son of a doctor, who was similarly preoccupied with craft and skill. Aristotle's recurrent references to the practices of medicine and house-building show a wealth of detailed observation of and great respect for the types and typology of the workplace. Nor was his interest purely taxonomic. For, in the *Posterior Analytics* 2.19 and Metaphysics A 1, beginning from a starting point close to Wittgenstein, he devised an account of thought and concept mastery, which was (in its turn) the basis for his account of the meaning of linguistic expressions.[8] Thus, he sought to describe a route to mastery of realist notions (or so I shall suggest) which focused on aspects of skill and practice to which Wittgenstein (for whatever reason) failed to attach sufficient importance.

Let me begin by introducing you to Aristotle's three distinct types of craftsmen.

---

[7] Some of David Pears's formulations suggest just such a position. Thus, for instance, he writes: 'It is not that language has to meet some external standard of accuracy to be a standard of measurement ... nor that an internal standard is independent of the world in which it originated. ...' (*The False Prison. A Study of the Development of Wittgenstein's Philosophy*, 2 vols., Oxford: Oxford University Press, 1987-88), ii. 459). Here, the picture seems to be one in which both we and the natures of things make a significant contribution to the full account of concept mastery. But, elsewhere, he interprets Wittgenstein as regarding philosophical theories that talk of 'the natures of things' as 'empty' (*The False Prison*, i. 16), the more radical position sketched at the end of the previous section. Bill Child argues convincingly (loc. cit., above n.4). that the latter passages represent Pears's understanding of Wittgenstein's position.

[8] Here I rely on an account of Aristotle's views that I have set out in greater detail elsewhere: *Aristotle on Meaning and Essence*, Oxford: Oxford University Press, 2000, chs. 4-6.

Low-level artisans (981a5-24)

This worker is described as 'like a natural force' (*Metaph.* 981b2ff.) and compared to an animal (980b25ff.). He has been trained to carry out a few techniques by his instructor, which he does without understanding what he is doing or why. He need not have a language. He may have been trained not to do certain things and to stop himself if he begins to do so. But if so, he would be stopped solely by the operation of a causal mechanism set up by his trainer, not by the force of reason. If asked why he was doing what he was doing, the best he could say would be 'My trainer told me to do it this way' or 'My trainer told me not to do that'. Outside the techniques he has been trained to implement, he has no idea of what to do. He is limited both in his range of operation and in the use he makes of reason in his activities.

Empirical doctors: people with experience (981a24-b2, 5-18)

Aristotle's empirical doctor has the ability to reason as follows: 'This treatment worked for Kallias and for Sokrates when they had this disease. ... so it may well work for Kleon, since he seems to have the same disease' (see 981a7ff.). The empirical doctor has the ability to see new cases as like previous ones and so to extend their skills to new cases beyond those so far encountered. Further, they are able to give primitive justificatory stories to explain why they are doing what they are doing: 'This worked there ... so, since this is like that, it may well work here'. In these ways, the empirical doctor is less tied to the conditions of her original instruction than the low-level artisan. However, in other respects, her understanding of what she is doing is limited. For her idea of the disease with which she is dealing is exhausted by her ability to recognize some cases as members of that kind. She may describe it as 'that phenomenon, the one of which these are cases, the one which I can treat in this way', with no further general idea of what the kind is.

Her epistemic condition can be contrasted with that of the third member of Aristotle's work-team: the master craftsman.

Master craftsmen

The master craftsman can explain why we act in one way rather than another. He has the ability to teach because he can explain why one way is the right way to act and another not, not simply on the basis of past success, but in the light of his grasp on the nature of the wood or illness in question. Thus, he will know what can and cannot be done to and with certain types of wood, what types of wood are good for what types of purpose, and what is required for the artefacts he is aiming to produce. He can explain why we should use this type of wood rather than this one. Thus, he will have a grasp on a variety of types of wood: what each is good for, what can be done with one and not another.

For these purposes, the master craftsman will need to have an understanding of the nature of the wood. For he is interested in knowing where he can improve his skill and achieve a goal, and where he cannot. In the latter case, the best reason for thinking that no extension of his skill could effect a given change is that the wood could not allow it to occur: if you tried that, the wood, given its nature, has to break.[9] Similarly, the master craftsman will have the ability to devise new methods and new products: give him the wood, and he can tell you what can and cannot be done with it.

The master craftsman's understanding gives him the ability to criticize the empirical craftsman. Thus, he will say, for example,

'This is a better way to do that ... because ...'
'That method will never work properly because ... there will always be problems ...'
'This difference between these two pieces of wood is not important ... they are both basically similar ... but that one is, because the two woods involved differ in the following ways.'

It is this type of understanding that gives the master craftsman his authority on the building site. He need not be better than the 'empiric' at carrying through particular tasks. It is rather that he has a better understanding of the kinds involved, which he can use to criticize and correct his own and others' practice. Nor is his role limited to criticism: for he can vindicate what empirical craftsmen do and do not do, and explain why they can do some things and not others. Thus, he may sometimes say: 'Given the nature of this wood, we cannot do any better than this'. Other times, he may say: 'Given the nature of the wood, it would be better to stain it this way rather than that.'

Aristotle's interest in builders is not, as I noted above, limited to providing a taxonomy of different style of artisans, as for a catalogue of different types of worker one might wish to employ. Rather, his taxonomy is set up to provide an account of how we arrive at thoughts about the relevant kinds. The master crafts-man's thoughts about types of wood are distinct from those of the empirical worker. For he will have a grasp on a type of wood (or illness) which is fully general, not constitutively linked to any particular cases. Similarly, the master craftsman will have the concept of the kind elm or ash, as one kind, with its own distinctive nature, standing in a nexus of similar kinds (see *Posterior Analytics* 100a15-b5).

It is important to note that the master craftsman is not required to be able to give a complete definition of the nature of the wood involved, such as a scientist might attempt. Indeed, it is unlikely that he will even attempt to do this, impressed as he will be by how much he continues to find out about the wood (in varying circumstances ...). He may well think that there is more to the nature than he has

---

[9]   While the master craftsman may be unaware of (or even sceptical of) the possibility of there being a fundamental scientific essence that explains the rest, his grasp of the kind is not just of its phenomenal (observational) properties. For he has a grasp on its nature, on what can and cannot be done with the kind.

already discovered. Nor need he have any idea that there is a scientific essence of the wood. Indeed, he may even be sceptical about the possibility of there being such an essence, one unifying feature from which all the rest follow. Still less need the master craftsman possess any mysterious direct intuition or inspirational insight into the nature of the objects with which he is dealing. For his knowledge will arise (in readily comprehensible ways) from reflection on his own and others' successes and failures as lower-level craftsmen. His understanding will arise naturally from the lower-level skills he shares with others (*Metaph.* 981a24-b1).

Thoughts of the type possessed by the master craftsman are the basis for Aristotle's account of propositions, claims which can be assessed as true and false (without qualification), in line with his famous dictum 'A proposition is true if and only if it says of what is that it is and of what is not that it is not' (*Metaph.* 1011b27). The concepts which the master craftsman possesses are the ingredients of propositions of this type.[10] Since Aristotle is often taken as a founding father of realism, such concepts are, we should assume, the ingredients for propositions with realist truth-conditions about illnesses or types of wood. We can see why this is so. The master craftsman's concepts reflect his understanding of the nature of the phenomena with which he is dealing. His understanding allows him to see a grounding for our practices of action and discrimination in the nature of the woods or illnesses with which he is dealing. Armed with this understanding, he can explain why we have certain ways of acting and not others, and underwrite certain of our discriminations and not others.

The master craftsman's grasp on the nature of objects and kinds is richer than that enjoyed by the empirical doctor. It is not merely that he finds it appropriate to act in one way and not another. Rather, he can explain why it is appropriate to do so, given his understanding of the distinctive nature of the types of wood available to him. His understanding of the objects and properties involved in these cases goes beyond the simple thought 'It is the type of thing to which I can do this, or the type that looks like that one'. For he has (and is entitled to have) a grasp on the nature of the wood, in terms independent of what he can do with it, which explains why he should act in one way and not another. It is this that appears to give him the ability to underwrite our discriminatory practices in a recognizably realist way. Given his knowledge, the concepts formed on its basis will similarly reflect his realist perspective.

Consideration of Aristotle's three types of craftsmen encourages us to raise two questions:

1. Which of these craftsmen most closely approximates to Wittgenstein's model of one who has mastered the relevant techniques of language?

---

[10]   For Aristotle's account of the connections between thoughts and propositions, see (for example) *De Anima* 432a11-13, *De Interpretatione* 16a3-9,10,14. These issues are discussed in *Aristotle on Meaning and Essence* (above, n.8) 80-87 and 110-146.

2. Is Aristotle really entitled (in the area under consideration) to claim to have provided a route to realist truth-conditions?

I shall sketch an answer to these two questions in the next two sections, and seek to defend it against objections in the penultimate section.

V. Which of these Craftsmen is Wittgenstein's?

Wittgenstein's remarks on mastery of a practice are scattered, employed with different opponents in mind in different contexts. Some may regard it as inappropriate to see him as offering even a sketch of what mastery of a practice consists in. However, one of the merits of David Pears's work on these topics is that it leads us to focus on the type or types of practitioner Wittgenstein had in mind in these different contexts. What model did he employ for mastery of a practice? Was he right to use just the model he did?

Level 1: Low-level artisans

Sometimes it appears as if Wittgenstein has only the lowest-level artisan in mind. Quite apart from his discussion in the early sections of the *Investigations*, he writes in the beginning of the *Brown Book*: 'Let us imagine a society in which this [the slab-language] is the only system of language. The child learns this language ... by being trained to its use. I am using the word "trained" in a way strictly analogous to that in which we talk of an animal being trained to do certain things' (*BB* 77). If context is required for the child to count as understanding, this will be made up of the same type of low-level activity. Nor are these remarks confined to discussions of slab-languages. In *Remarks on the Foundation of Mathematics* (p. 345) he compares our learning to follow a rule with chimpanzees learning a sequence, and later (*RFM* 394) speaks of human beings being trained or conditioned to act in a certain way. In this frame of mind, Wittgenstein can compare our mastery of a rule with the way in which a mechanism works (*RFM* 422). We are taught to perform a certain technique, and to recognize when we are doing it right or wrong by our trainer. Indeed, at this stage the applications of 'right' and 'wrong' are fixed by their role in teaching: 'The word "right" makes the pupil go on, the word "wrong" holds him back' (*RFM* 405). The pupil knows that he is acting rightly when he is implementing the technique he has learned. Indeed, this is all his grasp of acting rightly need consist in. There need be no extension beyond the simple techniques he has been trained to internalize in this way.

Level 2: Empirical skill

Not all of Wittgenstein's remarks on rule-following correspond to the pattern set by the low-level artisan. Sometimes his characterization of following a practice describes a stage like that attained by the empirical doctor. Thus, Wittgenstein sometimes emphasizes the incompleteness of certain rules, like those of chess or traffic (*Z* 440). In a similar style, in the passages cited above he compares mastery of a term with mastering the art of cooking. There is not one technique involved here. Rather the skilled cook needs to be able to see what needs to be done in a variety of different situations, some unforeseen when he acquires the skill. Further, he can justify what he is doing in terms of its producing the right results. In these cases, what is grasped goes beyond the examples (*PI* §208). The same seems true of Wittgenstein's account of face and mood recognition, to which I shall shortly turn. In these cases, too, the rules are unbounded. (See *PI* II. 227.)

Level 3: The elusive master craftsman

At some points it appears that Wittgenstein goes beyond the extendable discriminatory capacities invoked at level 2. Thus, he sometimes refers to our grasp of the point of activity involved.

> I am inclined to distinguish between the essential and the inessential in a game too. The game, one would like to say, has not only rules but also a *point*. ...
>
> It looks as if the use of [a] piece had a *purpose*. ..., and as if the purpose were that one should be able to recognize the piece and know how to play. – Are we talking about a physical or a logical possibility here? If the latter then the identity of the piece is something to do with the game.
>
> If I understand the character of the game aright – I might say – then this isn't an essential part of it.
>
> ((Meaning is a physiognomy.)) (*PI* §§564ff.)

Wittgenstein's idea seems to be this: the point is enshrined in the rules of the game in such a way that we grasp it and the rules simultaneously. It is not that the point explains why the rules are as they are. It is rather that the point and the rules are laid down together. Thus, the master understander will grasp simultaneously the rules of the game and their point. The point of the game is not to be seen as some type of abstraction from the rules.

Wittgenstein introduces his analogy with physiognomy to capture this idea. In understanding facial expressions, one will (in his view) grasp simultaneously *both* the correct descriptions of varying facial expressions *and* the overall mood of the person as expressed in the face. There is not some more underlying mood one can grasp by itself and use to explain why the face is as it is. Nor is the underlying mood understood by inference from correct facial descriptions. Rather, there is no grasping what the facial expression is without grasping the mood, and no grasping the mood without grasping the correct description of the facial expression.

Example

The goal of facial recognition may be to recognize sad (or happy) people by their facial expressions ... but there may be no way of specifying who such people are without reference to their characteristic facial expressions ...

The happy ones are like this: ☺

In a similar way, there is no grasping the point of a linguistic rule without correctly grasping the rule, and (at least in unbounded cases) no grasping the correct description of the rule without grasping its point. In this picture, the master craftsman will see how the rules and the point of the activity fit together, and how these jointly (partially) determine the nature of the pieces themselves (what words are used for fixing their identity).[11] But, he will not be able to use the point to justify the rules, because rules and point are equally basic in the relevant scheme of justification.

Wittgenstein's remarks make it clear that, in his view, there is nothing beyond the rules that can be used to justify or criticize the rules themselves. Our rules and concepts are not underwritten by an independent reality. In this way, grammar is autonomous, free from the dictates of a further reality. There is no further justification that can be required, since we can make no sense of a notion of what is really the case beyond that which our skilled judges take to be the case. Our practices are not to be explained or grounded in anything beyond themselves. As David Pears remarks, 'there is no need and no room for any further support or explanation of our practice.'[12]

VI. Aristotle's and Wittgenstein's Master Craftsmen Compared: The Road To Realism

There are striking similarities and striking differences between Aristotle's and Wittgenstein's accounts of our mastery of skills. Wittgenstein appears to move freely, in his account of mastery, between levels 1, 2, and 3 in Aristotle's hierarchy of skilled workmen.[13] However, some of his remarks may be regimented and

---

[11] Perhaps this insight is gained by one who 'commands a clear view of the use of our words', who has 'a perspicuous representation' of the relevant subject matter, and can 'see connections' (*PI* §122). If so, the conceptual master craftsman will grasp the inter-connections between our rules, the point of our rule-governed activities, and the identity of the concepts we employ. The interpretation of these remarks is the subject of lively debate between Gordon Baker ('*Philosophical Investigations* Section 122: Neglected Aspects', in R.L. Arrington and H.-J. Glock (eds.), *Wittgenstein's Philosophical Investigations*, London: Routledge, 1991, 34-68) and P.M.S. Hacker (*Wittgenstein's Place in Twentieth Century Analytical Philosophy*, Oxford: Blackwell, 1996, 312 n.90).

[12] *The False Prison* (above n.7), ii. 518.

[13] For a somewhat different approach to Wittgenstein's views on these topics, see Rush

clarified in the light of Aristotle's tripartite classification. Thus, one might suggest that, at the most primitive stage, we have the level 1 rule follower, the low-level artisan, bound to a few simple, bounded, techniques which can be followed mechanically. At the next, 'empirical', level we find people with extendable techniques who can reason about what to do on the basis of past experience. At the highest level we find the master craftsmen, who possess some grasp on the point of the activity, which they can use to guide their practice in difficult cases. If this suggestion is correct, Wittgenstein can allow for different types of rule followers at varying levels of intellectual sophistication.

While detailed discussion of Wittgenstein's account of the mastery of a rule lies beyond the scope of this chapter, enough has been said to indicate that Aristotle's master craftsman is, in fundamental respects, different from Wittgenstein's. Aristotle's craftsman (as we saw above) grasps what can and cannot be done with certain kinds of wood, and the goals that can be set for work with varying types of wood. Given this understanding of the wood, he can explain why some practices are fine as they are and why others should be changed or modified. Through his work he has come to realize when and where he is up against limitations to what he can do that stem from the nature of the objects he is dealing with. This realization is embedded in his description of what he is doing:

> 'Here we are working with the grain ... here we have to be very careful because the stress is close to what the wood can take ... we must find a different way because I can feel the strength of the resistance in the wood to this way of doing things ... if we go on we will break or damage the wood.'

or again

> 'Don't you see the pressure in the wood ... let's try and respond to it by doing something along these lines ...'.
> 'Maybe we can use the strength in the wood this way to achieve a given effect ...'.
> 'Perhaps the wood can be stained with this type of mixture to bring out its natural warmth ... show more of its natural texture ...'
> 'Don't you feel how the wood is reacting ... this is why the other technique did not work ... and why it may be better to do it in some other way ... by using the type of material we used to deal with that type of hard wood over there ...'.

Rhees's *Wittgenstein and the Possibility of Discourse*, ed. D.Z. Phillips, Cambridge: Cambridge University Press, 1998. Rhees understands Wittgenstein as modelling his account of language mastery on the skills of level 1 artisans, and criticizes him for doing so. While I agree with Rhees that Wittgenstein consistently emphasizes the importance of level 1 skills, I am not convinced that this exhausts his story. Rhees makes several interesting suggestions, differing from those sketched here, about what should be added to stage 1 skills to account for language mastery.

In these ways, Aristotle's master craftsman can vindicate certain of our rules and practices by reference to the nature of the wood, and can recommend setting up others. For his understanding of the wood allows him to grasp the limitations imposed on him by nature and on what can be done, given those limitations. It is not merely that he finds it natural (part of his second nature) to act in given ways. It is rather that he can justify proceeding in some ways and not others by pointing to his knowledge of what can and cannot be done, given his understanding of the subject matter with which he is engaging. Indeed, it is this grasp that leads him to act in certain ways rather than others.

In these cases, his standard for correctness is grounded in the understanding he has gained of the nature of the wood with which he is confronted. He can use his grasp of the nature of the wood to legitimize certain ways of acting and to rule out others. In contrast with Wittgenstein's master craftsman, Aristotle's is able to provide further support for and explanation of our practice. For he will grasp why some things work and some do not. It is not just that the Aristotelian master craftsman has a good way of describing what he does using terms like 'working with the grain ...'. It is rather that he can justify his acting in this way on the basis of his understanding of the wood.

In similar style, Aristotle's master craftsman can vindicate (or criticize) the discriminations made by the empirical or low-level craftsmen. Thus, he can correct or underwrite their systems of classification on the basis of his deeper grasp on the nature of the wood. Thus, although two pieces of wood may look or react similarly in certain cases, the master craftsman will be able to correct the practice of classifying them together if he knows that their natures are different: they react differently elsewhere, and this is important because one type of wood has a different type of grain from the other. In other cases, he will be able to underwrite our practices of classification and vindicate our using some of the concepts we do. Neither way is he merely saddled with the practices we have or happen to find natural. Rather, he has an understanding of the nature of the wood that allows some of our practices to be judged by some external standards. Indeed, from this perspective, the questions 'Which are the right rules?' or 'Which are the right concepts?' are not fantasies. Rather, the master craftsman can explain and vindicate our having certain rules and concepts on the basis of his grasp of the different types of wood he encounters and understands.

The differences between Aristotle's and Wittgenstein's master craftsmen appear important. For Aristotle's master craftsman seems to possess the intellectual resources required for an explanatory vindication of our practices favourable to a realist account. He needs to understand which aspects of (for example) the wood cannot (in principle) be changed, because they are part of its nature. He needs to be able to distinguish (at least in thought) between those aspects that we can hope to change by improving our skills and those where all our attempts are bound to be futile. The latter idea cannot be secured simply by noting the fact of repeated past failures, for such failures are consistent with the hope of future success (if only we could improve our techniques). For this idea, he needs the idea of the limits of what he (or an even greater craftsman) can achieve. Sometimes, no doubt, he can see how, with more time, better instruments, or better-prepared wood, something that is not now possible could be done. But in other cases, he will realize that something cannot be done, no matter how far our techniques improve. Here he will see that we are limited not by our own lack of skill but by the nature of the wood itself an invariable, something which (as he will see) cannot be changed. Although the master craftsman's interests arise out of practical questions about how things can best be made or what can be done with wood of this type, he is forced in seeking to answer these to look for the truth about the nature of the kinds around him. Similar answers will also be needed to explain to his students why they should follow certain practices and not others, where they should experiment and where experimentation is hopeless. In these ways, the master craftsman, beginning from essentially practical concerns, is led to construct a realist representation of the kinds around him. (I shall consider below the issue of how far the master craftsman's understanding of wood can extend to a master understander's grasp of other phenomena.)

The master craftsman's understanding of the kinds he encounters enables him to vindicate some of our craft practices and criticize others. Indeed, the type of vindication suggested seems to allow for the possibility of legitimizing our use of certain of our concepts in the way the realist originally envisaged. For we can now see how the structure of the world can determine some of the concepts we possess, the meanings of some of our linguistic expressions. If so, these linguistic expressions will be correctly used when and only when they reflect (or represent) the structure of the world. It is possible to characterize here a real difference between realism (so understood) and its rivals: for the former will aim to vindicate our practices (in the areas under discussion) on the basis of an understanding of the kinds around us, while the latter will think such a project to be mistaken (or impossible). Thus, for the realist, the source of various possibilities and impossibilities will lie in the kinds around us, not in our practices (conceived by the idealist as independent of the kinds around us) nor in the inextricable network of practices and objects (sketched near the beginning of the chapter).[14]

It is important to note that Aristotle's model of concept mastery is not the super-idealized Platonist model that Wittgenstein attacked, in which the criterion for linguistic practice is completely independent of actual practices, a standard completely independent of our unrolling sequences of application of the terms.[15] Nor is the standard detached from all contemporary setting or attached by definition to a fantasized and forever inaccessible sequence of correct applications.[16] For the master craftsman's perspective is not at all independent of our actual practices,

---

[14] It remains an open question how far the model of realism sketched here can be applied to vindicate realist claims in such areas as ethics, aesthetics, or the philosophy of logic.

[15] The requirement suggested by David Pears, *The False Prison* (above n.7), ii. 442.

[16] See ibid. 531.

detached from all contemporary setting; nor is it attached solely by definition. His results will only be visible from a perspective rooted in our actual practices. Indeed, the relevant standard can only be grasped from a perspective entrenched within our practices, even though it is not a standard which is based on what we find it natural to do. It is a standard visible only from within our practices, even though it is not constituted simply by our adherence to those practices. For it embeds, in a way completely removed from the super-idealized one Pears characterizes, a basis for assessing and vindicating the rules and concepts we employ in a given area.

VII. Does Wittgenstein have Good Reason to Sideline Aristotle's Master Craftsman?

I should like to consider three objections to the suggested deployment of Aristotle's master craftsman in the defence of a form of realism. My replies are intended merely to indicate how the position in question might be defended in detail.[17]

1. Internality

Objection. Surely, the master craftsman's judgments are internal to our practices. They do not really hold up an independent standard by which to judge our practices. For the master craftsman's judgments arise out of our practices and contain reflections on the nature of our practices. They would not be available to anyone who was not brought up and trained in our practices. So, we must conclude, not even here does language conform to some external standard of accuracy. It is not itself measured by an external reality.

Reply. This objection trades on an important ambiguity in the notion of what is *external*. On the one hand, it is correct to insist that the master craftsman's judgments do not express a standard which can be grasped from a perspective independent of our practices. He himself needs to be trained in these practices, his reflections only make sense as reflections on these practices, and his authority arises from his understanding of our practices. In this sense, his judgments are not 'external' to our practices. However, it does not follow that his judgments are wholly constituted by our practices, by what we find it natural to do. Indeed, it is because his judgments are 'external' in the second sense that he can (in some cases) criticize or reform our practices and in other cases explain and vindicate them. For a master craftsman's understanding of (for example) the wood provides him with

---

[17] There are other objections which need to be considered (e.g. those concerning the possibility of alternative concepts: see *PI* ii. xii).

some degree of explanatory vindication of our practices. He is not merely saddled with what we find it natural to do.

The relevant ambiguity in the notion of 'external standard' can be brought out as follows:

(A) External standard 1: a standard which can be grasped from a perspective wholly independent of our practices. In this sense, the grasper is an Archimedean figure, one whose perceptions and thoughts are not based (in any way) on what is parochial to us or our practices.[18]

(B) External standard 2: a standard that is not wholly constituted by our practices, by what we find it natural to do.

Although the master craftsman's understanding fails to grasp a standard that is external in the first sense, it can nonetheless grasp one that is external in the second. The latter is what is needed if he is to be able to underwrite some of our practices in a realist way, by pointing to natures with which we engage in acting and which serve to explain why we sometimes act successfully and sometimes fail to do so. Further, the master craftsman may on occasion be able radically to criticize or even 'debunk' our practices by showing that they are not in fact grounded in natures of the relevant type, but spring from our mistaken beliefs or prejudices. In these ways, he achieves a degree of distance from his practices sufficient for the possibility of a realist vindication of some of our practices (even though he does not possess an external standard of the type the Platonist envisaged).[19]

2. *Can the master craftsman really provide a realist justification for any of our practices? Does the idea of 'nature' not beg the question in favour of realism?*

Objection. Surely, the master craftsman is just an 'empirical' craftsman who happens to engage in some further theoretical speculation about what is involved in the practice itself? More specifically, is not his idea of the nature of (for example) wood merely the result of some theoretical speculation on his part, speculation which does not arise directly from what he does? Of course, the idea of nature he introduces is one that is favourable to realism. But this is solely because he assumes a realist theory in giving his explanation for our practices. He is no more entitled to this than is any other realist theoretician. Nothing has been said to vindicate his introduction of this type of theory. All we have to go on are the practices of the

---

[18] For such a view, see Bernard Williams' *Descartes. The Project of Pure Enquiry*, Harmondsworth: Penguin, 1978.

[19] For a similar distinction, see John Campbell's 'A Simple View of Colour', in J. Haldane and C. Wright (eds.), *Reality, Representation and Projection*, Oxford: Oxford University Press, 1993.

ordinary, stage 2, craftsmen. Just look at these and you will see that there is no need for the realist account that has been offered. The theoretical idea of nature does not really inform the craftsman's activities. It is merely the invention of theoretical philosophy.

Reply. In this objection, as stated, it is simply assumed that the master craftsman's knowledge is 'just more theory'. At this point the objector is as guilty of begging the question as his realist opponent. But the latter has an advantage since the realist concept of nature seems to be directly embedded in the behaviour of the master craftsman, in the descriptions he offers of what he is doing and of why he acts as he does. For he will say such things as

'I am now working with the grain of the wood, but over there I was going against it. That is why I had all those problems.'
'There is no point in trying to do any more of that. Can't you see that we are working against the grain?'
'Why don't we try to do it this way ... there is some chance the wood will allow us to get away with it?'

These descriptions reveal the extent to which the master craftsman's actions manifest his grasp on the nature of the wood. The correct description of his intentional actions reveal his developed practical knowledge of what he is doing and of why he is doing it. Further, the master craftsman is making explicit what is involved in the practical knowledge of the lower level craftsmen. Thus, he will say things such as

'Don't you see what we were doing when we did this? We were working with the grain, with the wood.'
'Don't you see where we were going wrong? We were working against the grain.'
'Don't you remember that difficulty we had with the wood, where we could not find a way round and felt that we were up against something we could not alter? Well, that was because we were trying to straighten out a knot in hard wood. We were right to feel that there was really no way round that difficulty.'

In these ways, the master craftsman is engaged in making the practical knowledge of ordinary craftsmen explicit. He is not merely assuming the idea of a nature as a theoretical entity and explaining what occurs in terms of that. Rather he is bringing out an idea already implicit in his and his colleagues' activities, what they know of the wood they are acting on, even when they do not describe it in these terms. The idea of nature he invokes in his explanations is driven by practice, not by theory. While more needs to be said about the nature of his practical knowledge, it seems that the master craftsman can offer a non-question-begging justification of his beliefs about the nature of the wood. At least, the latter is not a purely theoretical postulate resulting from a prior commitment to realism.

3. Aristotle's model is inappropriate for language mastery. It may be all right for our grasp of certain concepts, but it is not relevant to an account of language mastery.

Wittgenstein makes a number of comments in this direction. Thus, for example, in *Zettel* he writes:

> Why don't I call cookery rules arbitrary, and why am I tempted to call the rules of grammar arbitrary? Because 'cookery' is defined by its end, whereas 'speaking' is not. That is why the use of language is in a certain sense autonomous, as cooking and washing are not. You cook badly if you are guided in your cooking by rules other than the right ones; but if you follow other rules than those of chess you are *playing another game*; and if you follow grammatical rules other than such and such ones, that does not mean you say something wrong, no, you are speaking of something else. (*Z* 320)[20]

Or again,

> Language is not defined for us as an arrangement fulfilling a definite purpose. (*Z* 322)

But this point must be handled with great care. For while it may be true that language as a whole is not defined as being for a certain purpose, particular parts of our language, such as may be concerned with cooking or carpentry, will presumably reflect our interests in cooking and carpentry, and contain concepts designed for that purpose. For these interests will guide our discriminations of various types of wood or metal, the basis for our concepts of these types of phenomenon. Indeed, natural kind terms will, on the Aristotelian model, be introduced on the basis of our practices as carpenters, builders, or farmers. For in these ways, we gain access to the nature of the objects with which we deal. These cases are, unlike chess rules, constrained by natures and objects. In this domain, so far from making up our rules as we go along, we are constrained by the way things are. While it may well be that Aristotle's model is inappropriate for certain parts of language, it applies to those aspects which parallel our thinking about natural kinds and the practical skills that affect them. There may indeed be some parts of language that function like chess, where there is no room for a master craftsman of the type we have been considering. No doubt, in those areas it will be inappropriate to search for realism-conferring natures as the basis for our concepts. But these areas seem quite distinct from those, involving natural kinds, with which we have been concerned. While

---

[20] See also Wittgenstein's comments recorded in *Wittgenstein's Lectures, Cambridge 1930-32, from the notes of John King and Desmond Lee*, ed. D. Lee, Oxford: Blackwell, 1980, 57. There he says 'The rules of grammar are arbitrary in the sense that the rules of a game are arbitrary. We can make them differently. But then it is a different game.'

there may well be no external 'point' for the language as a whole, there may be such 'points' for certain sections of the language.

Objection. But, even in the areas on which you focus, there is still a major dis-analogy between Aristotle's master craftsman and any potential master of language. For a master craftsman can step outside his actual practice of a craft or skill (such as carpentry) and describe it in language. But no one can step outside their language and from the outside describe anything at all. For when we talk, we must presuppose a network of meaning relations obtaining between language and the world. We cannot simultaneously turn our backs on these meaning relations and still describe them (or anything). Perhaps we cannot even say meaningfully what these meaning relations are, since any attempt to do so must presuppose them.[21]

Reply. The degree of independence from his practice achieved by the master crafts-man must not be exaggerated. For the language he uses to describe his craft will be derived (in the ways already indicated) from the practice of his craft. Things would have been very different had the language he used to describe craft practice been a purely scientific one, capable of being understood without any engagement with the relevant craft. But this is not the case envisaged. Indeed, one may doubt whether there is a scientific language of this type, one which can be understood without prior engagement with notions such as length, space, or matter, notions derived from our everyday skilled interaction with the world.

The master craftsman is engaged in seeking to make explicit what is pre-supposed in his own practices. He cannot speak meaningfully about such features without already engaging in and relying on the practices we are seeking to describe. Indeed, in certain cases, he is presupposing the existence of certain practices in speaking as he does. In these ways, the master craftsman closely resembles the language master. Perhaps neither can say what the relevant practices are without presupposing them. If so, both are only making explicit what is involved in the practices they follow. But, while their judgments are both internal (in this sense) to their respective practices, both are capable of justifying and criticizing certain aspects of their respective practices. Neither is merely constrained by what they find natural to do given their practices.

VIII. Interim Conclusions

Wittgenstein sometimes noted that he had never read a word of Aristotle. Had he done so, he would have found someone who, unlike the Augustinian Platonist he

---

[21] See e.g. Merrill Hintikka and Jaakko Hintikka, *Investigating Wittgenstein*, Oxford: Blackwell, 1986, 1-2.

attacks, agreed with him in seeing conceptual thought and meaning as arising out of lower levels of activity (in the ways described). In representing Augustine as a central target, he overlooked the emphasis placed within the Aristotelian tradition on experience and on levels of purposive activity below the level of conceptual thought. For, unlike Augustine, neither Aristotle nor Wittgenstein was content to begin an account of meaning by assuming that a fully developed realist language is already in place. Nor did either countenance the possibility of the Archimedean, wholly external standard of assessment for our practices on which the Platonist insisted.

There remains an important difference between Wittgenstein's and Aristotle's account of these issues. Aristotle's emphasis on the role and significance of the master craftsman holds out the possibility of a position that respects Wittgenstein's concern with practice while simultaneously defending some of the claims of classical realism, which, it seems, he wished to reject. Indeed, Aristotle did not merely gesture towards the possibility of such a position. He did a great deal to show how it could be developed and defended.[22]

---

[22] This chapter leaves open several issues that require further examination. Apart from specific questions of Wittgenstein exegesis, these concern the precise characterization of level 2 skill and the differences between the understanding of the master craftsman and that of the scientist-metaphysician (both in Aristotle's account and in reality). More specifically, more needs to be said about the master craftsman's grasp on the natures of kinds, when this does not essentially involve any understanding even of the existence of the kind's scientific essence. For further discussion of this topic, see *Aristotle on Meaning and Essence* (above n.8) 149-61. Earlier versions of this chapter were read at Birmingham, Manchester, Oslo, Sussex and York Universities and at a research seminar organized jointly by the Universities of Berne and Geneva. I am grateful to those who participated in these discussions, and also to John Campbell, Bill Child and Olav Gjelsvik for their comments on the earlier version. It was an honour to present these ideas at the S.V.Keeling Lecture in 2001.

Chapter Eight

From Necessity to Fate: a Fallacy?*

Sarah Broadie

I begin with the ancient Stoics, end with the Aristotelians, and in between shall draw together some thoughts not ascribed to anyone in particular.

I. Introduction

The Stoics were universal determinists. That is, they held that whatever takes place is and always has been inevitable or necessary, given its antecedent causes.[1,2] This doctrine provoked one of the catchier bits of ancient reasoning, the Lazy Argument. Paraphrased for the modern ear, it goes: for any event E, (1) if the world is such that it is inevitable that E will occur, then E will occur no matter what else happens; and if the world is such that it is inevitable that E will not occur, then E will not occur no matter what else happens; but (2) (according to Stoic determinism) either the world is disposed in one of those two ways or it is disposed in the other. So (3) either way, the outcome will be whatever it will be no matter what else happens. Consequently, even if the occurrence of E is preferable to its non-occurrence or *vice versa*, nothing that anyone does with a view to producing the one or blocking the other can make the slightest difference. For example, if you, a sick person, are going to recover from your illness, then you will recover regardless of whether you get medical help. If, on the

---

*   Reprinted from *The Journal of Ethics* 5 (2001) 21-37, 'From Necessity to Fate: A Fallacy?', by Sarah Broadie, © Copyright Kluwer Academic Publishers: with kind permission from Kluwer Academic Publishers.

1   See A.A. Long and D.N. Sedley, *The Hellenistic Philosophers*, Cambridge: Cambridge University Press, 1987 (hereafter, 'LS'), §55 J-N (vol. 1, 336-8). The most comprehensive and penetrating study of Stoic determinism is Susanne Bobzien's *Determinism and Freedom in Stoic Philosophy*, Oxford: Oxford University Press, 1998, of which see especially ch. 5, 'Fate, Action, and Motivation: the Idle Argument'.

2   The formulations in this paper take no account of the fact that Chrysippus, the major figure of early Stoicism, defended a sense of 'necessary' such that not everything inevitable (because fated), is necessary; nor of the fact that he seems to have distinguished 'that which is necessary' from 'that which is necessitated'. See Bobzien, 122-43.

other hand, you are going to die from your illness, then you will die from it whether or not you get medical help. Either way, it is pointless to try to get medical help.[3]

The Stoic Chrysippus was quick to counter the Lazy Argument.[4] He rejected its first premiss, reasoning that if (for example) your recovery is the inevitable outcome, then determinism entails that such earlier events as are naturally required for this outcome have always been inevitable too because of antecedent causes. If, as would normally be the case, your recovery depends on your receiving medical help, then your receiving it, and therefore your taking whatever action is necessary for getting it (since it is assumed in the example that getting it depends on you), will also have been caused. Perhaps you go for help on impulse, or because reflectively it seems the wisest thing to do, or because you yield to someone else's advice. But whichever of these psychological antecedents obtains, it too has always been inevitable, just as it has always been inevitable that you would take the action you will take, and will recover in consequence. On this account there is no reason at all to think that you will recover regardless of what you do.

The universal determinist, then, does ask us to believe that in this world it has always been inevitable that you would act as you do, and therefore always inevitable that you would decide or otherwise come to act in that way. And this may be a hard belief for common sense to take on board. But there is another proposition which is not merely hard to believe, but is repugnant, intolerable and outrageous, namely that *in general* the outcome of your action would have been just the same even if the world had been such that in it you acted in the opposite way under the circumstances. However, as Chrysippus showed, the Stoic determinist definitely does not ask us to believe the intolerable proposition. So, since it is the intolerable proposition that yields the lazy conclusion that action in general is pointless, Stoicism is not vulnerable to the Lazy Argument.

We can illustrate Chrysippus's point by an example which Aristotle uses to explain the idea of dependence.[5] It is impossible in Euclidean geometry that the inner angles of a triangle add up to more or less than two right angles. Because of this, the internal angles of a quadrilateral necessarily add up to four right angles, since a quadrilateral is composed of two triangles. It follows that if, *per impossibile*, the internal angles of the triangle added up to three right angles, then given the original relation of triangle to quadrilateral the internal angles of the quadrilateral would add up to twice three = six right angles. The fact that it is impossible for the angles of the triangle to add up to three right angles should not,

---

3   Cicero, *On Fate* 28-30, LS §55 (vol. 1, 339-40; vol. 2, 340-41). The paraphrase substitutes 'it is inevitable that' for Cicero's 'it is your fate that' to reflect the fact that the argument means to derive fatalism in the modern sense (= 'the fated result will occur no matter what else') from determinism. Note that the Lazy Argument does not assume that all events are predetermined. It is just meant to apply to any that are.

4   Ibid.

5   *Eudemian Ethics* 2.6 1222b31-6: *The Complete Works of Aristotle, the Revised Oxford Translation*, ed. J. Barnes, Princeton: Princeton University Press, 1984, p.1936.

and does not, make it the slightest bit tempting to conclude that if, *per impossibile*, they did, the angles of the quadrilateral would not, so to speak, follow suit but would still add up, as they actually do, to four right angles.

What does contemporary philosophy have to say on this matter? Well, even if not on the sub-atomic level, on the level of human actions and events of immediate practical significance determinist doctrine is as alive and kicking today in some quarters as it was in the age of Chrysippus. Its modern sympathizers, like Chrysippus,[6] find the challenge of reconciling universal determinism with intuitions about human *freedom* and *responsibility* a fruitful source of serious business. However, reconciliation is one of those things that are necessary only when there is some reason to suspect they may be impossible; so the same question continues to stimulate incompatibilist answers too. But on both sides of that debate, no philosopher today of any skill or training sees the *Lazy Argument* as posing a difficulty for determinism. All, it seems, agree that universal determinism is at least consistent with the general efficacy of human action, and that any argument to the contrary is obviously based on a fallacy.

But in taking stock of things alive and kicking, we must also concede that in some quarters the Lazy Argument is still one of them. Which of us introducing a class to the theory of universal determinism has not had to face the student who responds: 'But if that's true, there's no point in doing anything!' Perhaps we remember making just that response ourselves when we first heard about the theory; and perhaps also remember our teachers patiently explaining to us, as we in turn explain to our own students, that the response is a fallacy. From the premiss that something had to happen, given the way things were, it simply does not follow that the same thing would have happened no matter what else had been the case, and that action was therefore pointless. To think otherwise, we may tell our students, is an 'elementary' fallacy.

These students are in rather good company. The Lazy Argument was endorsed by the great Aristotelian commentator, Alexander of Aphrodisias, and something like it had already been endorsed by Aristotle himself. Writing about a hundred years before Chrysippus, Aristotle declares:

> These and others like them are the absurdities that follow if it is necessary for every affirmation and negation (either about universals spoken of universally or about particulars) that one of the opposites be true and the other false, and that nothing of what happens is as chance has it, but *everything is and happens of necessity. So there would be no need to deliberate or to take trouble, thinking that if we do this, this will happen, but if we do not, it will not.*[7]

And against determinism Alexander argues:

---

6   LS, §62, vol. 1, 386-94.
7   *On Interpretation* 9 18b26-32: *Revised Oxford Translation*, 29 (italics added).

> If ... we are going to be persuaded that [all things come to be of necessity and] we are not in control of anything, [then] we will leave aside many of the things that ought to be done by us both on account of having deliberated about them and on account of eagerly undertaking the efforts involved in what is done; we will have become lazy with regard to doing anything of our own accord, on account of the belief that what ought to come about *would* come about, even if we did not exert ourselves about what needed to be done.[8]

The fact that Aristotle makes a move resembling the Lazy Argument,[9] and that Alexander follows with the Lazy Argument itself, may simply betoken confusion on the part of these philosophers. But it also prompts one to wonder whether the Lazy Argument, or something like it, might not have genuine force after all. The rest of my discussion will elaborate this suggestion.

First, let us clarify some terms.

> Determinism with respect to an actual event E (or non-event, not-E) is the view that it was always necessary that E would / would not occur.

> Fatalism with respect to actual E (or not-E) is the view that E would / would not have occurred no matter what else occurred beforehand.

> Futilism with respect to E (or not-E) is the view that rational effort on our part regarding E/ not-E is pointless. ('Rational effort' covers deliberation on whether to bring about E or not, and efforts to implement the conclusion of deliberation).

We should distinguish several grounds for being a 'futilist' with regard to E / not-E: that is, for judging it pointless to make a rational effort concerning E / not-E.

> (i) Whatever we decide/ try to do (or let happen), the empirical result will be the same.

> (ii) Whatever we do (or let happen), the value achieved will be the same.

> (iii) Epistemically we are in no position to prefer that E occur rather than not, or *vice versa*.

A futilistic attitude towards E / not-E may be adopted for empirical and in

---

[8]   *On Fate*, XXI 191,17-24, in *Alexander of Aphrodisias on Fate*, with translation and commentary by R.W. Sharples, London: Duckworth, 1983. Since Alexander must have known the Chrysippan rebuttal of the Lazy Argument, his revival of the latter suggests that he does not consider the rebuttal completely effective. As we shall see (Section IV below), the rebuttal cannot be mounted within an Aristotelian framework.

[9]   Aristotle moves straight from 'everything is necessary' to 'there is no point in deliberat-ing or taking trouble', whereas in Alexander the inference is mediated by the assump-tion that if everything is necessary, the same outcome occurs no matter what we do.

principle alterable or avoidable reasons. For example: (i) Once Aida and her lover are entombed, the result will be the same whether or not they reconcile themselves to their premature deaths. (ii) Two identical bowls of soup are equally available to the man driven by hunger. Nothing is gained or lost by his consuming this rather than this, or by consuming them in one order rather than the other. (iii) People often decline to vote because they feel they know too little to judge whether candidate A's victory and candidate B's defeat is preferable, or the reverse. Here, however, I am only concerned with putative cases in which the reason for futilism is in principle unchangeable and inescapable: for short, cases of 'in-principle futilism'.

It is clear from the explanation of the terms that fatalism with regard to E / not-E constitutes a type-(i) ground for the corresponding in-principle futilism. I now want to ask whether determinism with regard to E / not-E entails or logically supports any kind of in-principle futilism with respect to E / not-E.[10]

We have already seen that determinism with regard to E / not-E does not in general imply a corresponding fatalism. The implication fails for Stoic determinism, as Chrysippus showed. And in this respect modern causal determinism is like Stoic determinism. For when we teach determinism today, we save it from the charge of entailing fatalism by an argument that is essentially the same as the one Chrysippus gave. Consequently, it seems fairly clear that neither Stoic nor modern determinism provides a type-(i) ground for in-principle futilism. For it is difficult to see why one would endorse such a ground for futilism with regard to a given E / not-E if not because one is fatalistic about it. So, in general, the determinist as such has no more reason to be a futilist[11] on the first ground than to be a fatalist concerning any event. Nor is there any reason to think that determinism commits one to the second ground for futilism.

However, in what follows I shall argue first[12] that causal determinism as we understand it today and as the Stoics understood it, entails the third ground for futilism. It follows that this sort of determinism *approximates to* fatalism in so far as it shares the latter's capacity to generate futilism. I shall then argue[13] that a distinctively *Aristotelian* determinism with regard to an event E brought about my action entails fatalism with regard to E. In sum, this lecture is a two way attempt to vindicate the untutored reaction to determinism: 'If that's true there's no point in *doing* anything.'

To pave the way for these arguments, let us first engage with the topic of *fate*.

---

[10] The present discussion will not be exhaustive. For one thing, the list of grounds for futilism may be incomplete.

[11] I.e. in principle. This is now to be understood throughout.

[12] Section III, below.

[13] Section IV, below.

II. Fate

By 'fate' here, I do not mean what the Stoics meant, namely the pre-necessitation of things that we have been calling 'determinism'. I mean the pre-necessitation that is supposed to hold regardless of how one tries to get round it. How might fate in this narrower and seemingly more sinister sense come into anyone's picture? These days, no one respectable believes in fate (do they?) any more than they believe in general that action and choice are pointless. Why would one postulate fate, and what would one be postulating? Let us imagine some situations.

There is a soft-drinks vending machine, and someone wants a Coca Cola from it. He puts in money, pushes the Coke button, and the machine delivers his order. But somehow or other we who are watching know that even if he had put in a bid for Pepsi or Sprite or ginger ale, he would have been served a Coke. Is this fate? We are not in a hurry to think so, because we can easily hypothesize 'ordinary' explanations for what happened. Perhaps the machine is stocked only with Coke, so you get that whichever button you press. Alternatively, although the machine contains a variety of sodas, the man has an unconscious tropism towards Coke: whichever button he means to press, his hand ends up on the Coke button, whether he means it or not. We could think of explanations for this, neurological or psycho-logical; so no need to invoke fate.

Let us change the example. Let us suppose that someone wants to go to his class reunion. It is held every year, not always in the same place. Every year he plans to go, but something always crops up to prevent it. On one occasion he falls ill just beforehand. Another year, he misses the last flight because of exceptional traffic on the way to the airport. Next time, his plane is hijacked to Cuba. Or it has to land at the wrong destination because of weather. On another occasion, the Post Office loses a letter that announces to him (in timely fashion) a change in the reunion's date, so he turns up when it is over. And so on. He is not in general accident prone. It is just that the reunion seems to elude him systematically. Here we, and he, might begin to think him 'fated' not to get to it, even if we are aware of hardly knowing how to make sense of the thought. If we do find ourselves thinking in this direction, presumably this is because it makes even less sense to suppose that the person's failure to get to the reunion year after year is simply a string of coincidences. Nothing miraculous has happened. On each occasion, the failure has its own perfectly natural explanation. But if everything is perfectly natural, how is it that such different sequences all wind up in the same outcome – an outcome, moreover, which far from being the sort of thing one might expect to happen again and again, is the sort of thing that tends to happen quite rarely, the world being what it is?

The pattern we have suggests *purpose*. When the same result occurs over and over although what leads up to it is quite different each time, the result begins to seem like an end that is being aimed for. It is the mark of purpose that different methods are used to achieve it, reflecting differences in the circumstances. The person might not unreasonably come to think that even when he does not get the flu or break his leg at the last minute, when nothing makes him miss the plane, when the weather is propitious, when he has checked for a possible change of date or venue, etc., etc., even so, favourable as all these circumstances are, some other 'means' will be 'found' to thwart his endeavour – a perfectly natural means, of course. Not unreasonably, he might wonder whether next year, or the one after, the cause might not be a perfectly natural plane crash; and then he may think: 'I'd better stop trying to go; it will be my fault if engines fail or wings ice up, and a plane full of people falls out of the sky.' This sort of thinking is not irrational, given the facts. But of course these are fictional facts. We are making this story up so as to understand the meaning of 'fate'. If comfort is needed, can we not comfort ourselves with the thought that the likelihood of a situation developing in which a rational, enlightened, person might rationally invoke fate is at least as unlikely as the series of repeated failures to get to the reunion?

However, the repetition is not all that unlikely, if, as the protagonist begins to suspect, his non-appearance at the reunion *is* consistently purposed. But here we should pause to bring out the fact, implicit in the fictional situation so far, that the hypothesis that a natural or human purposive agent is responsible for the repeated outcomes is, from what we know of the circumstances, as far fetched as the hypothesis of coincidence. For I am assuming that 'the circumstances' include a complete lack of evidence for a single natural or human cause. In this situation, even the hard headed might find it least unreasonable to resort to talk of 'fate', meaning by this an agency concerning which all we know is that it has a certain purpose concerning the man and his reunion,[14] and is clever and foreknowing and powerful enough to carry out this intention no matter what. It is omnipotent with respect to this purpose, even if its unlimited power is limited just to this goal. Hence we cannot track the fate down as we could a natural or human agent, since then we might be able to hobble it or deflect its reach, or even discover what it is after and persuade it to act differently. Certainly, it would seem that, as far as fate is concerned, the man's not getting to his reunion is a matter of great significance; but there is no way – no natural way – of discovering what that significance is.

We can now pinpoint an important difference between the fatalism illustrated in the story, and determinism in its Stoic and modern forms. Determinism is universal-izable, fatalism is not. If the happening of some events is and always has been pre-necessitated (determinism), it does not follow that the same is not true for every other event. But if it is pre-necessitated that a given event E will happen somehow or other no matter what (fatalism), the events which on a given occasion pave the causal path to E are not such that they too would have happened no matter what. It is obvious in the reunion story that each time many things happen which would not have happened if particular conditions had been different. For example, if we imagine the protagonist stopping because of a red light *en route* to the airport, we assume that he would not have stopped at that point had the light been green,

---

[14]   The purpose, of course, might be not that he will never get to the reunion, but that he will get to it once in fifteen years, or only when some rare visitor is present.

ceteris paribus; and we do not assume that it would have been red no matter what moment he reached it. And if we allow ourselves to postulate an unpreventable purpose in order to explain the otherwise inexplicable pattern of events, it is because the pattern seems to show us a series of individually dispensable means to the same inevitable end. If we suppose that the events that are means on one occasion would have happened no matter what (for example, regardless of whether they led to the so called end), they no longer figure as means, but rather as ends in themselves.[15]

Perhaps we can now let go of the notion of fate. We invoked it to fill an explanatory gap which was only fictional, after all. And even if we ourselves were faced with the fictional events, we might insist, despite the absence of evidence, that the pattern must be due to a naturalistic cause. In that case, of course we would not be thinking of the failure to get to the reunion as something that will happen inevitably, no matter what. For a natural cause, if there is one, can in principle be identified and disabled so that it no longer has its effect. And if there is a natural cause (this includes human agency), we are under no temptation to ascribe mystical significance to the repeated outcome. If the cause is a human agent, then presumably the outcome is significant to him or her, but in ways that we can find out.

So far we have been considering fate as a conceivable explanation of a conceivable pattern of events. But if the latter is only *conceivable,* we can be forgiven for postponing a decision about whether we ourselves would postulate fate until such time as we ourselves are actually faced with such a set of facts. Sufficient unto the day – especially if the day in question is utterly improbable.

But even if we stay within familiar horizons, the idea of fate exercises a certain subliminal appeal. Consider some past event or conjunction of enormous cultural or personal significance. On the personal level, it is not unusual to be literally unable to imagine how one's life would have gone if twenty or however many years ago one had not met the 'significant other', or had never stumbled into one's line of work, or had had or not had children as the case might be. The concrete imagination takes its cue from our life as we have actually lived it, and when no alternatives can be pictured with comparable vivacity, as David Hume might have put it, it is as if for the concrete imagination there *are* no alternatives. So, looking back, it is as if I was bound to meet that person, to go to that place from which so much started. (Something of this mind-set coexists in many of us with the presumably more rational belief that alternatives were possible for the person I was then; I might have been luckier or unluckier. Since the more rational belief assumes the standpoint of me back then, e.g. wondering whether or not to accept what turns out later to have been a life-shaping invitation, it abstracts from the concrete consequential detail of the path actually taken, and so this path, or the initial stretch of it, appears as schematic as the alternatives.)

---

[15]   It may be correct to say that that the means are fated, given that the end is fated; but this is not to view the means *fatalistically*, i.e. to apply the Lazy Argument to them too.

Let us think briefly about history-shaping events and individuals; to each his or her own choice of example. Suppose that the Persians had permanently occupied Greece and Athens at the beginning of the fifth century BCE. Suppose that Plato or Aristotle had died in infancy. We cannot begin to imagine how Western history would have gone – how things would have been *now*, for instance. There is no point in even trying, any more than in trying to formulate a coherent alternative to '2 + 3 = 5' without changing the meanings. There is nothing to hang on to. This well-founded paralysis of the imagination expresses itself in the imaginational thought that there had to be a Plato who did what Plato did, and there had to be an Aristotle. Or, rationality off guard, we catch ourselves thinking that if the actual Plato (or 'Aristocles', as it seems his parents actually called him) had died as a child, another giant would have come in his place, to do essentially the same work. The other, we might think, would have been 'sent'; or the climate of the time was ready to bring such a figure forth. One way or another, the outcome would have been in important respects the same.

If, in the sort of context I have just tried to sketch, we fall back on the idea of a fated event or the fated contribution of some great person, it is not in order to explain the otherwise inexplicable. Rather, 'fated' now functions as a modal strengthener ensuring framework-status to the item in question. By fate, this actual, but by naturalistic standards no more than contingent, entity is guaranteed existence under all the alternatives felt by us to be culturally or personally possible.

It is time to turn to the two arguments promised earlier.

III. Showing that universal determinism gives ground for futilism

The argument is not complicated. Much of what we do, we do so that things will be better in some way than they would have been if we had not so acted, or so that they are more likely to be better. We base the judgment that things will be, or are more likely to be, better if we do D on a comparison with the way things would go if, *ceteris paribus*, we don't do it. Judgments about the way things would go if *ceteris paribus* we don't do D are based on induction. We can't be certain of them, but we can have good evidence for them, and that is sufficient basis for action. We also generally think that we can in principle make a reasonable judgment on whether things *would* be relevantly equal if we don't do D. This is important because we measure the actual gain achieved by doing it through comparison with how things would have been otherwise, not merely through comparison with how they are before we do it.

Now if, after doing D on the basis of the kind of comparison I have sketched, we were to become aware in retrospect that we lacked and still lack any grounds for making that comparison, then we should see ourselves as having done D in the dark, and as still not knowing what might have been gained or for that matter lost through our doing it. And if at the time of deciding whether to do D we had realized our ignorance with respect to the difference our doing it would imply, it would have been rational for us to conclude it pointless to deliberate on whether or not to do *D*; and if for some reason we had already started to do it, equally point-less to care whether or not we carried it through successfully, since we have no idea what, if anything, would be gained or lost thereby.

Suppose for example that I am driving, and I slow down to avoid hitting a neighbour's dog. I have quickly and, let us assume, by ordinary standards reason-ably, judged that it is safe to brake a bit and that my car will hit the dog if I don't. I briefly imagine the yelp of pain and then having to walk towards my neighbour's front door with a dead or injured dog in my arms. It is to forestall such distressing events at no cost that I act so as to avoid the creature. My reasoning assumes that whether I avoid it or not, a great deal in the situation will be the same either way. In both cases I shall be driving this car; the road conditions will be the same; the dog will be crossing the road until it is hit; it is my neighbour's adored companion; if I skid on braking I will not run into anything; the dog is not surrounded by a protec-tive force field; and much else. My reasoning is that if I don't brake, I will have harmed the dog gratuitously. This assumes that how things were up to the moment of braking is the same in many significant respects as how things would have been up to that moment had I failed to brake. It is on the basis of these features that I reckon the difference made by action rather than non-action and *vice versa*.

Now most determinists are like ordinary people in the way they reckon the net value, in a case like this, of braking to avoid the dog. They too compare the immediately foreseeable consequences of braking with those of not braking against a background of relevant circumstances the same either way.[16] It may look as if the comparison enables them, just as it enables the rest of us, to explain afterwards just what one did gain by braking on that occasion. In fact, however, or so I would argue, determinists are rationally disqualified from enjoying or offering any such explanation. They can say what would have been gained by braking *if*, in the absence of this event, other circumstances had been relevantly the same. They can say that braking in the actual situation stands for something better than any not-braking that might be supposed to occur in a relevantly similar hypothetical situation. But this leaves it open whether that is the situation one *would* have been in even if one had not braked. If we have no reason to believe it is, then we have no reason to hold that it *was* a good thing that I braked, and to be pleased that I did.[17] Conversely, if we are confident that the braking *was* a good thing, this is because

---

16   Most if not all real-life questions of moral and legal responsibility assume that in general, we can make reasonable judgments about the differences made by actions. When determinists try (as most do) to accommodate ordinary intuitions about responsi-bility to their doctrine, they show that they share the assumption.

17   We still have reason to hold the following: my braking would have been a good thing if, had I not braked, the rest of the situation had been pretty much as it actually was. But this does not justify my being pleased that I did brake, for unless we have reason to believe that the antecedent of the above conditional is true, we have no reason to believe that the actual braking *was* a good thing, and hence to be actually pleased about it.

we do not compare its results with those of non-braking on the mere *supposition* of similar conditions; rather, we consider it on the basis of an *assertion* that such conditions were in place and would have been in place whether there was braking or not. And we take that assertion to be justified. But it is justified only if one is justified in assuming that the common conditions and their causal antecedents were causally independent of the braking and *its* causal antecedents. This justification would be lacking if there were reason to think that things are connected in such a way that the hypothetical scenario in which I didn't brake is one in which a relevant common condition was absent. (For example: I only wouldn't have braked if I had been distraught or in a great hurry. My neighbour, who knows me well, was watching my demeanour as I loaded the car, etc., and she rightly judged that I was calm. But if she had seen reason to judge otherwise, she would not have let her dog out of the house. Here, my braking to avoid the dog and the dog's being there to be avoided are consequences of the same cause, my calm, and are related in such a way that the absence of either entails the prior absence of the cause and therefore the absence of the other.)

Again, one is not justified in assuming that the relevant actual conditions (relevant, that is, to its being a good thing that I braked) would have been in place whether I had braked or not if *one has no reason at all to believe that it is true that they would have been*. Now, in practical life we make this sort of assumption all the time, with a good deal of confidence. But certainly if we are determinists we are not entitled to such confidence. For the determinist, if the braking had not occurred, this would have been because the antecedent situation was different in some way from actuality, and this because of a difference in its antecedent, and so on. And causation being what it is, each of these differences would have bred subsequent effects, branching out into further effects and further differences. Moreover, at each stage there are different ways in which the antecedent might have been different enough to cancel the actual effect, and each of these different ways breeds its own ramifying set of different consequences. Not only can we not keep track of any given set of ramifications, but we cannot know which of them would have been, so to speak, *the* one that would have been realized in the world as it would have been if I had not braked for the dog. In fact that question makes no sense. In many examples one need back-track no more than a year from yesterday to find oneself drowning in ignorance of how the course of events today would have differed from the actual course were it the case that some humdrum event of yesterday had not occurred[18] – never mind back-tracking to the beginning of the world, as we are bound to if we are determinists.

But it is only the determinist who drowns, because of the doctrine that every stage is pre-necessitated by what went before. If and only if we understand the present as not so rigidly connected to the past, we can breathe easier and judge with reasonable confidence that events do make the differences they ordinarily seem to

---

[18] This argument has force even without chaos theory and the 'butterfly effect'.

us to make. Determinists, on the other hand, ought to refrain from such judgments, since they have no epistemic right to them if their theory is true. Indeed, if their theory is true it is pointless to care about doing something rather than something else, since the difference it makes for good or ill is a blind guess for all of us.[19, 20]

IV. Showing that Aristotelian determinism with respect to *E* entails fatalism with respect to *E*

The modern causal determinist typically holds that earlier conditions necessitate and explain the existence of later ones. We have seen that it is a mistake to infer from this that later ones would have occurred no matter what went before. But let us now consider determinism as it would be from an Aristotelian perspective. (Here it is enough to consider the pre-necessitation of some given event, without assuming that everything is thus determined.)

The Aristotelian typically holds that explanatory causal necessitation by one event of another runs from later to earlier. The later is the final cause, and the necessitation is in most cases hypothetical.[21] If there is going to be a house, materials for the roof and walls etc. must be assembled for the sake of it. If the fruit of a tree is to develop to the point where it can shed fertile seeds, the fruit must be sheltered from the sun; hence for the sake of the tree's reproduction there must be leaves growing in a certain position; and for leaves to grow where needed leaves must be made of relatively light material, not heavy matter that settles round the roots. For Aristotle, teleology is the most scientific approach to any subject matter that can sustain it. In the natural world, life-forms obviously provide the most promising subject matter. But, strange as it may seem to us, Aristotle even applies this scheme of later causally necessitating earlier to the movements and positions of heavenly bodies.[22] This is understandable, since for him the heavenly bodies are alive and instinct with intelligence and presumably purpose.[23] At any rate, causal necessitation of earlier by later is, for him, the scheme of choice, just as, no doubt, the reverse is the scheme of choice for us.

In the house and tree examples, an Aristotelian regards it as contingent whether

---

[19]   Sometimes, however, we act not so as to get something done, but simply so as to instan-
      tiate some form of conduct, such as keeping a promise. This sort of practical attitude
      may be available to the determinist. It will be an absolutely rigid deontology, since it
      can never take account of consequences.
[20]   In fact this should be a welcome conclusion for the ancient Stoics (although, as far as I
      know, they never drew it), because of their ethic of acceptance. Logically, I cannot
      regret running over the dog if I am convinced that there is no reason to think that things
      would have been better if I hadn't.
[21]   *Physics* 2.8-9: *Revised Oxford Translation*, 339-42.
[22]   *On Generation and Corruption* 2.11: ibid., 552-4.
[23]   *On the Heavens* 2.12 291b19-21: ibid., 481.

the end in question actually comes to be.[24] In the first place, the particular house or plant might not even have got started. Secondly, the processes of building and growth might have been interrupted before the end was reached. Buildings and trees are sorts of things that cannot grow or be produced except in dependence on an environment, which is also, necessarily, an arena for possible interference. Since builders are intelligent, they take account of this pervasive fact about building. And so, when it comes to growing, does the intelligence-like formative principle in the plant. Each is primed to pursue the end by varying, if necessary, the means in response to environmental challenges that arise. Otherwise, every challenge would bring the process to a halt. It is precisely because experience gives us reason to believe that, within certain necessary constraints, if the subject had not pursued its end in one way, it would have done so in another, that we see the process as purposive at all. In these cases it is the variety of ways of getting to the same result that leads us to postulate intelligence or something like intelligence as the guiding principle.

Compare this with Aristotle's heavenly bodies. We would have to have, as he had, a prior and independent belief that each heavenly body is governed by a distinct intelligence before we felt any inclination to look upon their movements as purposive. This is for two reasons. First, their movements are circular, continuous and everlasting.[25] Hence whatever position[26] we designate as an end led-up-to, the heavenly body does not stop there, but passes on as if that were no more an end-point than those preceding it. Secondly, according to Aristotelian physics, nothing about a heavenly body or its environment represents a possible threat to its single-minded progression. Its matter is such that it cannot decay or falter; its environment is such that it cannot be stopped or knocked off course. Thus its movement does not betray purposiveness by adjusting to potential obstacles, for potential obstacles are impossible up there. Even so, Aristotle applies the schema of purpose, declaring that a chronologically earlier stage must occur because a later one will, the former being a necessary antecedent for the latter. The case is like those of the house and the tree, except that here the necessity is absolute, not hypothetical, since the celestial movement has always been going on, and nothing can upset its continuation. In other words, if the later stage is to going to come about, what naturally leads up to it must, for the sake of it, come about first. But (since the movement is necessary and continuous), the later stage will come about, and will come about necessarily; and because of that, what leads up to it will come about necessarily too. And this is not only true now, but has always been so. That is to say: for as long as the movement has been going on (forever) it has always been

---

[24] Cf. *On Generation and Corruption* 2.11 337b30-34: ibid., 553.

[25] For Aristotle, this means 'temporally infinite in both directions'. But the present argument is not affected if we understand 'everlasting' as 'enduring for the whole of time' and take the entirety of time to be finite.

[26] E.g. a solstice; *On Generation and Corruption* 2.11 337b13-14: *ROT*, 553.

necessary that the particular later stage that we have in mind will come about, and therefore it has always been necessarily being led up to by whatever has to precede it.

Now imagine that someone proposes to the Aristotelian that some sublunary event, such as a particular house's getting finished, or someone's getting over an illness, is like the celestial positions in that its coming to pass is and always has been necessary. So this sublunary event is like the celestial positions in that its coming to pass has always necessarily been being led up to. Now if the completion of the house is an end, then its coming about is and always has been simply necessary, and by the teleological scheme every stage leading up to it has been for the sake of it. If, on the other hand, the completion of the house is and always has been necessary as a means to some further end, then every stage leading up to it has been for the sake of that end.

But such events are not celestial, and like all events down here they and what leads up to them unfold in an environment of potential obstacles. We would expect to see the leading-up adjusting to what would otherwise be obstacles and taking different forms at different stages to succeed. We say of the ordinary purposive agent building a house or trying to stay healthy that within a certain range of possibility the actual means he used were dispensable; if one way had failed, he would have taken a different route.

But now if the end's coming about has always been necessary, and has always depended on suitable antecedent means leading up to it, then the series of means stretches back into the infinite past. And if the end's coming about has always been necessary, and, as with sublunary ends in general, there are different ways in which it might come about, it has always been necessary that it will come about one way or another. Thus if a particular link in the actual chain of means had failed to materialize, as can happen with events down here, some other chain would have been followed, or some other link come into play instead. But then these are not means controlled or controllable by a human agent, since no human agent has such power over means as to make it true that the end will come about *of necessity*. And if a human agent controlled the means, the means-end series would have started from a particular human action or decision at a particular moment within history. But in that case it would not be true that it has *always* been necessary that the end will come about. We therefore have the pattern of purposive action engaged in by an agent that has been monitoring the stream of events from time everlasting so that from time everlasting they have always been being paid out in a way to side-step or compensate for every obstacle.

This, I submit, is the inevitable result of combining the determinist idea that it has always been predetermined that an event E will occur, with the Aristotelian assumption that earlier events happen because they lead up to an end that comes about later. Thus an Aristotelian faced with the suggestion that E's occurrence has always been pre-determined sees it as harbouring the following implications: (1) No *human* agent is responsible for ensuring that E will occur rather than not; and (2) if human decisions and efforts are involved, it is only as links in a chain of means to an end that would have come about in some other way had they been absent. So if, for example, the determinist tries to explain to the Aristotelian that when a human agent A voluntarily takes steps to bring about a state of affairs S – for example, that A recovers from illness – either it has always been necessary that A will recover or it has always necessary that A will die, the Aristotelian naturally infers that, whichever the outcome, it has always been pre-determined to occur if not by one chain of events then by another; hence it will come about just the same whatever A does or does not do.

Chapter Nine

Compassion and Terror*

Martha Nussbaum

The name of our land has been wiped out.

Hecuba, in Euripides, Trojan Women, 1322

Not to be a fan of the Greens or Blues at the races, or the light-armed or heavy-armed gladiators at the Circus.

Marcus Aurelius, Meditations 1.5.1

I

The towers of Troy are burning. All that is left of the once-proud city is a group of ragged women, bound for slavery, their husbands dead in battle, their sons murdered by the conquering Greeks, their daughters raped. Hecuba their queen invokes the king of the gods, using, remarkably, the language of democratic citizenship: 'Son of Kronus, Council-President of Troy, father who gave us birth, do you see these undeserved sufferings that your Trojan people bear?' The Chorus answers grimly, 'He sees, and yet the great city is no city. It has perished, and Troy exists no longer.' A little later, Hecuba herself concludes that the gods are not worth calling on, and that the very name of her land has been wiped out.

In one way, the ending of this drama is as bleak as any in the history of tragic drama. Death, rape, slavery, fire destroying the towers, the city's very name effaced from the record of history by the acts of rapacious and murderous Greeks. And yet, of course, it did not happen that way, not exactly. For the story of Troy's fall is being enacted, some six hundred years after the event, by a company of Greek actors, in the Greek language of a Greek poet, in the presence of all the adult citizens of Athens, most powerful of Greek cities. Hecuba's cry to the gods even imagines him as a peculiarly Athenian type of civic official, president of the city council. So the name of the land did not get wiped out after all. The imaginations of

---

* Reprinted from *Daedalus: Journal of the American Academy of Arts and Sciences* 132 (2003) 10-26, by kind permission of the editors. Also delivered as a Kristeller Lecture at Columbia University, April 2, 2002.

the conquerors were haunted by it, transmitted it, and mourn it. Obsessively their arts repeat the events of long-ago destruction, typically inviting, as here, the audience's compassion for the women of Troy and blame for their assailants. In its very structure the play makes a claim for the moral value of compassionate imagining, as it asks its audience to partake in the terror of a burning city, of murder and rape and slavery. Insofar as members of the audience are engaged by this drama, feeling fear and grief for the conquered city, they demonstrate the ability of compassion to cross lines of time, place, and nation – and also, in the case of many audience members, the line of sex, perhaps more difficult yet to cross.

Nor was the play an aesthetic event cut off from political reality. The dramatic festivals of Athens were sacred festivals strongly connected to the idea of democratic deliberation, and the plays of Euripides were particularly well known for their engagement with contemporary events. In this case, the audience that watched *The Trojan Women* had recently voted to put to death the men of the rebellious colony of Melos and to enslave the women and children. Euripides invites them to contemplate the real human meaning of their actions. Compassion for the women of Troy should at least cause moral unease, reminding Athenians of the full and equal humanity of people who live in distant places, their fully human capacity for suffering.

But did those imaginations really cross those lines? Think again of that invocation of Zeus. Trojans, if they worshipped Zeus as king of gods at all, surely did not refer to him as the president of the city council. The term πρύτανις is an Athenian legal term, completely unknown elsewhere. So it would appear that Hecuba is not a Trojan but a Greek. Her imagination is a Greek democratic (and, we might add, mostly male) imagination. Maybe that's a good thing, in the sense that the audience is surely invited to view her as their fellow and equal. But it still should give us pause. Did compassion really enable those Greeks to reach out and think about the real humanity of others, or did it stop short, allowing them to reaffirm the essential Greekness of everything that's human? Of course compassion required making the Trojans somehow familiar, so that Greeks could see their own vulnerability in them, and feel terror and compassion as for people related to themselves. But it's so easy for the familiarization to go too far: they are just us, and we are the ones who suffer humanly. Not those other ones, over there in Melos.

America's towers, too, have burned. Compassion and terror are in the fabric of our lives. And in those lives we do see evidence of the good work of compassion, as Americans make real to themselves the sufferings of so many different people whom they never would otherwise have thought about: New York firefighters, that gay rugby player who helped bring down the fourth plane, bereaved families of so many national and ethnic origins. We even sometimes notice with a new attention the lives of Arab-Americans among us, or feel a sympathy with our Sikh taxi driver when he tells us how often he is told to go home to 'his own country' – even though he came to the U.S. as a political refugee from the miseries of police repression in the Punjab. Sometimes our compassion even crosses that biggest line of all, the national boundary. Tragedy has surely led many people to sympathize with the women of Afghanistan in a way that feminists tried to get people to do for ages, without success. And other civilian victims of the violence, or people threatened by the violence, sometimes cause our imaginations to stop, briefly, before they rush back home to see what latest threat the evening news has brought our way.

The events of September 11 make vivid a philosophical problem that has been debated from the time of Euripides straight on through much of the history of the Western philosophical tradition. This is the question of what do to about compassion, given its obvious importance in shaping the civic imagination, but given, too, its obvious propensity for self-serving narrowness. Is compassion, with all its faults, our best hope as we try to educate citizens to think well about human relations both inside the nation and across national boundaries? So some thinkers have suggested. I count Euripides among them, and I would also include in this category Aristotle, and Rousseau, and Hume, and Adam Smith. Or is it a threat to good political thinking and to the foundations of a truly just world community? So the Greek and Roman Stoics thought, and before them Plato, and after them Spinoza, and Adam Smith. The enemies of compassion hold that we cannot build a truly wise concern for humanity on the basis of such a slippery and uneven motive; impartial motives based on ideas of dignity and respect should take its place. The friends of compassion reply that without building political morality on what we know and on what has deep roots in our childhood attachments, we will be left with a morality that will be empty of urgency – as Aristotle puts it, a 'watery' concern all round. This debate continues straight on into contemporary political and legal thought: in a recent exchange about animal rights, J.M. Coetzee invents a fictional character who argues that the capacity for sympathetic imagination is our best hope for moral goodness in this area. Peter Singer replies, with much plausibility, that the sympathetic imagination is all too anthropocentric, and we had better not rely on it to win rights for creatures whose lives lie at a great distance from our own.

I shall not trace the history of the debate in this lecture. Instead, I shall focus on its central philosophical ideas and try to sort them out, offering a limited defence of compassion and the tragic imagination, and then making some suggestions about how its pernicious tendencies can best be countered – with particular reference, throughout, to our current political situation. Let me set the stage for the analysis to follow by turning to Smith, who, as you will have noticed, turns up in my taxonomy on both sides of the debate. Smith offered one of the best accounts we have of sympathy and compassion, and of the ethical achievements of which this moral sentiment is capable. But later, in a section of the work entitled 'Of the Sense of Duty,' he offers a very solemn warning against trusting this imperfect sentiment too far when duty is what we are trying to get clear about. His concern, like mine, is with our difficulty keeping our minds fixed on the sufferings of people who live on the other side of the world.

> Let us suppose that the great empire of China, with all its myriads of inhabitants, was suddenly swallowed up by an earthquake, and let us consider how a man of humanity in Europe, who had no sort of connection with that part of the world,

would be affected upon receiving intelligence of this dreadful calamity. He would, I imagine, first of all, express very strongly his sorrow for the misfortune of that unhappy people, he would make many melancholy reflections upon the precariousness of human life, and the vanity of all the labours of man, which could thus be annihilated in a moment. ... And when all this fine philosophy was over, when all these humane sentiments had been once fairly expressed, he would pursue his business or his pleasure, take his repose or his diversion, with the same ease and tranquillity, as if no such accident had happened. The most frivolous disaster which could befall himself would occasion a more real disturbance. If he was to lose his little finger tomorrow, he would not sleep tonight; but, provided he never saw them, he will snore with the more profound security over the ruin of a hundred millions of his brethren, and the destruction of that immense multitude seems plainly an object less interesting to him, than this paltry misfortune of his own.

That's just the issue that should trouble us, as we think about American reactions to September 11. We see a lot of 'humane sentiments' around us, and extensions of sympathy beyond people's usual sphere of concern. But how often, both now and at other times, those sentiments stop short at the national boundary. We thought the events of September 11 are bad because they involved us and our nation. Not just human lives, but American lives. The world came to a stop – in a way that it never has for Americans, when disaster befalls human beings in other places. The genocide in Rwanda did not even work up enough emotion in us to prompt humanitarian intervention. The plight of innocent civilians in Iraq never made it onto our national radar screen. Floods, earthquakes, cyclones – and the daily deaths of thousands from preventable malnutrition and disease – none of these makes the American world come to a standstill, none elicits a tremendous outpouring of grief and compassion. At most we get what Smith so trenchantly described: a momentary flicker of feeling, quickly dissipated by more pressing concerns close to home.

Frequently, however, we get a compassion that is not only narrow, failing to include the distant, but also polarizing, dividing the world into an 'us' and a 'them.' Compassion for our own children can so easily slip over into a desire to promote the well-being of our children at the expense of other people's children. Similarly, compassion for our fellow Americans can all too easily slip over into a desire to make America come out on top, defeating or subordinating other nations. One vivid example of this slip took place at a baseball game I went to at Comiskey Park, the first game played in Chicago after September 11 – and a game against the Yankees, so there was heightened awareness of the situation of New York and its people. Things began well, with a moving ceremony commemorating the firefighters who had lost their lives, and honouring local firefighters who had gone to New York afterwards to help out. There was even a lot of cheering when the Yankees took the field, a highly unusual transcendence of local attachments. But as the game went on and the beer began flowing, one heard, increasingly, the chant, 'U–S–A. U–S–A,' a chant left over from the Olympic hockey match in which the U.S. defeated Russia, expressing the wish for America to defeat, abase, humiliate, its enemies. Indeed, the chant U–S–A soon became a general way of expressing the desire to crush one's enemies, whoever they were. When the umpire made a bad call against the Sox, the same group in the bleachers turned to him, chanting 'U–S–A.' Anyone who crosses us is an evil terrorist, deserving of extinction. From 'humane sentiments' we had turned back to the pain in our little finger.

With these Smithean examples before us, how can we trust compassion, and the imagination of the other that it contains? But if we do not trust that, what else can we plausibly rely on, to get ethical responsibility out of horror?

I shall proceed as follows. First, I offer an analysis of the emotion of compassion, focusing on the thoughts and imaginings on which it is based. This gives us a clearer perspective on how and where it is likely to go wrong. Second, I examine the counter-tradition's proposal that we can base political morality on respect for dignity, doing away with appeals to compassion. This proposal, at first attractive, contains, on closer inspection, some deep difficulties. Third, I return to compassion, asking how, if we feel we need it as a public motive, we might educate it so as to overcome, as far as we can, the problem that Smith identified.

II

Compassion is not just a warm feeling in the gut, if it is that at all. It involves a set of thoughts, quite complex. We need to dissect them, if we are to make progress in understanding how it goes wrong and how it may be steered aright. There is a good deal of agreement about this, among philosophers as otherwise diverse as Aristotle and Rousseau, and also among contemporary psychologists and sociologists who have done empirical work on the emotion.[1] (Daniel Batson of The University of Kansas should be mentioned with honour here, because he has not only done remarkable empirical work, he has also combined it with a conceptual and analytic clarity that is rare in social science research of this type. Candace Clark's sociological study is also exemplary.) Compassion is an emotion directed at another person's suffering or lack of well-being. It requires the thought that the other person is in a bad way, and a pretty seriously bad way. (Thus we do not feel compassion for people who lose trivial items like a toothbrush or a paper clip.) It thus contains within itself an appraisal of the seriousness of various predicaments. Let us call this the judgment of seriousness.

Notice that this assessment is made from the point of view of the person who has the emotion. It does not neglect the actual suffering of the other, which certainly should be estimated in taking the measure of the person's predicament. And yet it does not necessarily take at face value the estimate of the predicament this person will be able to form. As Smith emphasized, we frequently have great

---

[1]   In this section I am drawing on the analysis of compassion for which I argue at greater length in Nussbaum, *Upheavals of Thought: The Intelligence of Emotions*, New York: Cambridge University Press, 2001.

compassion for people whose predicament is that they have lost their powers of thought; even if they seem like happy children, we regard this as a terrible catastrophe. On the other side, when people moan and groan about something, we do not necessarily have compassion for them: for we may think that they are not really in a bad predicament. Thus when very rich people grumble about taxes, many of us do not have the slightest compassion for them: for we judge that it is only right and proper that they should pay what they are paying – and probably a lot more than that! The suffering of Hecuba and the Trojan women becomes the object of the audience's compassion directly, because it is understood that their predicament is really grave: slavery, loss of children, loss of city, are among the calamities all human beings typically fear.

So the judgment of seriousness already involves quite a complex feat of imagination: it involves both trying to look out at the situation from the suffering person's own viewpoint and then assessing the person's own assessment. Complex though the feat is, young children easily learn it, feeling sympathy with the suffering of animals and other children, but soon learning, as well, to withhold sympathy if they judge that the person is just a crybaby, or spoiled – and, of course, to have sympathy for the predicament of an animal who is dead or unconscious, even if it is not actually suffering.

Next comes the judgment of non-desert. Hecuba asked Zeus to witness the 'undeserved sufferings' of the Trojan women, using a Greek word, ἀνάξια, that appears in Aristotle's definition of tragic compassion. The tradition claims that we will not have compassion if we believe that the person fully deserves the suffering, just brought it on herself. There may be a measure of blame, but then, in our compassion we typically register the thought that the suffering exceeds the measure of the fault. The Trojan women are an unusually clear case, because, more than most tragic figures, they are hit by events in which they have no active share at all, being women. But we can see that non-desert is a salient part of our compassion even when we do also blame the person: typically we feel compassion at the punishment of a criminal offender, say, only to the extent that we think circumstances beyond his control are at least in good measure responsible for his becoming the bad person he is. People who have the idea that the poor brought their poverty upon themselves by shiftlessness and laziness fail, for that reason, to have compassion for them.

Next there is a thought much stressed in the tradition, which I shall call the judgment of similar possibilities: Aristotle, Rousseau, and others suggest that we have compassion only insofar as we believe that the suffering person shares vulnerabilities and possibilities with us. I think we can clearly see that this judgment is not strictly necessary for the emotion, as the other two seem to be. We have compassion for non-human animals, without basing it on any imagined similarity – although, of course, we need somehow to make sense of their predicament as serious and bad. We also imagine that an invulnerable god can have compassion for mortals, and it does not seem that this idea is conceptually confused. For the finite imaginations of human beings, however, the thought of similar possibilities is a very important psychological mechanism through which we get clear about the seriousness of another person's plight. This thought is often accompanied by empathetic imagining, in which we put ourselves in the suffering person's place, imagine the predicament as our own.

Finally, however, there is one thing more, not mentioned in the tradition, which I believe must be added in order to make the account complete. This is what, in writing on the emotions, I have called the eudaimonistic judgment, namely, a judgment that places the suffering person or persons among the important parts of the life of the person who feels the emotion. In my more general analysis of emotions, I argue that they are always eudaimonistic, meaning focused on the agent's most important goals and project. Thus we feel fear about damages that we see as significant for our own well-being and our other goals; we feel grief at the loss of someone who is already invested with a certain importance in our scheme of things. Eudaimonism is not egoism. I am not claiming that emotions always view events and people as mere means to the agent's own satisfaction or happiness. But I do mean that the things that occasion a strong emotion in us are things that correspond to what we have invested with importance in our account to ourselves of what is worth pursuing in life.

Compassion can evidently go wrong in several different ways. It can get the judgment of non-desert wrong, sympathizing with people who actually do not deserve sympathy and withholding sympathy from those who do. Even more frequently, it can get the judgment of seriousness wrong, ascribing too much importance to the wrong things or too little to things that have great weight. Notice that this problem is closely connected to obtuseness about social justice, in the sense that if we do not think a social order unjust for denying women the vote, or subordinating African-Americans, then we will not see the predicament of women and African-Americans as bad, and we will not have compassion for them. We'll think that things are just as they ought to be. Again, if we think it's unjust to require rich people to pay capital gains tax, we will have a misplaced compassion toward them. But finally, and obviously, compassion can get the eudaimonistic judgment wrong, putting too few people into the circle of concern. On my account, then, we will not have compassion without a moral achievement that is at least coeval with it.

My account, I think, is able to explain the unevenness of compassion better than other more standard accounts. Compassion begins from where we are, from the circle of our cares and concerns. It will be felt only toward those things and persons that we see as important, and of course most of us most of the time ascribe importance in a very uneven and inconstant way. Empathetic imagining can sometimes extend the circle of concern. Thus Batson has shown experimentally that when the story of another person's plight is vividly told subjects will tend to experience compassion toward the person and form projects of helping. This is why I say that the moral achievement of extending concern to others need not antedate compassion, but can be coeval with it. Still, there is a recalcitrance in our emotions, given their link to our daily scheme of goals and ends. Smith is right: thinking that the poor victims of the disaster in China are important is easy to do for a short time, hard to sustain in the fabric of our daily life, where there are so many things closer to home to distract us, and these things are likely to be so much more thoroughly woven into our scheme of goals.

Let us return to September 11, armed with this analysis. The astonishing events made many Americans recognize the nation itself as part of their circle of concern with a new vividness. Most Americans rely on the safety of our institutions and our cities, and do not really notice how much they value them until they prove vulnerable – in just the way that a lover often does not see how much he loves until the loved one is ill or threatened. So our antecedent concern emerged with a new clarity in the emotions we experienced. At the same time, we actually extended concern, in many cases, to people in America who had not previously been part of our circle of concern at all: the New York firefighters, the victims of the disasters. We extended concern to them both because we heard their stories, like a tragic drama being played out before us, and also, especially, because we were encouraged to see them as one part of the America we already loved and for which we intensely feared. When disaster struck in Rwanda, we did not in a similar way extend concern, or not stably, because there was no antecedent basis for it: suffering Rwandans could not be seen as part of a larger 'us' for whose fate we trembled. Vivid stories can create a temporary sense of community, but they are unlikely to sustain concern for long, if there is no pattern of interaction that would make the sense of an 'us' an ongoing part of our daily lives.

Things are of course still worse with any group that figures in our imaginations as a 'them' over against the 'us'. Such people are not only by definition non-us, they are also, by threatening the safety of the us, implicitly bad, deserving of any misfortune that might strike them. This is the sports-fan mentality so neatly depicted in my baseball story. Compassion for a member of the opposing team? You've got to be kidding. 'U–S–A' just means, kill the ump.

III

In the light of these difficulties, it is easy to see why much of the philosophical tradition has wanted to do away with compassion as a basis for public choice and to turn, instead, to detached moral principles whose evenhandness can be relied on. The main candidate for a central moral notion has been the idea of human worth or dignity, and the principle that has been put to work, from the Stoics and Cicero on through Kant and beyond, is the idea of acting, always, in such a way as to show respect for the dignity of humanity. We are to recognize that all humans have dignity, and that this dignity is both inalienable and equal, not affected by differences of class, caste, wealth, honor, status, or even sex. The recognition of human dignity is supposed to impose obligations on all moral agents, whether the humans in question are co-nationals or foreigners. In general, it enjoins us to refrain from all aggression and from fraud, since both are seen as violations of human dignity, ways of using a human being as merely a tool of one's own ends. Out of this basic idea Cicero developed much of the basis for modern international law in the areas of war, punishment, and hospitality.[2] Other Stoics used it to criticize conventional norms of patriarchal marriage, the physical abuse of servants, and many other aspects of Roman social life.

This Stoic tradition was quite clear that respect for human dignity could move us to appropriate action, both personal and social, without our having to rely at all on the messier and more inconstant motive of compassion. Indeed, for separate reasons, which I shall get to shortly, they thought compassion was never appropriate, so they could not rely on it. What I now want to ask is whether this counter-tradition was correct. Respect for human dignity looks like the right thing to focus on, something that can plausibly be seen as of boundless worth, constraining all actions in pursuit of well-being, and also as equal, creating a kingdom of ends in which humans are ranked horizontally, so to speak, rather than vertically. Why should we not follow the counter-tradition, as in many respects we do already – as when constitutions make the notion of human dignity central to the analysis of constitutional rights,[3] as when international human rights documents use similar notions.

Now it must be admitted that the notion of human dignity is not an altogether clear notion. In what does it consist? Why should we think that all human life has it? The minute the Stoic tradition tries to answer such questions, problems arise. In particular, the answer almost always takes the form of saying, look at how far we are above the beasts. Reason, language, moral capacity – all these things are seen as worthy of respect and awe at least in part because 'the beasts', so-called, do not have them, because they make us better than others. Of course they would not seem to make us better if they did not have some attraction in themselves, but part of their attraction surely also is their tendency to make us look better. Moreover, the claim that this dignity is equal relies especially heavily on the better-than-beasts idea. No matter how we vary in our level of rational and moral capacity, the idea seems to be, the weakest among us is light years beyond those beasts down there, so the differences that exist among humans in basic powers become not worth adverting to at all, not sources of differential worth at all. Dignity thus comes to look not like a scalar matter but like an all or nothing matter. You either have it, or, bestially, you do not.

This view has its moral problems, clearly. Richard Sorabji has shown how it was linked with a tendency to denigrate the intelligence of animals; and of course it

---

[2]   See my 'Duties of Justice, Duties of Material Aid: Cicero's Problematic Legacy,' *Journal of Political Philosophy* 7 (1999) 1-31.

[3]   Germany is one salient example. In a forthcoming book, James Whitman describes the way this central notion has constrained legal practices in Europe generally, especially in the area of criminal punishment. Dignity, he argues, is a non-hierarchical notion that has replaced hierarchical orders of rank.

has been used, too, not only by the Stoics but also by Kant and modern contractarians, to deny that we have any obligations of justice toward non-human forms of life. Compassion, if slippery, is at least not dichotomous in this way: it allows of extension in multiple directions, including the direction, as Coetzee said, of imagining the sufferings of animals in the squalid conditions we create for them. There is another more subtle problem with the dignity idea. It was crucial, according to the Stoics, to make dignity something that is radically independent of fortune: all humans have it, no matter where they are born or how they are treated. It exerts its claim everywhere, and it can never be lost. If dignity went up or down with fortune, it would create ranks and orders of human beings: the well-born and healthy will be worth more than the ill-born and hungry. So the Stoics understood their project of making dignity self-sufficient as essential for the notion of equal respect and regard.

But this move leads to a problem: how can we give a sufficiently important place to the goods of fortune for political purposes, once we admit that the truly important thing, the thing that lies at the core of our humanity, does not need the goods of fortune at all? How can we provide sufficient incentive to political planners to arrange for an adequate distribution of food and shelter and even political rights and liberties, if we say that dignity is unaffected by the lack of such things?[4] Stoic texts thus look oddly quietistic: respect human dignity, they say. But it does not matter at all what conditions we give people to live in, since dignity is complete anyway. Seneca, for example, gives masters stern instructions not to beat slaves or use them as sexual tools. But as for the institution of slavery itself? Well, this does not really matter so much, for the only thing that matters is the free soul within, and that cannot be touched by any contingency. Thus, having begun his letter on slavery in a way that looks radical, Seneca slides into quietism in the end, as his master scornfully says, 'He is a slave,' and Seneca calmly replies, 'Will this do him any harm?' (*Hoc illi nocebit?*)

Things are actually even worse than this. For the minute we start examining this reasoning closely, we see that it is not only quietistic, it is actually incoherent. Either people need external things or they do not. But if they do not, if dignity is utterly unaffected by rape and physical abuse, then it is not very easy, after all, to say what the harm of beating or raping a slave is. If these things are no harm to the victim, why is it wrong to do them? They seem not different from the institution of slavery itself: will they really do him any harm, if one grants that dignity is sufficient for eudaimonia, and that dignity is totally independent of fortune? So Seneca lacks not only a basis for criticizing the institution of slavery, but also a basis for the criticism he actually makes, of cruel and inhumane practices toward slaves.

---

[4] I deal with this question at greater length in 'Duties of Justice,' and also in 'The Worth of Human Dignity: Two Tensions in Stoic Cosmopolitanism,' forthcoming in *Power and Politics*, a festschrift for Miriam Griffin, ed. T. Rajak, Oxford: Clarendon Press.

Kant had a way of confronting this question, and it is a plausible one, within the confines of what I have called the counter-tradition. Kant grants that humanity itself, or human worth, is independent of fortune: under the blows of 'step-motherly nature' the good will still shines like a jewel for its own sake. But external goods such as money, health, social position are still required for happiness, which we all reasonably pursue. So there are still very weighty moral reasons for promoting the happiness of others, reasons that can supply both individuals and states with a basis for good thoughts about the distribution of goods.

The Stoics notoriously deny this, holding that virtue is sufficient for εὐδαιμονία. What I want to suggest now is that their position about human dignity pushes them strongly in this direction. Think of the person who suffers poverty or hardship. Now either this person has something that is beyond price, by comparison to which all the money and health and shelter in the world is as nothing – or she does not have something that is beyond price. Her dignity is just one contributor to her happiness, a piece of it that can itself be victimized and held hostage to fortune, in such a way that she may end up needy and miserable, even though she has dignity, and even virtue. This would mean that human dignity is being weighed in the balance with other goods; it no longer looks like the thing of surpassing, even infinite worth that we took it to be. There are, after all, ranks and orders of human beings: slavery and abuse can actually change people's situation with regard to their most important and inclusive end, εὐδαιμονία itself.

Because the Stoics do not want to be forced to that conclusion, they insist that external goods are not required for εὐδαιμονία: virtue is sufficient. And basic human dignity, in turn, is sufficient for becoming virtuous, if one applies oneself in the right way. It is for this deep reason that the Stoics reject compassion as a basic social motive, not just because it is slippery and uneven. Compassion gets the world wrong, because it is always wrong to think that a person who has been hit by fortune is in a bad or even tragic predicament. 'Behold how tragedy comes about,' writes Epictetus: 'when chance events befall fools.' In other words, only a fool would mind the events depicted in Euripides' play, and only fools in the audience would view these events as tragic.

So there is a real problem about how, and how far, the appeal to equal human dignity motivates. Looked at superficially, the idea of respect for human dignity appears to provide a principled, even-handed motive for good treatment of all human beings, no matter where they are placed. Looked at more deeply, it seems to license quietism and indifference to things in the world, on the grounds that nothing that merely happens to people is really bad.

We have now seen two grave problems with the counter-tradition: what I shall call the animal problem, and what I shall call the external goods problem. Neither of these problems is easy to solve within the counter-tradition. By contrast, the Euripidean tradition of focusing on compassion as a basic social motive has no such problems. Compassion can and does cross the species boundary, and whatever good there may be in our current treatment of animals is likely to be its work. We are able to extend our imaginations to understand the sufferings of animals who are cruelly treated. We are able to see that suffering as significant, as undeserved, and as part of our scheme of goals and projects. It is only that most of the time we do not make the effort to see in this way.[5] As for the problem of external goods, compassion has no such problem, for it is focused in its very nature on the damages of fortune: its most common objects, as Aristotle listed them in the *Rhetoric* (2.8 1386a4-16), are the classic tragic predicaments: loss of country, loss of friends, old age, illness, and so on.

But let us suppose that the counter-tradition can solve these two problems, providing people with adequate motives to address the tragic predicaments. Kant makes a good start on the external goods problem, at least. So let us imagine that we have a reliable way of motivating conduct that addresses human predicaments, without the uneven partiality that so often characterizes compassion. A third problem now awaits us. I shall call it the problem of watery motivation, though we might equally well call it the problem of death within life. The name 'watery' motivation comes from Aristotle's criticism of Plato's ideal city. Plato tried to remove partiality by removing family ties, and asking all citizens to care equally for all other citizens. Aristotle says that the difficulty with this strategy is that 'there are two things above all that make people love and care for something, the thought that it is all theirs, and the thought that it is the only one they have. Neither of these will be present in that city' (*Pol.* 2.4 1262b22-3). Because nobody will think of a child that it is all theirs, entirely their own responsibility, the city will, he says, resemble a household in which there are too many servants, so nobody takes responsibility for any task. Because nobody will think of any child or children that they are the only ones they have, the intensity of care that characterizes real families will simply not appear, and we will have, he says, a 'watery' kind of care all round (1262b15).

If we now examine the nature of Stoic motivation, I think we will see that Aristotle is very likely to be correct. I shall focus here on Marcus Aurelius, in many ways the most psychologically profound of Stoic thinkers. Marcus tells us that the first lesson he learned from his tutor was 'not to be a fan of the Greens or Blues at the races, or the light-armed or heavy-armed gladiators at the Circus' (1.5.1). His imagination had to unlearn its intense partiality and localism – and apparently the tutor assumes that already as young children we have learned narrow sectarian types of loyalty. It is significant, I think, that the negative image for the moral imagination is that of sports fandom: for in all ages, perhaps, that has been such a natural way for human beings to imagine yet other types of loyalty, to family, city, and nation. It was no accident that those White Sox fans selected a hockey chant as their way of expressing distress about the fate of the nation.

---

[5] See J.M. Coetzee, *The Lives of Animals*, Princeton: Princeton University Press, 1999, 35: 'There are people who have the capacity to imagine themselves as someone else, there are people who have no such capacity (when the lack is extreme, we call them psychopaths), and there are people who have the capacity but choose not to exercise it.'

The question is whether this negative lesson leaves the personality enough resources to motivate intense concern with people anywhere. For Marcus, unlearning partiality requires an elaborate and systematic programme of uprooting concern for all people and things in this world. He tells us of the meditative exercises that he regularly performs, in order to get himself to the point at which the things that divide people from one another do not matter to him. One side of this training looks benign and helpful: we tell ourselves that our enemies are really not enemies, but part of a common human project:

> Say to yourself in the morning: I shall meet people who are interfering, ungracious, insolent, full of guile, deceitful and antisocial ... But I, ... who know that the nature of the wrongdoer is of one kin with mine – not indeed of the same blood or seed but sharing the same kind, the same portion of the divine – I cannot be harmed by any one of them, and no one can involve me in shame. I cannot feel anger against him who is of my kin, nor hate him. We were born to labor together, like the feet, the hands, the eyes, and the rows of upper and lower teeth. To work against one another is therefore contrary to nature, and to be angry against a man or turn one's back on him is to work against him.[6]

Instead of seeing the enemy as an opponent, see him as a fellow human being, sharing similar concerns and goals, and engaged in the common project of making human life better. (Notice how close these thoughts actually are to the thought-content of an extended compassion.) Passages such as these suggest that a strong kind of even-handed concern can be meted out to all human beings, without divisive jealousy and partiality. We see ourselves not as team players, not as family members, not as loyal citizens of a nation, but as members of the human kind, and our most important goal as that of enhancing the life of the human kind.

Now even in this good case problems are lurking: for we notice that this exercise relies on the thoughts that give rise to the animal problem and the external goods problem. We are asked to imagine human solidarity and community by thinking of a 'portion of the divine' that resides in all and only humans: we look like we have a lot in common because we are so sharply divided from the rest of nature. And the idea that we have a common work relies, to at least some extent, on Marcus' prior denigration of external goods: for if we ascribed value to external goods we would be in principle competing with one another, and it would be difficult to conceive of the common enterprise without running into that competition.

But I have resolved to waive those two difficulties, so let me do so. Even then, the good example is actually very complex. For getting to the point where we can give such concern even-handedly to all human beings requires, as Marcus makes abundantly clear, the systematic extirpation of intense cares and attachments

---

[6]   2.1, trans. G.M. Grube, Indianapolis: Hackett, 1983. Cf. also 6.6: 'The best method of defence is not to become like your enemy.'

directed at the local: one's family, one's city, the objects of one's love and desire. Thus Marcus needs to learn not only not to be a sports fan, but also not to be a lover. Consider the following extraordinary passage:

> How important it is to represent to oneself, when it comes to fancy dishes and other such foods, 'This is the corpse of a fish, this other thing the corpse of a bird or a pig.' Similarly, 'This Falernian wine is just some grape juice,' and 'This purple vestment is some sheep's hair moistened in the blood of some shellfish.' When it comes to sexual intercourse, we must say, 'This is the rubbing together of membranes, accompanied by the spasmodic ejaculation of a sticky liquid.' How important are these representations, which reach the thing itself and penetrate right through it, so that one can see what it is in reality. (6.13)[7]

Now of course these exercises are addressed to the problem of external goods. Here as elsewhere, Marcus is determined to unlearn the unwise attachments to externals that he has learned from his culture. This project is closely connected to the question of partiality, because learning not to be a sports fan is greatly aided by learning not to care about the things over which people typically fight. (Indeed, it is a little hard to see how a Kantian project can be stable, insofar as it teaches equal respect for human dignity while at the same time teaching intense concern for the externals that go to produce happiness, externals that strongly motivate people not to treat all human beings equally.) In the quoted passage, however, the link to partiality seems even more direct: for learning to think of sex as just the rubbing of membranes really is learning not to find special value or delight in a particular, and this extirpation of eroticism really does seem to be required by a regime of impartiality. Not being a fan of the Blues means, too, not being a fan of this body or that body, this soul or that soul, this city or that city.

But getting rid of our erotic investment in bodies, sports teams, family, nation – all this leads us into a strange world, a world that is gentle and unaggressive, but also strangely lonely and hollow. Marcus suggests that we have two choices only: the world of real-life Rome, which resembles a large gladiatorial contest (see Seneca, *On Anger* 2.8), each person striving to outdo others in a vain competition for externals, a world exploding with rage and poisoned by malice, or the world of Marcus' gentle sympathy, in which we respect all human beings and view all as our partners in a common project, but in which the terms of the project do not seem to matter very much, and the whole point of living in the world becomes increasingly unclear. To unlearn the habits of the sports fan we must unlearn our erotic investment in the world, our attachments to our own team, our own love, our own children, our own life.[8]

---

[7]   Based on P. Hadot, transl. Michael Chase, *The Inner Citadel: the Meditations of Marcus Aurelius*, Cambridge, Mass.: Harvard University Press, 1998, with some modifications.

[8]   It is significant that this adopted child did not, as the movie *Gladiator* shows us, make a

And this means: something like a death within life. For only in a condition close to death, in effect, is moral rectitude possible. Marcus tries repeatedly to think of life as if it is a kind of death already, a procession of meaningless occurrences:

> The vain solemnity of a procession; dramas played out on the stage; troops of sheep or goats; fights with spears; a little bone thrown to dogs; a chunk of bread thrown into a fish-pond; the exhausting labor and heavy burdens under which ants must bear up; crazed mice running for shelter; puppets pulled by strings... (7.3)[9]

(This, by an emperor who was at that very time on campaign in Parthia, leading the fight for his nation.) And the best consolation for that bleak conclusion comes also from the thought of death:

> Think all the time about how human beings of all sorts, and from all walks of life and all peoples, are dead ... We must arrive at the same condition where so many clever orators have ended up, so many grave philosophers, Heraclitus, Pythagoras, Socrates; so many heroes of the old days, so many recent generals and tyrants. And besides these, Eudoxus, Hipparchus, Archimedes, other highly intelligent minds, thinkers of large thoughts, hard workers, versatile in ability, daring people, even mockers of the perishable and transitory character of human life, like Menippus. Think about all of these that they are long since in the ground ... And what of those whose very names are forgotten? So: one thing is worth a lot, to live out one's life with truth and justice, and with kindliness toward liars and wrongdoers. (6.47)

Because we shall die, we must recognize that everything particular about us will eventually be wiped out. Family, city, sex, children, all will pass into oblivion. So really, giving up those attachments is not such a big deal. What remains, and the only thing that remains, is truth and justice, the moral order of the world. In the face of the looming inevitability of our end, we should not mind being dead already. Only the true city should claim our allegiance.

Marcus is alarming because he has gone deep into the foundations of cosmopolitan moral principle. What he has seen is that impartiality, fully and consistently cultivated, requires the extirpation of the eroticism that makes human life the life we know. The life we know is unfair, uneven, full of war, full of me-first nationalism and divided loyalty. But he sees that we cannot so easily remove these attachments while retaining humanity.[10] So, if that ordinary erotic humanity is unjust, get rid of it. But can we live like this, once we see the goal with

---

principled rational choice of the best man to run the Empire. In real life, Marcus chose his worthless son Commodus, tripped up yet once more by the love of the near.

[9] Translation from Hadot/Chase (1998).

[10] One might compare the imagery of ancient Greek skepticism. Pyrrho, frightened by a dog (and thus betraying a residual human attachment to his own safety) says, 'How difficult it is entirely to divest oneself of the human being.' Elsewhere he speaks of the skeptic as a eunuch, because he lacks the very source of disturbance.

Marcus' naked clarity? Is justice not something that must be about and for the living?

IV

Let me proceed from now on on the hypothesis that Marcus is correct: extirpating attachments to the local and the particular does deliver to us a death within life. Let me also proceed on the hypothesis that we will reject this course as an unacceptable route to the goal of justice, or even one that makes the very idea of justice a hollow fantasy. (This is Adam Smith's conclusion as well: enamoured as he is of Stoic doctrine, he thinks we must reject them when they tell us not to love our own families.) Where are we then placed?

It looks as if we are back where Aristotle, and Adam Smith, leave us: with the unreliability of compassion, and yet the need to rely on it, since we have no more perfect motive. This does not mean that we need give up on the idea of equal human dignity, or respect for it. But insofar as we retain, as well, our local erotic attachments, our relation to that motive must always remain complex and dialectical, a difficult conversation within ourselves as we ask how much humanity requires of us, and how much we are entitled to give to our own. But any such difficult conversation will require, for its success, the work of the imagination. If we do not have exceptionless principles, if, instead, we need to negotiate our lives with a complex combination of moral reverence and erotic attachment, we need to have a keen imaginative and emotional understanding of what our choices mean for people in conditions of many different kinds, and the ability to move resourcefully back and forth from the perspective of our personal loves and cares to the perspective of the distant. Not the extirpation of compassion, then, but its extension and education. Compassion within the limits of respect. How might such an extension be arranged?

The philosophical tradition helps us identify places where compassion goes wrong: by making errors about fault, about seriousness, about the circle of concern. But the ancient tradition, not being very interested in childhood, does not help us see clearly how and why it goes especially badly wrong. So to begin the task of educating compassion as best we can, we need to ask how and why local loyalties and attachments come to take in some instances an especially virulent and aggressive form, militating against a more general sympathy. To answer this question we need a level of psychological understanding that was not available in the ancient Greek and Roman world, or not completely. I would suggest (and have argued elsewhere) that one problem we particularly need to watch out for is a type of pathological narcissism in which the person demands complete control over all the sources of good, and a complete self-sufficiency in consequence. Nancy Chodorow long ago argued that this expectation colors the development of males in many cultures in the world. Recent studies of teenage boys in America, particularly the impressive work of Dan Kindlon and Michael Thompson, in their book *Raising*

Cain,[11] has given strong local support to this idea. The boys that Kindlon and Thompson study have learned from their culture that men should be controlling, self-sufficient, dominant. They should never have, and certainly never admit to, fear and weakness. The consequence of this deformed expectation, Kindlon and Thompson show, is that these boys come to lack an understanding of their own vulnerabilities, needs and fears, weaknesses that all human beings share. They lack the language in which to characterize their own inner world, and they are by the same token clumsy interpreters of the emotions and inner lives of others. This emotional illiteracy is closely connected to aggression, as fear is turned outward, with little real understanding of the meaning of aggressive words and acts for the feelings of others. Kindlon and Thompson's boys, some ten years later, make the sports fans who chanted 'U-S-A' at the ump, who think of all obstacles to American supremacy and self-sufficiency as opponents to be humiliated.

So the first recommendation I would make for a culture of respectful compassion is a Rousseauian one: it is, that an education in common human weakness and vulnerability should be a very profound part of the education of all children. Children should learn to be tragic spectators, and to understand with increasing subtlety and responsiveness the predicaments to which human life is prone. Through stories and dramas, they should get the habit of decoding the suffering of another, and this decoding should deliberately lead them into lives both near and far, including the lives of distant humans and the lives of animals.

As children learn to imagine the emotions of another, they should at the same time learn the many obstacles to such understanding, the many pitfalls of the self-centred imagination as it attempts to be just. Thus, one should not suppose that one can understand one's own sister, without confronting and continually criticizing the envy and jealousy in oneself that pose powerful obstacles to that understanding. One should not imagine that one can understand the life of a person in an ethnic or racial group different from one's own, or a sex different from one's own, or a nation, without confronting and continually criticizing the fear and greed and the demand for power that make such interactions so likely to produce misunderstanding and worse. What I am suggesting, then, is that the education of emotion, to succeed at all, needs to take place in a culture of ethical criticism and especially self-criticism, in which ideas of equal respect for humanity will be active players in the effort to curtail the excesses of the greedy self.

At the same time, since we have spoken of greed, we can also see that the chances of success in this enterprise will be greater if the society in question does not overvalue external goods of the sort that cause envy and competition. The Stoics are correct when they suggest that overvaluation of external goods is a major source of destructive aggression in society. If we criticize them to the extent of encouraging people to love their families, their friends, their work, their local

---

[11] Dan Kindlon and Michael Thompson, with Teresa Barker, *Raising Cain: Protecting the Emotional Life of Boys*, New York: Ballantine Books, 1999.

context, even, to a certain extent, their nation, this does not entail the overvaluation of money, honour, status, and fame that Seneca saw at Rome and that we see in America now. Obviously enough, the urge for control over the sources of good is more pernicious when the good includes these highly competitive elements. If people care primarily for friendship, good work, and, let's even hope, social justice, they are less likely to see everything in terms of the hockey match, and more likely to use Marcus' image of the common work or project. Because this project is not a Stoic one, there will still be important sources of good to be protected from harm, and there will still be justified anger at damage to those good things. But a lot of occasions for anger in real life are not good or just, and we can do a lot, as a society, to prune away the greedy attachments that underpin them. Kindlon's next book, after *Raising Cain*, is a study of rich teenagers in America. It provides an alarming portrait of the greed and the overvaluations of a certain class in our nation, and its tales of children who humiliate others because they do not have the same expensive ski vacations or expensive designer clothes is a chilling illustration of how overvaluation is connected to destructive violence. There would be a great deal to be said about how education could address these problems, but I shall not attempt to say it here.

Instead, I want to turn back to Euripides, reflecting, in concluding, about the role of tragic spectatorship, and tragic art generally, in promoting good citizenship of the sort I have been advocating here. Tragedies are not Stoic: they start with us 'fools,' and the chance events that befall us. At the same time, they tend to get their priorities straight. Thus, the overvaluations I have just been mentioning usually are not validated in tragic works of art. When people moan and groan about a social slight, or the loss of some money, that is, more often at least, an occasion for comedy. The great Athenian tragic dramas, to stick with those, revolve around attachments that seem central and reasonable: to one's children, one's city, one's loved ones, one's bodily integrity, one's health, one's freedom from pain, one's status as a free person rather than a slave, one's ability to speak and persuade others, the very friendship and company of others. The loss of these things is worthy of lamentation, and the tragic dramas encourage us to understand the depth of these losses and, with the protagonists, to fear them. In exercising compassion the audience is learning its own possibilities and vulnerabilities: as Aristotle said, 'things such as might happen' in a human life. At the same time, often, the audience learns that people different in sex, race, age, nation experience suffering in a way that is like our way, and that suffering is as crippling for them as it would be for us.

Such recognitions have their pitfalls, and I have identified some of them in talking about *The Trojan Women*. We always risk error in bringing the distant person close to us: we ignore differences of language and of cultural context, and the manifold ways in which these differences shape the inner world. But there are dangers in any act of imagining, and we should not let these particular dangers cause us to admit defeat prematurely, surrendering before an allegedly insuperable barrier of otherness. When I was out in the rural areas of Rajasthan, visiting an education project for girls, I asked the Indian woman who ran the project (herself, by the way, from Delhi) how she would answer the frequent complaint that a foreigner can never understand the situation of a person in another nation. She thought for a while and said, 'I have the greatest difficulty understanding my own sister.' In other words, there are barriers to understanding in any human relationship. As Proust said, any real person imposes on us a 'dead weight' that our 'sensitivity cannot remove.' The obstacles to understanding a sister may in some instances be greater than those to understanding a stranger. At least they are different. And of course there still other and equally great obstacles to understanding our own selves. All we can do is to trust our imaginations, and then criticize them (listening if possible to the critical voices of those we are trying to understand), and then trust our imaginations again. Perhaps out of this dialectic between criticism and trust something like understanding may eventually grow. At least the product will very likely be better than the obtuseness that so generally reigns in human relations.

As Euripides knew, terror has this good thing about it: it makes us sit up and take notice. Tragic dramas cannot precisely teach anything new, since they will be moving only to people who at some level already understand how bad these predicaments are. But they can awaken the sleepers, reminding them of human realities they are neglecting in their daily political lives. The experience of terror and grief for our towers might be just that, an experience of terror and grief for our towers. One step worse, it could be a stimulus for blind rage and aggression against all the opposing hockey teams and bad umpires in the world. But if we cultivate a culture of critical compassion, such an event may, like Hecuba's Trojan cry, possibly awaken a larger sense of the humanity of suffering, a patriotism constrained by respect for human dignity and by a vivid sense of the real losses and needs of others. And in that case, it really will turn out that Euripides was right and Hecuba was wrong: the name of the Trojan land was not wiped out. It lives, in a work of the imagination to which we can challenge ourselves, again and again.

Index of Passages Cited from Ancient Authors

Meno 72CD, 75BC 21
Phaedo 40; 101CE 21
Philebus 45; 47E1-48A2, 50E4 93
    n.11; 51A-53D 40 n.3
Protagoras 351D-357E 40 n.2
Republic 40, 51, 71; 1 338C, 343C 1;
    339ff. 2; 347E 3; 351ff. 1; 352D 3;
    2 357-8 2 and n.2; 358C 3 nn.3,4;
    359D-360C, 360E-361D 3; 362D 4;
    367B 2, 4; 368D 14; 3 406BE 41
    n.6; 407E 41-2 and n.9; 4 434D-
    445E 40 n.1; 5 476A 21 476C 9;
    479 9-10; 6 485 9,16; 492 15; 505A
    9; 506E 11; 508B 9; 7 517B 11;

    520ff. 16; 532-3 11
Symposium 206A 7 n.7; 206E2-5 7;
    210AB 7-8 and n.9; 210E 8 and n.9;
    211B 8 n.9; 212A 7,10; 215-17 7
Theaetetus 167C 24
Timaeus 70-1, 78; 47AB 40-1 and n.4;
    47B 41 n.5

SENECA
    On Anger 2.8 155

THUCYDIDES
    1.11 74; 2.65.8 75; 3.82.7, 8.9.3 74

General Index